The STRONG PEOPLE

A HISTORY OF THE PORT GAMBLE S'KLALLAM TRIBE

The Port Gamble S'Klallam Tribe
Kingston, WA

Page i

Published by Port Gamble S'Klallam Tribe
31912 Little Boston Road NE
Kingston, WA 98346-0280

ISBN: 978-0-615-71105-8

Contents

Preface with Acknowledgements

This book was written for the Port Gamble S'Klallam people.

The most vivid and valuable source material for this book came from Port Gamble S'Klallam elders: some were interviewed in the mid-1970s, some in 1994 for the publication *Pride Is Our Heritage,* and some during oral history projects in 2005 and 2008. Their memories, pride, tenacity, love, and wisdom form the foundation of this book, and we are deeply grateful to each and every one of them. More quotes from the 2005 oral history project can be found in the publication *Our Lives.*[1]

The most recent oral history project was limited in scope and unable to include the voices of all elders; therefore, important memories are missing from this book. One person's recollection of an event or era often differs from another person's. The same can be said for written sources of information, whether that source is an anthropologists' ethnography, a government official's letter, or a missionary's memoir: each document presents the observer's point of view and may not reflect other perspectives. In writing Port Gamble S'Klallam history, we have attempted to weave together oral histories and primary source documents to present a story that is as accurate as possible. Future interviews and research will add to and perhaps change aspects of what is presented here.

We have tried to personalize Port Gamble S'Klallam history by incorporating specific familial details into a well-rounded representation of all Port Gamble S'Klallam families. Today's tribal members trace their ancestry back to a core of fourteen families on the tribe's 1939 Base Roll: Anderson, Charles, Fulton, Garrison, George, Henry, Jackson, Jones, Lambert, Purser, Sparks, Sullivan, Tom, and Webster. For some families, more information was available than for others due to differences in historical and anthropological records. Researching family history is always a work in progress, and we hope this book will encourage tribal members to dig even deeper into their family histories than we have managed.

Individuals' Indian names have not been included in the book because they are the property of the person's family. Tribal members are welcome to research their family's names in the Port Gamble S'Klallam archives.

This book represents an unusual collaboration. The Port Gamble S'Klallam History Book Committee guided every stage of the book's development, and different committee members wrote different chapters. Each chapter stands in the style of its author. We have not attempted to homogenize the writing from chapter to chapter. However, both the committee and several community members extensively reviewed the content of each chapter to ensure that the facts and perspectives reflect the Port Gamble S'Klallam Tribe as much as the individual authors.

For their painstaking review and feedback on chapter drafts, we thank Rose Purser, Karen James, Josh Wisniewski, Juanita Holtyn, and members of Holtyn's 2009 Northwest Indian College History class: Steven Adams, Shallee Graff, John Melovidov, Mathew Ives, Marian Sparks, Keri Bailey, Julianna Sullivan, and Lindsey Fulton. We tried to incorporate as many suggestions as possible. If we have overlooked or misrepresented anything, the error lies with the committee, not our reviewers.

Thanks also to community members who shared their baseball memories at a pie social organized by Sharon Purser and documented by Francine (Jones) Swift. And to Floyd Jones, Jake Jones, Russell Fulton, Skip George, and Harry Fulton III for their significant contributions to the Mill chapter.

The Port Gamble S'Klallam Tribal Council and tribal administration generously supported this project over several years by permitting staff members to extend their already-overworked schedules to include work on this book. In addition, many staff and committee members donated their time to the project.

The History Book Committee received support from several people who were not able to participate fully as committee members, but whose advice was generously given when requested: elder Rose Purser; Cultural Director Marie Hebert; former Director of the Oral History Project, educator, and present Tribal Council member Francine (Jones) Swift; Self-Governance Coordinator Greg Anderson (who authored part of Chapter 10); and former Tribal Attorney Tallis King George.

S'Klallam artist Jeffrey Veregge created the cover and other design work in the book, along with the help of Collin Oliphant and Dylan Haubrich. We were fortunate to have such a talented man help us prepare the book for the publisher. Chas Hoppe performed the book's final technical edit. We used a number of elder photos Seattle photographer John Stamets shot in 1992 for a tribal exhibit called "Pride Is Our Heritage." We appreciate the work of these five men.

The Port Gamble Foundation provided invaluable staff support to seek project funding, assist with content preparation and editing, and work with the publisher.

We appreciate and thank the following funders who helped to underwrite the production of this book: the Port Gamble S'Klallam Tribe and its Community Awards Program, the Genographic Legacy Fund, the Nisqually Indian Tribe Charitable Fund, the Potlatch Fund, the Siletz Tribal Charitable Contribution Fund, and the Squaxin Island Tribe One Percent Charitable Contribution Commission.

We are also deeply indebted to the late Candi (Jones Ives) Seachord, whose years of excellent research into family genealogies and vision for a tribal history book helped launch this project.

We thank you all.

The Port Gamble S'Klallam Tribe History Book Committee:

Ron Charles, Denise Comstock, Joan Garrow, Ted George, Ron Hirschi, Emily Mansfield, Laurie Mattson, Sharon Purser, Billie Jo Reynolds, and Gina Stevens

The Context for Port Gamble S'Klallam History

Ted George

Our Native American customs, beliefs, traditions, and values—though often similar—were not always universal among all our Native Nations. Indian histories must acknowledge that there is a vast array of indigenous variances that reflect the uniqueness of each group.

Native American cultures arose from thousands of years of communal living, and may offer today's world the best answers to a troubled humanity. The ancient wisdom of health practices, relationships, and preservation of the quality of life has been frequently acknowledged by researchers for its basic and singular simplicity. Author Vine Deloria and others have cited this. For example, concepts from the Iroquois Confederacy have influenced both the United States Constitution and the current structure of the United Nations.

However, most sources and references were crafted by non-Indians whose translations of events and experiences reflected Euro/Anglo-Saxon understandings of what they witnessed.

Our histories must accurately reflect our particular cultures from our own sources. Each tribe must communicate its local relevance, central themes, and focus in its own words.

The view of Indian people as savage, uncivilized barbarians—or as noble princes—are distorted or romanticized sentimentalities that do not serve true Indian people well.

Dispossession of land, removal from homes, relocation, and efforts to civilize and Christianize Indians were common and are central to all of our stories. They are now recognized as among the most inhumane and tragic errors committed by the United States government, and the shame and consequences of these violations still exist.

Within this larger context, the Port Gamble S'Klallam history must be told.

Introduction

Ron Charles

Years ago, former tribal attorney Tallis King George began a concerted effort to collect every bit of information pertaining to the history of the Port Gamble S'Klallam Tribe from a variety of sources, hoping to someday turn that material into a book. A few years ago, a committee was formed, and its members have been working diligently since then to accomplish this daunting task. We hope the readers will find the book interesting and informative, and that it will be looked at with pride by the tribal members of today and tomorrow. If this tribal history provides a foundation of knowledge and pride for our young people, its purpose will have been accomplished.

When referring to our people, I personally use the term "Klallam." It is what I was used to growing up. The Tribe's name has been also spelled "Clallam." The original word was *nexʷƛ̕áyəm̓*. In recent years, the Port Gamble and Jamestown tribes went back to the name used in the Treaty of Point No Point, "S'Klallam." The Lower Elwha Tribe continues to use "Klallam."[2]

Much of the history of the early S'Klallams living in the Port Gamble area was never recorded, but it is safe to say that the residents of *nexʷqíyt* were puzzled and dismayed to find that, under the terms of the 1855 Treaty of Point No Point, they were expected to pick up and move sixty miles away to the Skokomish Reservation. They wondered what sense it made for them to pack up and go to this unfamiliar place, where they were not even sure if they could eke out a subsistence living, and where they were very likely to get a less than enthusiastic welcome from the Twana, who were already crowded into a small area.

Why would they leave the Port Gamble area, when they were just getting accustomed to the white man's ways, working at the many jobs in and around the mill, where their conscientious work greatly pleased the mill owners?

Further, would this forced move to Skokomish prove to be their people's death knell, the loss of their very identity as members of the S'Klallam Nation? Given those choices, it was an easy decision to stay near their jobs, in the area where many of their dead were buried. The people would take their chances with the federal government and hope they would not force them to move in the future.

No real effort was ever made to compel the S'Klallams to move, and the influential mill men could very well have had something to do with all that, as the Indians came to be very important to the mill operation. In those early days of the Port Gamble mill, the young, footloose white men of that era would prove to be quite unreliable, and could be gone in a heartbeat if an exciting new venture sparked their interest. On the other hand, the S'Klallams were hard workers and tended to stay put.

During the approximately eighty years that the village of *nexʷq̓íyt* was occupied, it is clear that, despite the harsh living conditions in the cold, damp climate on Port Gamble Bay; despite the deadly toll from epidemics like tuberculosis; despite the continued loss of their favorite fishing, hunting, and gathering places to the influx of settlers; and, finally, despite having to live through some of the worst of economic times, these folks chose to stay. They stayed under some trying circumstances, but over the years their leaders would resolutely continue to remind recalcitrant government officials of treaty promises not kept and the S'Klallams' anger at not having a homeland of their own.

Over the years, the federal government would make half-hearted efforts to appease the S'Klallams, promising them allotments of land on other Northwest reservations, but these offers were always flatly rejected by their leaders, who refused to budge from the lands where so many of their people lay buried. The Port Gamble people were forced to wait eighty long years before the federal government relented, and offered them 1,300 acres of land on Port Gamble Bay.

The successful S'Klallam quest for a homeland turned out to be somewhat of a bittersweet victory, however, because a few short years later, the Kitsap County government ordered the tribe to abandon and burn their old village of *nexʷqíyt*.

After more than eighty years of being lashed by strong winds and floodwaters, the old village had fallen unquestionably into disrepair. Nevertheless, the event was especially traumatic for the old folks, as they watched the only home they had ever known unceremoniously set afire. It was indeed a sad day.

It was a victory, nonetheless, because these tough and resilient people had won despite formidable odds, and had convinced a skeptical federal government that they did indeed deserve a homeland of their own.

As we wrote this book, as we took time to examine our tribe's history, it became crystal clear that today's tribal members can look back with pride, knowing that the treaty rights we enjoy, the right to live on these beautiful lands on Port Gamble Bay, and our very right to exist as a tribe are all benefits that we possess today because of the actions taken years ago by our S'Klallam ancestors at *nexʷqíyt*. And, so it is to those who came before us, with a huge debt of gratitude, that we dedicate this book.

Port Gamble S'Klallam Historical Timeline

Pre–1792
S'Klallam people live on Strait of Juan de Fuca and travel seasonally to Hood Canal, the San Juan and Whidbey Islands, and other locations undisturbed by Europeans.

1792
Arrival of Captain Vancouver. (Spanish ships had come along the coast and into the Straits before Vancouver.)

1833–1859
S'Klallam trade with the Hudson's Bay Company at their post at Ft. Nisqually.

1842–1844
S'Klallam meet French Catholic priests on Whidbey Island. Some convert to Christianity.

1853
Founders of the Puget Mill Co. arrive on Port Gamble Bay. Later, S'Klallam on the west side of the Bay move across to Point Julia. S'Klallam begin working at the mill.

1855
Treaty of Point No Point. S'Klallam, Chemakum, and Twana cede aboriginal territory in exchange for reserved land; reserved fishing, hunting, and gathering rights; and other promises.

1855–1856
Treaty War. S'Klallam do not participate.

1859
Indian Agent requests reservation for the S'Klallam at Clallam Bay. No reservation is established.

1860s–1870s
Houses are built by Puget Mill Co. on Point Julia for S'Klallam who work at the mill. Later, a Catholic church and a school

Page xiii

Port Gamble S'Klallam Historical Timeline

are also built in the village. Many S'Klallam families live in the village on the Spit until 1940.

◻ 1886
Port Gamble S'Klallam families begin purchasing land on the east side of the Bay.

◻ 1886–1900s
Boarding school era: some S'Klallam children are sent to Tulalip or Cushman boarding schools.

◻ 1909–1913
Port Gamble S'Klallam try to buy land on the Bay from Puget Mill Co., which refuses to sell. By now, S'Klallam families own over 200 acres on or near Port Gamble Bay.

◻ 1912–1915
S'Klallam consider taking allotments at Quinault, on the condition that they could sell them and use the money for

homes at Port Gamble. When the U.S. does not agree to their conditions, they refuse to leave Port Gamble Bay.

◻ 1914–1918
World War I

◻ 1917
U.S. buys land in Coontown for a tribal day school that is never built.

◻ 1920–1925
S'Klallam lobby U.S. for $10,000 per person for settlement of treaty claims.

◻ 1925
Congress passes S'Klallam Claims Settlement bill of $400,000. Each S'Klallam receives $722.

◻ 1926–late 1930s
Much of the land owned by

Port Gamble S'Klallam Historical Timeline

S'Klallam families is lost to Kitsap County for failure to pay taxes, mainly during the Depression.

☐ **1929–1930s**
Great Depression.

☐ **1934**
Indian Reorganization Act is passed with money for new reservations. Port Gamble S'Klallam is highest priority of Tulalip Agency.

☐ **1936**
Land is bought from McCormick Lumber Co., including 1,231 acres and tide lands.

☐ **1938**
Port Gamble S'Klallam Reservation is proclaimed.

☐ **1939–1940**
Houses and a water system are built on the bluff. The village

at Point Julia is burned to the ground.

☐ **1940**
Shaker Church gets lease from U.S. for former school site.

☐ **1939–1945**
World War II.

☐ **1951**
The S'Klallam Tribe (all three groups) file an Indian Claims Commission case against the United States for compensation for land ceded under the Treaty of Point No Point.

☐ **1950–1953**
Korean War.

☐ **1953**
Congress adopts the Termination policy. 1950s is also a period of relocation of Indians to urban areas. Port Gamble

S'Klallam History

S'Klallam are not as affected as many other tribes by these policies.

☐ **1965–1975**
Vietnam War.

☐ **1970**
"Indian Self-determination" policy is announced. This includes money for tribal economic development, Indian health, and Johnson-O'Malley education funds.

☐ **1974**
The "Boldt" decision upholds treaty fishing rights.

☐ **1976**
Final Indian Claims Commission decision awards roughly $400,000 to the S'Klallam Tribe as a whole.

☐ **1992**
Port Gamble S'Klallam Tribe is among the first 15 tribes in the U.S. to implement the BIA Self-Governance Demonstration Project.

☐ **1994**
Treaty shellfishing rights are affirmed by federal court ruling.

☐ **1996**
Port Gamble mill closes permanently, ending nearly 150 years of employment of Port Gamble S'Klallam people.

☐ **2010**
Through Self-Governance and hard work, the Port Gamble S'Klallam Tribe's annual budget surpasses $5 million in revenues for the benefit of the Port Gamble S'Klallam people.

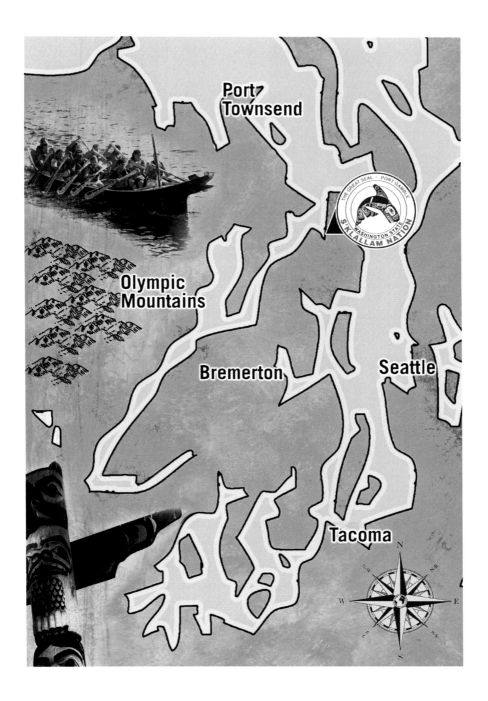

Port
Townsend

THE GREAT SEAL · PORT GAMBLE
WASHINGTON STATE
S'KLALLAM NATION

Olympic
Mountains

Bremerton

Seattle

Tacoma

N
NW   NE
W   E
SW   SE
S

CHAPTER 1

The S'Klallam Migration to Port Gamble Bay

Ron Charles

*"You can stay, but I'm going [to Port Gamble Bay].
I can paddle and I'm going!"*

–Emma (Sly) Henry to James Henry about
leaving Clallam Bay and Jamestown

Prior to the coming of the explorers, traders, and settlers to the Northwest, the people of the large and powerful S'Klallam Nation were scattered in villages along the north shore of the Olympic Peninsula. Thirty-one S'Klallam settlements ranged from the Hoko River on the west to Port Gamble Bay on the east, according to research by the Lower Elwha Tribe.[1] A settlement on Port Gamble Bay was not one of the thirteen winter villages identified by anthropologist Erna Gunther, nor was it among the shorter list of S'Klallam villages named in the preamble of the Treaty of Point No Point. But S'Klallam oral history includes Port Gamble Bay as an important settlement site before and around treaty times.

Like other northwest coast people, the S'Klallam traveled almost constantly, drawn by lands and waters that provided their livelihood, and by friends and relatives that lived in neighboring areas. S'Klallam people lived in many places over the course of a year—in temporary camps along

The S'Klallam Migration to Port Gamble Bay

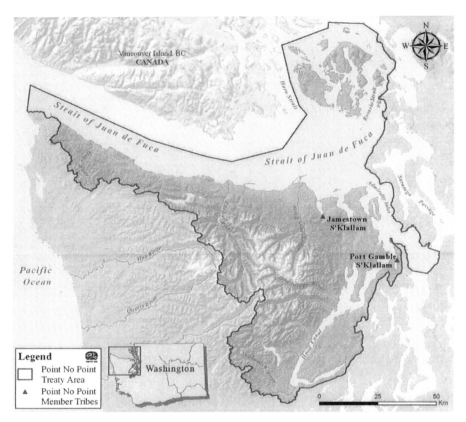

Map of our Point No Point Treaty area. Our ancestors occupied the Port Gamble area along with some Chemakum people. Map courtesy of Point No Point Treaty Council.

travel routes; in settlements where they returned every year for weeks or months at a time to fish, hunt or gather; and in permanent villages where they spent the winter. When S'Klallam ancestors passed along stories of living on Port Gamble Bay before treaty times, their meaning may have encompassed any of these possibilities.[2]

Around treaty times, the area surrounding Port Gamble Bay and the mouth of Hood Canal was used by several Native groups, including S'Klallam, Twana (Skokomish), Chemakum, and Suquamish.[3] As noted anthropologist Barbara Lane concluded:

The S'Klallam Migration to Port Gamble Bay

It appears that by the mid-nineteenth century the eastern Clallam were in close contact with both their Chemakum neighbors and the Twana-speaking people living on Hood Canal. According to the accounts written in the 1850s and 1860s, the Clallam were encroaching on what formerly had been regarded as Chemakum territory. By treaty times, both groups, Clallam and Chemakum, were sharing sites around Port Townsend and Port Gamble.[4]

We don't know exactly when S'Klallam ancestors first began to stay on Port Gamble Bay. They probably shared camping or temporary settlement sites on Port Gamble Bay with the other groups who used the area.[5] An archaeological study found evidence of continuing use of Point Julia for most of the last 1,000 years, but did not identify which Indian people had used the area that long ago.[6] The important thing is that S'Klallam ancestors eventually occupied the Port Gamble Bay area along with some Chemakums who were assimilated into what ultimately became known as the Port Gamble S'Klallam Tribe.[7] They called their settlement on the east side of the Bay *nexʷqíyt*.

The S'Klallam Nation, having occupied their lands on the Olympic Peninsula for many, many years, may not even have known about the contention brewing regarding "ownership" of what the British and Americans called the Oregon Territory, or what the land-hungry settlers had in mind. Until 1846, the United States and Great Britain jointly claimed what was known as the Oregon Territory, and by the time President Polk made his inaugural address in 1845, his expansionist attitude led him to proclaim clear title to the Territory for the U.S. By 1846, the two countries had agreed to divide the Territory along the 49th parallel from the crest of the Rocky Mountains to the Puget Sound region. This was done without consulting the area's original inhabitants.

By 1848, Congress created the Oregon Territory, which included all the lands north of California, south of the 49th parallel, and west of the Continental Divide. In 1853, the Washington Territory was formed to include everything north of the Columbia River and west of the Continental Divide.

The S'Klallam Migration to Port Gamble Bay

The S'Klallams had inhabited their lands on and near the Olympic Peninsula for thousands of years, and were expert at harvesting the fish, shellfish, berries, wild game, and other natural resources. They preserved these resources in order to survive year-round in what was sometimes a harsh winter environment.

Isaac Stevens was appointed the first governor of the Washington Territory, and one of his first duties was to obtain clear title to the lands from the tribes, something the government had failed to do before creating the Donation Land Act. Stevens quickly accomplished most of what he was sent out to do in a series of treaties with the Northwest tribes between 1854 and 1855.

The village at Point Julia, about 1940. The absence of trees on the bluff is evident, apparently having been logged by the mill company before the land was sold for the reservation. Note that the new houses up above were already built, so this photo had to have been taken shortly before the village was burned. Photo courtesy of the Port Gamble S'Klallam Archives.

The S'Klallam Migration to Port Gamble Bay

As more of the "Bostons" (as the Natives referred to the Americans) arrived by the early 1850s, many lured by the promise of free land, successful timber companies began to move their sawmill operations from the east coast to the Puget Sound area, where the virgin old-growth forests remained almost untouched. Puget Sound was still part of Oregon Territory in 1852, and under the Oregon Donation Land Law a single man could lay claim to 320 acres of free land.[8]

In the summer of 1853, owners of the Puget Mill Co. arrived at Port Gamble, where they quickly decided to erect a sawmill. A history of the logging industry described what took place:

> Talbot and Walker found their mill site on the east bank of Hood Canal, a natural channel that George Vancouver had discovered in 1792. In sheltered Gamble Bay, the water was deep enough for ocean-going ships and there was a flat, sandy spit of land big enough for mill buildings. "Teekalet," for brightness of the noonday sun, was the Indians' name for the place.[9]

While the Puget Mill Co.'s understanding of the meaning of "Teekalet" was apparently well-intended, the actual word, *texexq e'ultx*, means "skunk cabbage" in Suquamish.[10]

A 1937 *Seattle Times* article told this version:

> The grandfathers and great-grandfathers of the Clallam Indians, who live in Little Boston today, once lived across the cove from the sandpit on the site of what is today Port Gamble. They were there when the schooner Julius Pringle came into the cove, her hold full of mill machinery, in 1853. Puzzled by the presence of Indians, in their efforts to build a New England town in the West, the two Yankees probably decided to accept them as gracefully as possible. They built Little Boston, across the arm of the bay, for the Indians, and because industry was the keynote of their lives, put the Clallams to work in the mill.[11]

The S'Klallam Migration to Port Gamble Bay

*The village on Point Julia, probably around the late 1800s. Some
buildings appear in disrepair by this time. Tribal members who
worked in the mill used canoes to get back and forth from work.
Photo courtesy of the Seattle Times.*

In 1919, Indian Agent Charles E. Roblin wrote:

> The S'Klallam reportedly began performing tasks around the
> mill and selling the dogfish oil that lighted it soon after its
> construction. They helped keep the mill running during the late
> 1850s as white men joined the gold rush on the Fraser River.[12]

The decision by the Puget Mill Co., in the early days of the mill
operation, to help build the housing on the Spit for the S'Klallams only
a short distance away from the mill was indeed a wise one, for the
Indian workers would form the backbone of the mill's workforce for
almost 150 years. The S'Klallams, however, were always reminded that
those houses, and all the surrounding lands, now belonged to the Puget
Mill Co., and the company had no interest in selling any of it.

Written records of the earliest residents of the new village at Little Boston
do not exist, but Chief "Cookhouse" Charley (b. ca. 1844), was a member
of a family that likely was present when the mill operators came looking
for a mill site. Chief Charley's son, Sammy Charles, was born at the village
on the Spit in 1879, and in a 1947 *Seattle Post-Intelligencer* interview, he
passed down the Charles family's account of what transpired between

the S'Klallam and the would-be builders of the mill at Port Gamble:

> Chief Charlie was the last of the headmen; there have been no
> Little Boston chiefs since. The Bostons said that they wanted to
> put a sawmill there, and would the Indians please move to the
> other side. There were inducements. There would be lumber,
> free lumber, and all that the Nooksclime [S'Klallam] needed to
> build big houses. They could have the trimmings for firewood,
> fine firewood, and all they wanted.[13]

In March 1854, Josiah P. Keller, Puget Mill Co. partner and manager, noted
that "sundry Indian lodges" comprised part of the village at the mill site
itself and that he had "plenty of Indian neighbors."[14] Large parcels of
land around the Bay, including most of the current reservation, were
conveyed to Pope and Talbot in 1863 by Daniel Bagley of the University
of Washington Board of Commissioners, under the university land grant
selection process. Both this process and Bagley's role in conveying land
to his friends in the timber industry was of questionable legitimacy.[15]

The beautiful Northwest, with its bounty of old-growth forests, proved
to be a bonanza for Port Gamble mill owners Pope and Talbot, and as
reported in *The Loggers*: "Both men died millionaires—Pope in 1878
and Talbot in 1881—and the solid organization they passed on would
prosper for many years."[16]

Thus, the building of these Point Julia houses by the mill owners
to ensure they would always have a good steady workforce would
eventually set in motion the process that would bind this community
of S'Klallams together and, in the 1930s, enable them to convince the
federal government to establish a reservation for them. The village
became known as Little Boston. The Indian Reorganization Act of 1934
brought with it the opportunity to purchase 1,300 acres in and around
Point Julia, which the mill owners finally were willing to sell.

The S'Klallam Migration

By the time the mill owners were setting up their mill operation at Port Gamble, the S'Klallam way of life was experiencing radical change. The strange new diseases, the disastrous effects of liquor's introduction to their society, and the general trauma of watching a seemingly endless stream of light-skinned people march into their heretofore relatively tranquil lives must have prompted the S'Klallams to seek different ways to eke out a living in this new world.

For the most part, S'Klallams could ensure a decent quality of life by working at the many Northwest mill operations, harvesting seasonal crops in places like the Puyallup Valley, and continuing to rely on the area's abundant natural resources. Unfortunately, diseases such as tuberculosis were prevalent, and the short life span of many of Little Boston's residents ensured a low population in the village.

The first S'Klallams to live in the newly constructed Boston-style homes on the Spit likely drew the attention of friends and relations from other parts of the Olympic Peninsula as they made their way to their traditional fishing places on Hood Canal. After stopping by and reconnecting with friends and relations at Little Boston, some would elect to stay and seek work at the mill. As Louisa Sparks said in an interview, "The S'Klallam came while traveling home from the canal fishing and stayed because of the sawmill."[17] Echoing Sparks, anthropologist Erna Gunther wrote, "Little Boston was settled by Clallam Bay and Elwha people who stopped to work at the saw mill in Port Gamble when they returned from the fishing season on Hood Canal."[18]

These later arrivals added much to the strong social fiber of the burgeoning Port Gamble S'Klallam community, because they all seemed to be strong, adventuresome folks who took the initiative to make a better life for their families. These later arrivals to Port Gamble came from several different areas, and all would eventually assimilate themselves into the community, and, as was the Indian custom, they were recognized as tribal members.

Tyee Jack (b. 1838) and his two wives who were sisters, Mary (b. 1830) and Nancy (b. 1854), came from Clallam Bay and moved to Port Gamble for work at the mill. They were likely among the earliest residents. Tyee Jack is recognized in the 1877 census as one of the "Headmen." His son, Peter Jackson, would go on to be an important leader for the Port Gamble community during the early part of the 1900s, as the S'Klallams continued to press the government for land of their own.[19]

Tommy Tom and his wife Nellie may have also been early residents at Little Boston. Nellie once described an incident when the mill owners first arrived (see Chapter 4) that suggests she may have been present. Tommy Tom worked at the Seabeck mill, but the couple left Seabeck when the mill burned in 1886. They moved permanently to Port Gamble, where Tommy found work at that mill, taking in and raising their nephews, Harry and James Fulton, after Nellie's sister, Susie Fulton's death.[20]

Joe and Josie (Pulsifer) Anderson and children. Joe was a Port Gamble Klallam leader who would serve on the S'Klallam Claims Committee. Photo courtesy of the Port Gamble S'Klallam Archives.

One-Armed Peter and his wife, Mary, were also early residents of the community at Little Boston, though their original home is not known. Their son, Joseph Anderson (b. 1862), was raised on the Spit.[21]

Louise Butler Webster, a Chemakum woman, was born at Point No Point in 1855 while her people, from nearby Port Townsend, gathered for the Treaty signing. Her father's name was William. Louise married James Webster, a S'Klallam man also known as Chemakum Jim, and they were living at Port Townsend when the government burned their houses in 1871. The couple was forced to move to the Skokomish Reservation, which they found not to their liking, so they soon moved to Port Gamble, where James found work as a longshoreman.[22]

The S'Klallam Migration to Port Gamble Bay

Louise Webster's brother, George Adams (b. 1857), also moved to Port Gamble, where he later married Mary Ann Williams. Mary Ann had a relative who was chief of a village at the east end of Clallam Bay and buried at Little Boston.[23]

James Webster Sr. (b. 1868), son of Louise and Chemakum Jim Webster, acquired four acres of land on Indian Island next to *pačwi'ləs* (Prince of Wales), the son of the S'Klallam leader *čičməhȧn* (Duke of York).[24] The government later bought the land from him. Webster then moved to Port Gamble and bought land north of Point Julia.[25]

Just as the Websters were burned out of their Port Townsend village, *qatáy,* in 1871, so was the family of Eddie George (b. 1863). After their Port Townsend homes were burned, it appears that the family moved to Dungeness, where Eddie's father, George appears on the 1877 census. Eddie George and his wife, Lucy Emore (b. 1866), lived on Scow Bay before moving to Little Boston to work in the mill.[26] Their many descendants today live on both the Port Gamble and Suquamish reservations.

PORT TOWNSEND VILLAGE IS BURNED

S'Klallam author Mary Ann Lambert described the burning of the village in Port Townsend in 1871, witnessed by Eddie George, in *The Seven Brothers of the House of Ste-Tee-Thlum:*

"Orders had come to *Cheech-ma-han* (Duke of York), *E' ow-itsa's* nephew, that all Clallams living at Port Townsend had to relinquish their aboriginal domain and be permanently transferred to the Skokomish Reservation. A day was set for the Clallams to load their personal belongings into canoes—and leave their ancestral homes for once and for all by paddling out to a waiting steamboat, which was to tow them to their new home at the head of Hood Canal. There was no alternative for the Indians. This was a command from the government—from the great white fathers at Washington, D.C. and Olympia, so they were informed—and had to be obeyed. One Clallam refused to go, saying, 'I was born on this soil, a Clallam, and I will die here a Clallam as my forefathers have done.'

History repeated itself in 1940 when government officials burned the village at Pt. Julia.

When the fifty canoes, more or less, reached the waiting steamer in Port Townsend Bay they were tied to her stern, one canoe behind the other, forming a long line of canoes. Ironically enough one connects this event to a prison chain gang. When this long line of canoes had begun to move, in tow of the side-wheeler, and were about to round Marrowstone Point, some of the Clallams looked back for the last time to their beloved *Kaw-tie* (*qatáy,* Port Townsend). What they saw was enough to sadden the most stout-hearted—the village was in flames, having been set on fire, by order of Uncle Sam.

Eventually the shore of Skokomish was reached . . . but in less than five days every Clallam canoe, stealthily, by cover of night, returned to *Kaw-tie* and to a heap of ashes which was once their home."[27]

The S'Klallam Migration to Port Gamble Bay

Ruth Martinez (b. 1915, d. 2002) told the story of her grandparents, James and Emma (Sly) Henry, who moved from Clallam Bay to Port Gamble, probably in the 1880s:

Ruth Martinez, whose grandparents, James and Emma (Sly) Henry, moved from Clallam Bay to Port Gamble, probably in the 1880s. Photo courtesy of the Port Gamble S'Klallam Tribe.

> When they came from Clallam Bay, Grandpa wanted to stay at Jamestown and she [Grandma Emma (Sly) Henry] wanted to go. She said, "You can stay, but I'm going. I can paddle and I'm going with the others." The others had already paddled away, so Grandpa said, "You can't go alone. It'll be hard to make a living by yourself." She said, "Well, somehow I'll manage, but don't worry about it." "Well," he said, "Put it that way, I just fell in love. I'll stay and go with you." So they came on to Port Gamble then, and Grandpa was always glad that they did! [28]

A S'Klallam man named Old Solomon came to the Port Gamble area from Dungeness around 1880, and soon bought land north of the Spit. Solomon's wife, Susie, had been previously married to Howard Chubby of Jamestown. She brought with her to the marriage and to Port Gamble her daughters, Dora and Emily.[29] Solomon's daughter, Alice, would eventually marry Harry Fulton Sr., and they produced two children before Alice's untimely death. After her death, Harry married Angie, a Skokomish woman, and they had eleven more children, all raised at the house in Coontown. Old Solomon sold half of his property to his friend, Eddie George, in 1911.[30]

The S'Klallam Migration to Port Gamble Bay

In the mid-to-late 1800s, many of the white mill workers originally hailed from East Machias, Maine. One of them, James Fulton, married Susie, a S'Klallam woman. James worked at the Seabeck mill, and Susie was the sister of Nellie Tom, whose husband Tom also worked in the Seabeck mill. At some point, James abandoned his family, who eventually moved up to Little Boston, perhaps when the mill at Seabeck burned down in 1886.

Harry and Angie Fulton, with some of their family at the old house in Coontown around 1940. Photo courtesy of Ron Charles.

S'Klallams George and Mary Littleman homesteaded twenty acres of land on the south end of San Juan Island in the 1880s. George and Mary's two surviving daughters moved to Port Gamble, where Mary (the younger) married James Fulton, and Susie married Thomas Charles.

Charley Jones (b. 1864) and his brother, Jacob (b. 1869), were the sons of Mary, a S'Klallam woman, and her Skagit husband, who probably came to Port Gamble to work in the mill. Mary may have met her husband in the camas meadows or fishing camps on Whidbey Island, where both S'Klallam and Skagit people made seasonal trips.

In 1890, Jacob Jones had not yet married, and was living with his brother Charley at Little Boston. Around 1898, Jacob had the good fortune of marrying the much sought-after Jenny Dexter, who had recently divorced her elderly husband, *Niatum* Dexter. *Niatum* had been a "sub chief" at Elwha in 1877.[31] He later lived in Hadlock. Jenny thought he potlatched too much, giving away their wealth. Jenny was now living at Port Gamble with her children.[32] Jenny's father was S'Klallam, and her mother was Makah/S'Klallam.

Paul Kane painting of a Klallam canoe during a storm on the Strait of Juan de Fuca. Image courtesy of the Stark Foundation.

Charley Jones and his wife, Lucy, were the parents of Louisa Pulsifer. Lucy was Cowitchan and Snohomish, but lived on the Skokomish Reservation. Charley spent time in both Skokomish and Port Gamble after his marriage.

Henry Lambert was born around 1869 and raised around the Port Angeles area before going to Port Gamble to work at the mill. Henry's father, Cultus John, was an Elwha Klallam "sub chief" in 1878. Henry's mother was Snohomish.[33]

George Sparks was the son of a Port Ludlow mill worker, Charlie Sparks, from Maine, and his wife Fannie, a S'Klallam or Chemakum. George longshored in Port Ludlow and came to Port Gamble in 1893, when the Port Ludlow mill closed for a year.[34] Louisa Sparks, George's wife, had a father named Skookum John who lived at Little Boston in 1877 and gave potlatches at New Dungeness. Louisa's mother's father was chief at New Dungeness. Louisa had three siblings at Jamestown: Mrs. John Cook, Mabel Hall, and Henry Johnson.[35]

The S'Klallam Migration to Port Gamble Bay

Richard Purser was a Canadian Indian who moved to the Port Gamble area and married Julia John, a Suquamish. The two lived in the village where Dick carved canoes in a shop on the Spit.[36] Their son, Ed Purser, came back to Little Boston after serving in the Canadian Army during World War I. Today, many of their descendants are members of the Port Gamble S'Klallam and Suquamish Tribes.

George Howell was born in 1864 to a S'Klallam mother and a white father. His father, Dan Howell, was charged with selling whiskey to the Indians at Port Gamble in 1856, but George apparently had a stronger connection with his mother's people than with his father's ways. George lived at Jamestown before coming to Little Boston.[37] George's wife, Nancy, was S'Klallam but it is not known where she was from.

It is clear to see that the people known today as the Port Gamble S'Klallam Tribe are descended from a combination of the few S'Klallams present when the mill builders came in 1853 and the many others from all over S'Klallam territory who would come to Port Gamble to find work and community.

Pre-treaty Travel

In pre-treaty times, S'Klallam and other Northwest tribal seafaring nations routinely traveled incredible distances by canoe. They thought nothing of traveling many miles to attend a celebration, harvest crops, go fishing, or find trading partners. They were experts at working the tides, currents, and winds to their advantage, and when conditions would not permit travel, they would simply stop and rest. The Reverend Myron Eells said this about their canoe travel: "The canoes are the friends of these Indians as much as the horse is of the Indian of the prairie, or of the Arabian, or the sledge is to the Eskimo."[38]

Eells and his brother, Edwin, who was the Indian Agent at Skokomish, would sometimes hire S'Klallam canoes to ferry them to various Indian communities. In describing the S'Klallams he hired, Reverend Eells said, "The Clallams are better navigators than the Indians further up [south] Sound, as they live on the Strait of Fuca, where there is less protection from the ocean winds than in the upper [southern] Sound."[39]

The S'Klallam Migration to Port Gamble Bay

Edwin Eells once hired a S'Klallam crew to take him on a long journey out to visit the Makah people, for whom he had supervisory responsibility as Indian Agent. Perhaps unfamiliar with the ferocity of storms in the wintertime in the Strait of Juan de Fuca, he set out in the dead of winter. On the way back, somewhere west of Port Angeles, they were hit by a terrific storm, and Eells was sure he would perish. The S'Klallams, he reported, kept up a wild chant as they maneuvered the canoe skillfully through the storm, and guided him to safe water. He was very grateful, for he was sure he was going to die that day.[40]

S'Klallam canoes carried skillful paddlers across the Strait of Juan de Fuca to visit relatives on Vancouver Island, through the San Juan Islands for seasonal fishing, and south to Fort Nisqually to trade with the Hudson's Bay Company.[41] Anthropologist Barbara Lane commented in a 1977 report:

> Extensive trade was carried on among Indian groups in western Washington in order to acquire food stuffs, raw materials, and manufactured goods not available locally. The trade existed because different localities had different resources.[42]

The canoe was the primary mode of travel, and S'Klallams considered walking to be their least preferred method of travel.

Many of the S'Klallams lived in their so-called permanent homes perhaps six months out of the year, but when the time came to travel to their temporary villages for the salmon season, the entire household would put their belongings in the canoe and ship off. Some of the S'Klallam people from as far away as Clallam Bay would embark on the annual trip to Hood Canal, which became their second home until they were finished drying salmon, picking berries, and performing other seasonal activities.

In later years, the S'Klallam joined many other natives from around the Northwest in becoming the first migrant workers on the Puyallup Valley farms that were developed in the mid-to-late 1800s. In an interview, Irene (Fulton) Purser (b. 1900) remembered a trip to Puyallup she took in the early 1900s to harvest hops with her grandparents. According to Purser, shortly after returning from picking hops they left again for a long camping trip in Brinnon to catch and dry fish. She also reported that her family made yearly trips to Port Townsend in July to watch the canoe races.[43]

The village at Point Julia, *nexʷqíyt,* was apparently an important site for visitors from both near and far. In September 1854, there was reportedly a large gathering on the Spit, when between 1,000 and 1,500 people in two hundred canoes assembled to attend a potlatch by a man known as Bonaparte.[44]

In 1856, a large contingent of northern Indians frightened the residents of Port Gamble, who sent word to the gunship, Massachusetts, stationed in Olympia. The northern Indians were Stikene, Homagais and Kake Tlingit people from the then-Russian Territories, according to the commander of the ship.

The Massachusetts, with its navy sailors and superior weaponry, soon arrived and got into a skirmish that resulted in the deaths of twenty-seven northern Indians and one Port Gamble resident. The surviving members of the northern Indians were subsequently escorted to Victoria and sent back home.[45]

Approximately a year later, a group of these same northern Indians, still angry over their defeat at what became known as "The Battle of Port Gamble," came back and took revenge by killing Colonel Isaac Ebey on Whidbey Island.

Canoe travel by the Northwest tribes must have been very routine, as commonplace as our shopping trips to the city today. It also appears that, when invited, the invitee felt an obligation to show up. Much singing, dancing, and gift giving took place. Considering the many large gatherings at Little Boston over the years, Port Gamble must have been a very convenient meeting place.[46]

The end of an era came in 1940, when the now dilapidated old village on the Spit was burned to the ground by a group of Kitsap County and federal officials in a well-intended effort to facilitate a seamless move into the twenty new houses that had been built with loan funds assembled by then-Congressman Warren Magnuson. Despite the good intentions, watching the only homes they had ever known go up in smoke must have been a bitter pill to swallow for those residents.

A way of life was gone. The Port Gamble S'Klallam would be hereafter expected to live their lives the way the rest of America lived, forsaking even more of their traditional ways. It is not surprising that many of them were devastated. In describing the events, Harry Fulton Sr. recalled a S'Klallam elder, Mrs. Mary Ann Adams, singing a tribal song in her chair, crying as her old village burned.[47]

CHAPTER 2

The Treaty of Point No Point: Rights that Live Today

Gina Stevens

*"Parents have a duty to care for their children. This duty includes providing love, guidance, education, a safe and healthy environment, financial support . . . access to S'Klallam family . . . and **an opportunity to exercise S'Klallam treaty rights."***[1]

T he S'Klallam signed the Treaty of Point No Point on January 26, 1855, well over a century ago, and the rights the S'Klallam reserved in their treaty are very much alive today.

Treaty rights are so important to the Port Gamble S'Klallam people that even the tribe's Family Code, adopted in 2002, explicitly recognizes that parents have a duty to provide their children with an opportunity to exercise those rights. To date, S'Klallam people have reserved and fought to exercise treaty rights in practice, by statute, and in the court system for over one hundred and fifty five years.

However, to say S'Klallam people have reserved and exercised their treaty rights is a crudely oversimplified and inadequate statement of what those rights mean. In fact, the S'Klallam people's very identity is inseparable from those rights. Recently, the tribe conducted a series of interviews with individual tribal families to develop an Indian Child Welfare practice manual, and when asked if the tribe as a whole could serve as a child's permanent home, one couple said:

> [It's] very important to keep the kids within the tribe. . . . [Its very important that] they get to know their culture, and clams, and fish . . . and the beach, they need all of that in their lives, and if they're off reservation, they wouldn't have that.[2]

The couple associated the tribe and its culture with clams, fish, and the beach, and identified these things as a *need* in the life of a S'Klallam child.

What is a treaty? What treaty rights did the S'Klallam reserve, and why are they so important? Treaties are agreements between sovereign nations. Indian governments used treaties to confirm and retain rights such as the sovereign right of self-governance, fishing and hunting rights, and jurisdictional rights over their lands. The federal government used Indian treaties to secure land cessions from the Indians. Treaties did not, as is commonly assumed, *grant* rights to Indians from the United States. Tribes did cede certain rights to the United States government, but they *reserved* the rights they never gave away.[3]

In 1855, the S'Klallams, Skokomish, and Chemakums assembled together to meet with representatives of the federal government to consider whether to sign a treaty or not. The ultimate goal of the federal government was to acquire land and concentrate the Indians onto reservations:

> It is however proposed, if practicable, to remove all the Indians on the East side of the Sound as far as the Snohomish; as also the S'Klallams to Hoods Canal, and generally to admit as few Reservations as possible, with the view of finally concentrating them in one.[4]

The Treaty of Point No Point: Rights that Live Today

Settlers had continued to arrive and move into the Pacific Northwest and began to encroach upon the territory of the numerous established tribes. The interaction between the settlers and the Indians led to a great deal of hostility, forcing the government's perceived need to extinguish Indian title to the lands in order to keep peace between the Indians and settlers.[5]

Acquiring title to the land was the federal government's ultimate goal, but it is equally clear that the tribes did not want to give up their land. A Skokomish leader speaking at the Point No Point Treaty Council was likely voicing the concern of all the Indians present:

> I am not pleased with the idea of selling at all. I want you to hear what I have to say. All the Indians here have been afraid to talk, but I wish to speak and be listened to. I don't want to leave my land. It makes me sick to leave it. I don't want to go from where I was born. I am afraid of becoming destitute.[6]

It is easy to understand why the S'Klallams may have been "afraid to talk." In *Shadows of Our Ancestors*, editor Jerry Gorsline notes that the S'Klallam were generally quiet during the treaty discussions because a Klallam village had been shelled by a ship as a punitive measure sometime prior to the discussions.[7]

The hostility between the non-Indians and tribes was very real—as was everyone's desire for the land—but it appears that the federal government knew that hostility alone was not enough of a driving factor for the tribes to consider giving up everything. The federal representatives also promised the tribes: (1) compensation for their lands; (2) a place to live on the Skokomish Reservation; (3) schools; (4) doctors; (5) their own homes; and, (6) after giving the tribes presents, the promise of more after the treaty was signed.[8] It's not clear the tribes fully understood the two-day treaty discussions, as the meetings were conducted in the Chinook Jargon, and translators had to interpret for each respective tribe. The Chinook Jargon was a trade language commonly used as a way around the "diversity and forbidding complexity of northwest tribal languages."[9]

The Treaty of Point No Point: Rights that Live Today

In spite of the hostility, all the promises within the treaty, and the incomprehensible language, it is clear the S'Klallam people recognized the need to retain their right to hunt, fish, and gather—to preserve the S'Klallam way of life. During the treaty discussions, Chief *čičməha'n* [*Chits-a-mah-han*] of the S'Klallam people, also known as the Duke of York, said:

I am happy since I have heard the paper read and since I have understood Gov. Stevens— particularly, since I have been told that I could look for food where I pleased, and not in one place only. . . . We are willing to go up to the Canal since we know we can fish elsewhere— we shall only leave there to get salmon, and when done fishing will return to our houses.[10]

S'Klallam clam basket. Stephen DeCoteau illustration, courtesy of the Port Gamble S'Klallam Tribe.

The treaty article reserving these rights states:

> The right of taking fish at usual and accustomed grounds and stations is further secured to said Indians, in common with all citizens of the United States; and of erecting temporary houses for the purpose of curing; together with the privilege of hunting and gathering roots and berries on open and unclaimed lands. Provided, however, that they shall not take shell-fish from any beds staked or cultivated by citizens.[11]

Ultimately, the S'Klallam, Skokomish and Chemakum ceded or surrendered approximately 750,000 acres of land to the federal government, but reserved their aboriginal right to hunt, fish, and gather.

Who were the S'Klallam treaty signers, and could they have possibly known their diligence to reserve hunting, fishing, and gathering rights

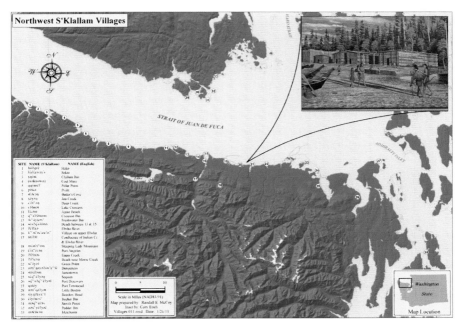

S'Klallam village sites pre-treaty signing.
Map courtesy of the Lower Elwha Klallam Tribe.

in 1855 would continue to be the livelihood of the S'Klallams over 150 years later? One of the S'Klallam treaty signers is listed as *Tuls-met-tum*, Lord Jim, a S'Klallam sub-chief.[12] It appears this signer was the grandson of Chief *Ste-tee-thlum* the Younger, and the uncle of Susie and Mary Littleman, who came to Little Boston and married into the Fulton and Charles families.[13]

Chief *Ste-tee-thlum* the Younger was sixteen years old in 1777, when he married a Nanimo princess, *Tsus-khee-na-kheen*, and together had seven sons and one daughter. *T'what-ski*, the third son of Chief *Ste-tee-thlum* the Younger, and the uncle to the S'Klallam treaty signer, was well known for his prowess as a hunter and fisher. His popularity grew and fostered jealousy among other tribes, and as a result, members of the Haida Tribe sought to shame him by capturing and enslaving him. Ironically, *T'what-ski* outsmarted the would-be captors when he appealed to their hunger with the smell of salmon cooking over an open fire and made a quick escape while they were distracted.[14]

From Chief *Ste-tee-thlum* the Younger's time in 1777, to the signing of the treaty in 1855, and up through today, the vital importance of fishing and hunting—later enshrined as rights in the treaty—is well documented. It's hard to imagine the S'Klallam treaty signers were thinking ahead a century and a half when they reserved their hunting, fishing, and gathering rights in writing; however,

Claude "Skip" George and Benny Anderson, 1939, happily carrying their catch of salmon. Photo courtesy of the Seattle Post-Intelligencer Collection.

it's abundantly clear that treaty rights have been and continue to be an inherent and consistent way of life that has spanned centuries and generations of S'Klallam people.

Fishing rights in particular have been at the forefront of publicity and controversy. One only has to look to the "fish wars" of the 1970s and the Boldt decision to find well-documented years of hard won battles for the tribes.[15] Washington State tribes had always fished, but when fishing became lucrative and non-Indians began to dominate the industry, the State of Washington attempted to regulate Indian fisheries practices, leading to years of litigation. U.S. District Court Judge George Boldt's ruling held that the United States' mid-1850s treaties with Washington tribes provided that Indians always were entitled to half the salmon and steelhead harvest in their traditional fishing grounds off-reservation. Boldt ruled that Washington State had virtually no authority over tribal fishing; in fact, the tribes ceded fishing rights to non-Indian settlers—not the other way around. The decision also established tribes as "co-managers" with the State over Washington's salmon fisheries resources.[16]

The Boldt decision was no easy victory for Washington tribes, and while fishing rights have been at the center of disputes for decades, it's important to note that hunting rights are equally important. In the early 1990s, the Point No Point Treaty Council—an organization made up of the Skokomish Tribe and three S'Klallam Tribes—commissioned Dr. Barbara Lane to analyze the Treaty of Point No Point hunting provision. Lane stated:

> The off-reservation hunting and gathering provisions in the treaties made in Washington Territory in 1854-55 represent a departure in part from prior United States treaty policy. In contrast to earlier treaties in other parts of the country, the Washington Territory treaties contain no language limiting Indian access to off-reservation lands for hunting and gathering purposes, to lands ceded under a given treaty.[17]

Dr. Lane concluded that the limiting language was omitted intentionally: the treaty negotiators and Indians alike understood that the Indians travelled seasonally to procure resources in a variety of localities.[18] If the Indians' hunting and gathering had been restricted to the reservations established under the treaties or even to the areas of land the tribes ceded, they likely would not have signed the treaty.

Hunting is on par with fishing as an inextricable part of S'Klallam life. And while hunting and gathering hasn't been fought over or litigated to the same extent as fishing, the Port Gamble S'Klallam Tribe equally regulates and manages hunting and gathering with the primary purpose of protecting, enhancing, and managing wildlife resources.[19]

S'Klallam people had a unique relationship with the wildlife resources: elk, deer, mountain goat, cougar, black bear, and other wildlife. To fail to protect, manage, and enhance wildlife resources today would be the equivalent of destroying a known quality of life. As the S'Klallam historically understood, "[Indian] People did not conceive of themselves

The Treaty of Point No Point: Rights that Live Today

Rose Purser with granddaughter, Brandy, in the mid 1970s enjoying shellfish. The practice of harvesting fish, shellfish, and game has brought families together for generations. Photo courtesy of the Port Gamble S'Klallam Archives.

as owners of the game in their territories, but rather saw themselves and the animals as co-inhabitants of the place."[20]

As recently as February 2010, the three S'Klallam tribes released a joint press statement in an effort to educate state citizens about the critical importance of managing wildlife:

> Tribal hunters do not hunt for sport. They hunt to put meat on their family's dinner table, or provide food for guests at traditional ceremonies. They also gather materials to make cultural artifacts, such as ceremonial drums constructed of cedar and elk skin. Wildlife in the Northwest is of inestimable value to its native people.

The Treaty of Point No Point: Rights that Live Today

The loss of habitat, human population growth, development, the increasing demand for resources, non-native species invasions, and a changing climate all present wildlife managers with challenges. We sincerely hope that the leaders of Washington State will realize that addressing these challenges requires cooperation, not confrontation.

Most important, we invite all citizens of Washington State and tribal alike to join us in ensuring that the world we leave for our grandchildren will be as rich in the abundance and diversity of wildlife as the one our grandparents left to us.[21]

It is disheartening that, 156 years after signing the treaty, the S'Klallam people must continue to explain to their non-Indian neighbors about a way of life that they have lived and sought to preserve since time immemorial. If the larger non-Indian community could understand the S'Klallam perspective, then perhaps the next 156 years could truly become years of collaboration.

The loss of fish and wildlife, and the loss of the ability to harvest and hunt is, in effect, the same as the loss of an entire people. Fishing and hunting is not something S'Klallam people do, it is who they are.

CHAPTER 3

"What Shall We Eat If We Sell Our Land?"[1]
The S'Klallam Natural World
Emily Mansfield and Ron Charles

S'Klallam Head Start Teacher: "What is your favorite season?"

John Aikman, Age 4: "Sockeye!"

In August 1906, six-year-old Irene Fulton left Little Boston with her Solomon grandparents in a large seagoing canoe, loaded with belongings and other family members. The only thing missing was Irene's mother, Alice, who had recently passed away. For over a week, the canoeing family arose in the early morning to take advantage of the tides and winds that would help push their heavy craft south through Admiralty Inlet and Puget Sound to the Puyallup River. If the wind came from the north, as it often does in August, up went the sail. Riding an incoming tide up the river, the family stopped at their camping destination in front of Cushman Hospital and hollered, "Canoe up!" A wagon appeared and hauled the canoe up onto the riverbank, where it would rest for several weeks, covered with mats, amid hundreds of other huge canoes that had come from as far away as Neah Bay, British Columbia, and Alaska. The wagon transported the family to the nearby hop fields, where they harvested the crop, visited with friends from other tribes, and earned some money. Often, the Solomons and other S'Klallam families arrived on the Puyallup early enough to work as strawberry or raspberry pickers before the hops harvest. After the harvest, they followed the tides back to Port Gamble Bay, stopping in along Seattle's waterfront on the way.[2]

Irene's childhood trip to the Puyallup hop fields was reminiscent of the seasonal travels her S'Klallam ancestors made every year to fill their canoes with dried fish, berries, and venison for their winter meals. By the early 1900s, seasonal work picking hops and berries had become part of the annual cycle of resources that traveling Port Gamble S'Klallam families relied upon during a typical year. Irene, at age 92, described the rest of the summer seasons of her childhood:

> And then we'd come home and just stay for maybe a week. Then we'd go up to Brinnon, and that's when they'd go and dry fish. They'd catch salmon on the river and dry it. Then we'd stay up there for a long time. Boy, we used to have good times![3]

Both before and during treaty times, S'Klallam families' lives revolved around the seasons, foods, and other resources that varied through the year. They fished, shellfished, hunted, and trapped. They gathered berries, roots, medicinal plants, and other foods and materials during their regular seasonal travels.

S'Klallam children learned early on that all of life was connected. As Clara (George) Jones told her children, the bounty of food provided by nature occurs in cycles that the observant person can expect:

> When the salmonberries came out in the spring, the clams were the fattest. When the tides were big, you could get sea urchin and barnacles off the rocks. Then the *sxʷaʔya 'səm* [soapberry] was green and ready and there were little grunt fish under the rocks.[4]

Everyone knew that certain low-tide locations during the spring and early summer yielded the best sea urchins. Smelt, herring, ducks, and codfish all came in at a certain time, a certain season. Families usually ate traditional food in its season.[5]

Because the Port Gamble S'Klallam came from different pre-treaty S'Klallam villages before settling at Port Gamble Bay, their ancestors traveled seasonally to hunt, collect marine resources, and gather plants in all the areas used by S'Klallam people. The Elwha and Dungeness Rivers supported some of the largest salmon runs in the region. Elk hunts took groups of S'Klallam hunters to the passes in the center of the Olympic Mountains. The waters and beaches of the Strait of Juan de Fuca yielded halibut, salmon, ducks, marine mammals, and dozens of other fish and shellfish. Both the S'Klallam and other Indian people would set up camps on San Juan Island to take advantage of the rich Salmon Bank off the island's southeast side, repeating the process in other areas of the San Juans. Whidbey Island camas fields drew whole families of both S'Klallam and other groups, and Hood Canal's salmon fisheries and hunting and gathering resources attracted S'Klallam from villages as far away as Clallam Bay to join their Twana friends and relatives.[6]

S'KLALLAM FISHERIES[7]

Fish	**Time**	**Method**
Spring salmon	*Mid April – July*	Trap, trolling, gillnet
Spring salmon	*Late July*	Gillnet, trap
Humpback	*August – end of October*	Trap, spear, line
Silver salmon	*May – November*	Trap. line, gillnet, spear
Dog salmon	*Follow silvers*	
Steelhead	*Dec., Jan., Feb.*	Trap, line in river
Halibut	*April – September*	Line
Ling cod	*April – September*	Line, spear close to shore
Flounder	*April – September*	Speared from canoe
Herring	*Mid Feb. – late March*	Rakes; eggs harvested on kelp and on branches placed in Port Gamble Bay
Smelts	*September*	Hole dug on beach
Sandlance (aka Candlefish)	*Sept. – late Oct.*	Dug and picked up on beach

When the S'Klallam signed the Treaty of Point No Point in 1855, they fully expected to continue their traditional ways of obtaining and using the bountiful resources of their homeland and the vast areas where they hunted, fished and gathered. For the first sixty years after the treaty, for the most part, they were able to do so.

Many generations of S'Klallam traveled to Hood Canal during the summer and fall. Often the whole village went. Some went to Hamma Hamma, some to Brinnon, some to Tahuya, and some to Seabeck. There they caught and smoked salmon while visiting with their Twana-speaking friends and family. Even Chehalis and Squaxin people came to the mouth of the Skokomish River when they heard S'Klallam were there. The families also gathered huckleberries and hunted in the mountains during these trips. On their return, they bound two canoes together with planks, forming a platform to carry their new supply of goods.[8]

Seabeck was one of the favorite annual fishing places of the Port Gamble S'Klallam old timers. They traveled here for their winter supplies, fishing in the river at Seabeck and the creeks to the north and south. S'Klallam, Chemakum, and Twana often gathered at Seabeck, where they would gamble and sing with friends and relatives to fill the hours when they were not fishing.[9] The lagoon at the head of Seabeck Bay was called *dE'bEdEb,* "The place where you hear the sound of dancing feet" (now, Nick's Lagoon).[10]

Irene (Fulton) Purser's trips to Hood Canal, the hop fields, and other locations followed the ways of her immediate ancestors—ways her grandfather, Solomon (b. 1850) had learned from his parents and grandparents. As much as they could, Port Gamble S'Klallam people continued the traditional seasonal patterns that had defined S'Klallam life for centuries.[11] But by the time Irene's generation reached adulthood, their freedom to maneuver was drastically shrinking.

By the early 1900s, Washington State had banned the use of fishing nets and Indian fishing weirs in rivers. The state also determined that, off the reservations, Indian fishermen were required to follow the state's regulations. At first, the new laws may not have been uniformly enforced against Indians in undeveloped areas of either the Straits or Hood Canal. But as the non-Indian population grew and development increased in these areas, so did state interference with Indian fisheries.[12]

Port Gamble S'Klallam families were still camping on Hood Canal during the childhoods of Kate (Anderson) Moran (b. 1908), Martin Charles (b. 1914), and Dorothy (Day) George (b. 1922). Kate and Martin both recalled camping and fishing at Brinnon. Martin said:

Irene (Fulton) Purser.
Photo courtesy of John Stamets.

> The whole tribe used to go camping up in Brinnon and made their smokehouses with cedar branches. They'd build up little saplings and put the branches on top and smoke their salmon inside there.[13]

By the time Daisy (Garrison) Day Fulton took young Dorothy to Hood Canal, she was canning or salting the salmon right on the beach. Dorothy remembered that they would haul empty jars to their campsite. As soon as the jars were all filled with berries or salmon, the group would go home.[14]

According to Harry Fulton Jr. (b. 1915), these families made their last trip to their summer and fall encampments in the 1920s. By that time, the mid-Hood Canal population was rising, so the state began to curtail Indian fishing in the area.

S'KLALLAM ADAPT CHANGING ECONOMIES INTO THEIR LIFE WAYS

From their earliest contact with explorers, traders, and settlers, S'Klallam adeptly turned the newcomers' needs for resources to their own advantage. When sailors on the ships of Quimper (1790), Vancouver (1792), and Wilkes (1841) needed rations, the S'Klallam were there to trade fish, venison, berries, furs, and ducks for goods. When the Hudson's Bay Company at Fort Nisqually sought furs, S'Klallam people arrived in canoes loaded with pelts. When the Puget Mill Co. on Port Gamble Bay needed dogfish oil to grease its saws, S'Klallam gladly increased their credit accounts at the company store by providing the fish. S'Klallam fishing know-how helped stock the Hudson's

Photo sent to George Pulsifer, December 1916. In the new cash economy, S'Klallam families relied on seasonal work, traveling to labor in the hops and berry fields in the same way they traditionally traveled to harvest plants, fish, and game. Note that the girls seem to have hops draped over their shoulders. Photo courtesy of the Anderson/Moran family.

Bay Company salmon salting operation on San Juan Island and the cannery in Port Angeles.[15] These activities, like Irene (Purser) Fulton's childhood journey to the Puyallup hop fields in

1906, were examples of how S'Klallam adapted to the new cash economy in ways that least disrupted their traditional way of life in rhythm with the seasons.

Through the late 1800s and early 1900s, seasonal work in various resource industries was a natural extension of traditional S'Klallam resource travels. Seasonal labor supplied needed cash while leaving families free to pursue their own subsistence travels. Like the fisheries that preceded them, camps, hops, strawberry, and raspberry picking also provided a social gathering place for people from different tribes. Thelma Fulton and Alvin Oya's long marriage began with their meeting in the raspberry fields in Alderton.[16] These trips to the berry fields lasted at least into the late 1940s.

Even while Port Gamble S'Klallam children were enjoying their families' seasonal outings, their grandparents chafed at the state's fishing restrictions. The elders never forgot the promises made in the treaty and repeated to them by their elders. For example, in 1914, although their lack of land was the primary concern in negotiations with the federal government, Port Gamble S'Klallam leaders made certain to include in their demands the enforcement of their treaty right to fish, hunt, and gather.[17]

Even after the Hood Canal trips were only a memory, families still traveled together to areas closer to Port Gamble Bay, and they often camped for a week or more in the late spring, summer, and early fall. Today's Port Gamble S'Klallam elders vividly remember the few areas where they could fish for themselves inconspicuously and without state interference: Hansville/Point No Point, Twin Spits/Foulweather Bluff, Port Ludlow, and Whiskey Spit (Point Hannon on Hood Head). Although the places were limited, today's elders remember getting the same foods and materials at the same time of year as their ancestors.

When today's elders look back on their trips between the 1920s and 1940s, they remember them as fun times spent with grandparents and family. For example, Con Sullivan loved going with his grandfather, William George Sr., when he fished at Whiskey Spit. Sullivan camped with his Uncle Emore ("Ame") and others at Hansville, Twin Spits, and Skunk Bay. Whether they were carrying octopus, butter clams, rock cod from Port Ludlow, or ling cod from Foulweather Bluff, they never came back empty handed.[18]

Recalling his childhood in the 1930s and '40s, Ted George noted that around June every year they would see someone heading for Point No Point, and they would know the fish were in. Everyone packed up a canvas tent and blankets and went down to camp, cook over beach fires, and fish. At the time, there were no houses at the site.[19]

BILL GARRISON'S SALTED SALMON

Dorothy George remembered her Uncle Bill's method of salting salmon:

> [They salted] Silvers, kings, humpies, they called it. It's that
> pale fish. But I remember especially watching Uncle Bill do it.
> He knew when to salt them enough and then he used to take
> a potato and when it floated in the salt water, then it was all
> set. And he didn't touch it any more until he wanted some for a
> meal. Then he'd get some out and soak it in fresh water, drain
> it, soak in some more fresh water. He did that three times and
> by the third time, he was done soaking, it was just like fresh fish.
> He used a five-gallon crock pot. [The time of year you do that is]
> usually when you first start catching salmon.[20]

Even when some families' seasonal travels were constrained by full time millwork, they would still go camping at nearby fishing and gathering spots during the two-week mill shutdown. For instance, Rose Purser remembers once camping in a tiny shack with her grandparents and other families at Port Ludlow, where there was nice, dry sand.[21]

Before homes were built in the area, almost any kind of seafood could be gathered at Port Ludlow. People would tie up at a big rock in the Port Ludlow Bay, where a ledge allowed them to fill their boats with all kinds of seafood. Christine Charles remembered refusing to eat the sea cucumbers![22]

During the summer fish camps, many S'Klallam like Irene (Jackson) Purser hold vivid childhood memories of their grandmothers, mothers, and aunties baking bread in the sand.[23] Susie (Dick) Charles cooked on the beach for everyone camping nearby. Her daughter, Christine, remembered her delicious sand-baked bread:

> She used to make bread, it's like how you bake powder biscuits. She used to make a hot fire and that sand gets really hot after it goes for quite a while. She'd flip that sand over and put that dough on that sand that she'd cover up with the other sand. That hot sand. And I don't remember how long she left it there, and she'd take that sand off and she'd pick up that bread, it'd be done. The sand didn't stick to it, there'd be some sand there, but she'd just brush it off. That tasted good![24]

Skip George's grandma also made blackberry jam at the beach to go on the hot bread![25]

One way S'Klallam families adapted to the state's restrictions on their fishing activities was to visit relatives on reservations with rivers. When Rose Purser's family lived in Centralia, they used to travel to Skokomish when the fish were running in the Skokomish River. There, they visited her great-grandmother (Angie Peterson Fulton's mother), camped in tents, and fished with relatives, usually other Fultons from Port Gamble. These activities provided canned, smoked, and salted salmon for the winter.[26]

In a similar vein, one summer when Foster Jones had no longshoreman work, he took his boys to Quinault to fish Dolly Hyasman's net. Dolly was Foster's cousin, and a close enough relative that the Joneses were welcome. Russell Fulton Jr. went to Neah Bay every summer to troll for salmon with the Makahs.[27]

TROLLING

After development and state enforcement curtailed Indian fisheries on Hood Canal and on other rivers, the Port Gamble S'Klallam had to resort to trolling for salmon in the waters around Port Gamble Bay and Point No Point. Trolling was certainly not a new practice; ancestors had trolled for salmon even when greater numbers could be caught at the mouths of streams or on the rivers. George Sparks (b. 1866), for example, was adept at trolling and received the same Indian name as a great troller of early times. Around the turn of the century, Sammy Charles made his own trolling spoons from sheets of brass, copper, and nickel. He advised younger fishermen to go out trolling either just before daylight or just after dark.[28]

A Hansville resident recalled watching Sammy row his skiff off Point No Point, trolling for salmon with just a hand line. She said it was funny to watch the non-Indian fishermen follow right behind him, trying to emulate his every move because they knew Sammy was the best troller around. But they never could catch the big kings like Sammy did, as he must have possessed secrets he could only have learned from many years of fishing at the point.[29]

Like Sammy Charles, Russell Fulton Sr. trolled with plugs and spoons while rowing. Later, Russell Fulton Jr. trolled the ocean waters off Neah Bay, displaying the same skill as his father, although his boat and gear were modern. Despite the contrast in methods, both men possessed the same S'Klallam know-how.[30]

The S'Klallam Natural World

During and after the 1930s, while the state kept an alert eye open to arrest Indians fishing for salmon, other species were less restricted. S'Klallam people had always relished a wide variety of seafood and knew how to fish for it. Now, without a whole winter's supply of dried salmon from Hood Canal, families began to rely more upon other species. Ivan George's parents fished for lingcod and rock cod at Twin Spits.[31]

Christine Charles' mother, Susie (Dick) Charles, waded in hip boots for cockles and crab. She raked the crabs into a galvanized tub that she dragged on a rope. Sometimes she cooked the crabs in saltwater right on the beach, and in the tub where she caught them.[32]

Dorothy (Day) George's grandfather, Bill Pulsifer[33] from Skokomish, used to tease her S'Klallam family because they ate grunt fish, so named because when a fisherman (or child) poked around for them under a rock, they made a loud noise.[34] According to Gene Jones, elders esteemed "grunters" for their spiritual qualities: when a person was close to death, eating three grunters gave them back their will to live.[35]

Octopus fishing was a big event. To catch them, most people traveled to Lip Lip, on the southeast side of Marrowstone Island.[36] Martha John described how S'Klallam fished for devilfish, as octopuses were called:

> To catch devilfish, you take a long stick and tickle them. They live under a big rock. Most Indians know where to find them. Devilfish are very curious so when they are tickled, they come out from under the rock and then they can be clubbed on the head.[37]

Gertrude Adams' father went to Washington Harbor to lure a *st'ix̌ʷaʔc̓*—devilfish—out from under its rock. He'd bring it right home for her mother to cut up and boil.[38]

The specialized practice of flounder fishing was also passed down from one S'Klallam generation to the next, and is still remembered by today's elders. The area now known as Driftwood Keys was a favorite spot for flounder fishing. Skip George learned from his Uncle Ivan George:

> Me and Uncle Ivar used to go out spearing flounders at night.
> Used to put the headlamp on the bow of the boat on a stick . . .
> and Uncle Ivar'd stand up there in the bow of the boat and see
> them little flounders and go *thith,* spear them. The spear was
> long—it was about ten feet long.[39]

Martin Charles caught flounder by stepping on them. They were then
baked over alder limbs and eaten with little potatoes cooked in the hot
beach sand.[40]

Alice (George) Fulton (b. 1930) describes her experiences learning
about herring fishing from her grandparents:

> In the spring of the year, they'd be harvesting herring and
> they'd have tubs and tubs of it. We learned how to string herring
> on sticks and then they'd hang them and smoke them. The
> smokehouses were built with wide cracks between the boards
> and you could peek in and see all the fish hanging.[41]

Whether they were on a week-long camping trip or a day's outing,
wherever they went the S'Klallam got whatever was there—whether
it was fish, clams, game, berries, or medicinal plants. William Jones is a
living example of this S'Klallam trait. In his seventies, Bill is renowned
for his skills as hunter, fisher, and provider. He learned as a child to go
after everything possible. Even as a youngster, whenever he went out
he took his .22—or his shotgun if ducks were around—a clam fork, a
shovel, and his fishing gear. He'd come home with enough food for five
or six families.[42]

While families all had their favorite places to acquire resources away
from home, much of what Port Gamble S'Klallam people needed could
be found around Port Gamble Bay. The rich shellfish beds on the bay
were always close at hand, even when stormy winter weather kept
people off the water.[43]

Ivan George and his father, William, sometimes caught a couple of
salmon on the way to work at the mill. William then cleaned the fish

on his lunch break.[44] Victor and Bernard Tom, like many others, fished for salmon and trout in Middle Creek.[45] Irene (Fulton) Purser fished for black bass in Port Gamble Bay. Bennie and Martha George brought their children from George's Corner back to Little Boston to fish for cod. When the cod came in, the Georges knew they would meet all their friends and relatives out fishing on the water.[46]

But above all other marine resources, the Port Gamble S'Klallam relished their clams. With an abundance of shellfish in Port Gamble Bay and in the absence of a large salmon river on the reservation, the Port Gamble S'Klallam people gravitated toward shell fishing. They dug clams wherever they could, but Port Ludlow, Hazel Point, and Scow Bay were favorite twentieth century locations.[47]

In Port Gamble Bay, clams were available all year, but spring was the best time to go digging. Like most traditional S'Klallam women, Nancy Jackson dug clams and dried them on the warming oven of her wood stove. Her granddaughter, Irene (Jackson) Purser, recalled:

> We used to get sugar in sacks and she used to put them in little sacks. Five pound bags and then . . . she'd put brown paper bags up there and when they got dry she put them in a bag, tie 'em behind the stove and when she'd want clam chowder or something she'd go open the bag and make her chowder with it. Mother [Ellen (Moses) Jackson] used to can clams, but she used to dry them first. She did the same thing with blackberries.[48]

Martha George explained that in the old days clams were dried on an open fire. But her grandmother "got modern" and dried them in the oven. "The clams would have to be pounded with a hammer because they were so hard!"[49]

The rich shellfish beds in Port Gamble Bay helped many people through hard times. Port Gamble town residents at the turn of the century called Mary Jackson "Clam Mary" because of her routine of selling clams up and down their streets. Others also clammed commercially. It was something a person could do as soon as the tide went out, when there

In the Port Gamble S'Klallam community, no family gathering is complete without a clam bake. A few aspects of the preparation may have changed between the old ways—like this photo from the 1940s—and the new. For example, laying wet newspapers on the clam bed instead of seaweed; but the Port Gamble S'Klallam are still famous for their clam bakes. Photo courtesy of the Port Gamble S'Klallam Archives.

were no other jobs around.

For example, Ivan George remembered that all of the Georges dug clams to sell. They got seventy-five cents for two five-gallon cans of clams. In the 1930s, when a few dollars bought a box of groceries, clam digging was decent money.[50]

Martin Charles and Harry "Jum" Fulton Jr. sometimes caught a tub of crabs, cooked them and sold them for twenty-five cents each to the sailors on the ships across the Bay.[51]

For many, like Rose Purser, clamming was a regular part of the family's income. After she got married, Rose became a clam digger to supplement Rudy's sawmill income. When the tides were at night, they dug

The S'Klallam Natural World

by gaslight.[52]

Lloyd Fulton still camped at Hazel Point in the 1950s, digging clams for spending money. No one bothered him in those years.[53]

To this day, the Port Gamble S'Klallam are uniquely well known in Indian country for their traditional clambakes. Skip and Betty George recalled how clambakes were held on the beach during their childhood:

> We used to cut cedar branches off and cover up our clams with cedar branches and seaweed, and cook them that way on our clambakes. People wouldn't know how to do that anymore. But that's how we used to do it when we didn't have no burlap sacks. We used seaweed and cedar on the beach. Guess that's the old Indian way . . . the cedar didn't have all the pitch that the fir and hemlock has on it. So we used the cedar boughs. And the seaweed. I remember we used to go out on low tide and gather all the seaweed and make a big pile of seaweed.[54]

ELLEN (SIGO) GEORGE'S CLAM BASKET

Ivan George recalls his mother's method of making a clam basket:

Ellen Sigo George

She made them out of cedar limbs. You know they split the long skinny limbs and spread them and make baskets and fill the baskets up with cockles. Just walk out in the water and dunk `em a couple of times and the sand would run right through them. She would take a cedar limb and bend it around like that and then they'd tie and use that regular rope. . . . They used to get that rope in bales and they braided a lot of that rope right in with their baskets, you know around the edge of the top of the basket. And they'd sew the top of the basket clean around it with the big limb around it, the top. And then they'd put their clams in. The baskets come in handy for everything when you was fishing and everything.[55]

Ellen (Sigo) George, 1904. Photo courtesy of the Port Gamble S'Klallam Archives.

Treaty Fishing Rights on Trial

State regulation and increased development drove S'Klallam fishermen away from most of their former net fishing locations. Lloyd Fulton lamented the loss of camping areas to population growth:

> We used to camp over at Whiskey Spit and at Port Ludlow. Nobody would bother you. Nobody would kick you off the beach or anything....Times have really changed. You can't camp at any place anymore because homes are coming up all over.[56]

In spite of state regulation, people continued to fish, usually at nearby streams and always with the risk of getting a ticket from the state. Through the 1900s, a good chum run continued to make it to Seabeck every November, and so did Martin Charles. Charles gaffed chum salmon for smoking. He was adamant that it was his right to do so and he would have gone to jail, if caught. He insisted on going in broad daylight: "Everybody expects you to go at night. We'll go in the day!"[57]

Much like their ancestors, Charles and other tribal members never conceded that their fishing rights were lost. They continued to go secretly to their favorite streams in order to obtain their fish for smoking. The teenagers in the family were the "mules." Ron Charles' uncle dropped the boys off at the creek at the head of Liberty Bay in Poulsbo in the middle of the night with a gunnysack and a gaff. They were given the responsibility for spearing salmon for the family smokehouse.

Legal Chronology of S'Klallam
Treaty Fishing and Hunting[58]

1905   Elk hunting is banned by the state until 1933.

1915   Indians must follow state fishing and hunting regulations
off-reservation, except when fishing for family consumption
one half mile off shore in the salt waters bordering a
resevation, or in rivers that flowed through or bordered a
reservtion within five miles of reservation boundaries.

1964   Protest fish-ins staged at Frank's Landing. These were
followed by demonstrations and national attention over the
next decade.

1968   U.S. Supreme Court, in *Puyallup Tribe v. Department of
Game* upholds treaty fishing right but with the state's right
to regulate in a non-discriminatory way where "reasonable
and necessary." State continues its past practices of
arresting Indian fishermen.

1974   *U.S. v. Washington*—the Boldt decision—upholds the treaty
fishing right to fifty percent of the catch.

1994   *U.S. v. Washington* upholds treaty shellfish rights.

The S'Klallam Natural World

Throughout Washington State in the 1950s and '60s, Indian fishermen's frustration at the loss of their treaty rights grew. The Puyallup, Muckleshoot, and Nisqually Tribes embarked on a confrontational strategy to draw attention to the injustices all tribes encountered. Most of the protesters were dedicated groups of Indian people who had always tried to continue their fishing practices. However, the protest fisheries, or "fish-ins" (fisheries held with the express purpose of provoking state arrest) attracted more militant Indians, including out-of-state members of the American Indian Movement, and even a few non-Indian celebrities and thrill seekers. Indian people throughout Washington were of distinctly different minds about these tactics.

Although always supportive of regaining their treaty fishing rights, there was controversy among Port Gamble S'Klallam people over which tactics should be used. Most took a hands-off approach to the "fish-ins" because, in their lifetimes, they had only seen Indian people arrested for fishing violations. They were skeptical that radical efforts would gain anything.

Russ Fulton, Jr., and son, Jeff, 1970s. Prior to the Boldt decision, Russ purchased a state trolling license in order to avoid prosecution when commercially trolling in Neah Bay. Photo courtesy of Russell Fulton, Jr.

A few younger tribal members did get involved, although it was without their elders' blessings. In retrospect, one elder recently noted that Craig Purser should be acknowledged for his involvement in the fishing protests. "He was a militant but visionary voice."[59]

However controversial they were among the S'Klallam, the "fish-ins" and demonstrations did bring enough attention to the issue that in 1970, the United States sued the State of Washington over treaty fishing rights. Nine treaty tribes—mainly tribes with large rivers on their reservations—joined the lawsuit to affirm and enforce their treaty right to fish. The S'Klallam were not among the original plaintiffs in the case. After Judge Boldt issued his landmark decision in 1974 affirming the treaty right to catch fifty percent of the salmon, other tribes joined the case, including Port Gamble S'Klallam. In 1977, with the expert assistance of anthropologist Dr. Barbara Lane, Port Gamble S'Klallam proved to the court what S'Klallam elders had been insisting for over a century: that under the Treaty of Point No Point, the tribe had reserved the right to take fish in all of its usual and accustomed fishing locations.

Suddenly, tribal members found themselves legally able to fish commercially. But nearly a century had passed since their ancestors had fished the Strait of Juan de Fuca and Hood Canal for salmon. Besides, their traditional salmon fisheries were most often located either at the mouths of rivers or upstream. S'Klallam traditionally fished the Elwha, Dungeness, Dosewallips, Duckabush, and Hamma Hamma. No one had been taught how to fish commercially on the open waters with modern gear.

George Charles, a lifetime troller, went out and bought a gillnetter immediately after the Boldt decision. He encouraged his cousin, Ron, to apply for a new program at the BIA, where tribal members could borrow enough to get started in the fishing business. A lot of funds were available because many Indian people didn't understand the process or didn't have good credit. To his surprise, Ron got the loan and started to learn the business. For Ron Charles and others, the process was a lot of trial and error: they had to learn which boats worked well, which nets to use, and how and where to set nets. It took some time.

Bill Jones also quickly took advantage of the opportunity the Boldt decision opened. He bought a sixteen-foot boat with a thirty-five-horse motor and gillnetted for silvers around Quilcene. Through trial and error, he found that his 60-mesh net only went deep enough to catch fish in the early morning, when the fish came up closer to the surface. His brother, Bob, fared better with a bigger boat and a 120-mesh net.[60]

Ron Charles (far right) with other Northwest Indian Fisheries Commissioners: (left to right) Guy McMinds, Marvin Wilbur and Billy Frank, Jr. Charles worked on the Port Gamble S'Klallam Tribe's treaty fishing rights case, and he was actively involved in implementing the decision after it was handed down in 1974. In 1976, Charles was one of the five commissioners of the Northwest Indian Fish Commission, established after the Boldt Decision to assist member tribes in their role as natural resources co-managers. Photo courtesy of the Northwest Indian Fisheries Commission.

Skip George remembered that he had a lot to learn when he started fishing after the Boldt decision—not just about catching the fish, but about marketing them as well. He had no buyers, so he tried to sell the fish to people at the taverns. Soon, he found out he could make more selling smoked fish, so he learned how to smoke small pieces without having them fall off into the fire. When he was advised he could charge more, he said, "I don't care what they charge at the store. I'm giving them Indian prices! They was my fish, I can sell them at any price I want to sell them."[61]

In the years immediately following the Boldt decision, some white fishermen hired Indians with tribal fishing cards for one night at a time. The non-Indian "charter boat" would pocket most of the money and the catch counted against the Indian share. This practice was quickly outlawed.

Fishing was not only difficult at first for Port Gamble S'Klallam fishermen, but it was often dangerous. Many non-Indian fishermen reacted to the Boldt decision with defiance and violence. There were many accounts of non-Indians fishing illegally as an act of civil disobedience. Adding to the danger, Indian fishermen were greatly outnumbered by white fishermen. For example, when one Port Gamble S'Klallam fisherman came into the marina in Port Townsend, he was told not to land or he would be beaten up. There were stories of shots being fired. Some fishermen stopped going to rivers on the Straits because the harassment from sports fishermen was so bad.

State officials were complicit, sympathetic to the non-Indian fishers' cause. Governor Dan Evans even pleaded that he had no control over the situation. The tribes continually went back to Judge Boldt's courtroom and told of the unwillingness of the state to comply with Boldt's orders. For a time, the court actually took over the management of the Puget Sound fishery.

Even so, each year the western Washington tribes produced more fishermen, became more adept at regulating their own fisheries, received more legal backing by the courts, and finally achieved taking their fifty percent share of the salmon in the 1980s.

Meanwhile, the Port Gamble S'Klallam did not forget their treaty right to take shellfish. Historically, many families had made part of their living from clam digging in both the post-treaty economies and the traditional pre-treaty commercial trade. Unlike salmon fishing, where tribal fishers steered clear of confrontations with the state, Port Gamble S'Klallam shellfishers were far more assertive about their treaty right to harvest shellfish. They were often arrested, despite pleas from tribal leaders to not take their cases to state court, where bad law would be made.

Skip George remembered those days of harassment. For example, the sheriff once blocked him from accessing clam beds on Indian Island.

The S'Klallam Natural World

However, another time at Salisbury Point, he was stopped by an enforcement officer who knew him, knew he often dug clams for elders, and allowed him to exceed the limit to take clams to Auntie Dorothy and Uncle Ivar.[62]

Most shellfishing arrests did not end so pleasantly. Tribal leaders feared that if a shellfisher's case was appealed to the higher state courts, there would likely be an unfavorable ruling that would affect all future cases. Historically, state courts had not been friendly interpreters of Indian treaties. It became essential to the Port Gamble S'Klallam shellfishers that federal courts affirm their treaty right to shellfish. As a practical matter, this decision required all Washington treaty tribes to collectively file a shellfish version of the Boldt case. Port Gamble S'Klallam, along with the Suquamish, pushed the other tribes hard to go forward with the federal case.

When Judge Rafeedie upheld tribal shellfish rights in 1994, salmon fisheries were in a steep decline, with prices at an all-time low.[63] Boat owners found it very difficult to make a living salmon fishing anymore, but over the next few years many of them were able to switch their boats over to geoduck harvesting. The results produced pleasant surprises, and geoduck and crab proved to be lucrative fisheries.

Judge Boldt's affirmation of treaty fishing rights came with an important condition: each tribe had to manage and regulate its fishery. Not long after the decision, "Boldt Implementation Funds" came to the tribes through the BIA. The Skokomish, Lower Elwha, and Port Gamble S'Klallam Tribes pooled their money to form the Point No Point Treaty Council in 1974, which the Jamestown S'Klallam joined in 1981 after they became federally recognized.[64] The Treaty Council was charged with protecting treaty rights and practicing good fisheries management. In fact, it hired the first biometrician in the Northwest. The Point No Point Treaty Council became a model fisheries management agency and later took up the cause of treaty hunting rights protection as well.

As fisheries, and later shellfisheries, became an economic force in the Port Gamble S'Klallam community, the tribal government devoted more attention to fisheries management. In 1975, the tribe began an aquaculture project with salmon holding pools. A few years later, it entered an agreement with the state for a pen project raising coho. As the coho returned, many Port Gamble members developed a set net fishery in Port Gamble Bay.[65]

Of course, the treaty fishing right would be meaningless without fish. Therefore, co-management between the tribe and state and federal agencies was key to protecting that right. Co-management included environmental protection of fish habitats, a responsibility the Port Gamble S'Klallam Tribe embraced. Ron Hirschi, a tribal biologist in the 1980s, recounted one example of S'Klallam advocacy through the protection of salmon streams from the ravages of logging. One summer, Ron and Shawn DeCoteau were reviewing streams slated for logging:

> We went out and sampled to see if there were fish, then met with officials to go over possible ways of preventing damage to habitat. At that time, people were still pretty much anti-Indian and the role of the tribe, as a "co-manager," did not have much respect.
>
> Shawn and I had found fish in a small stream that was a tributary to Shine Creek. There was a hawk nest, so Shawn named this "Redtail Creek." We were to meet with officials from the Department of Natural Resources, Washington Department of Fish and Wildlife, and Pope & Talbot timber company. They all let us know the area was to be clear-cut because there was "no water on the site." At our meeting, Shawn very scientifically presented the data: we had walked the stream, sampled, and found fish for the entire length of the proposed clear-cut.
>
> Pope and the others demanded an onsite meeting. Shawn led the group along the small stream, showing them fish all along the way. Today, I drive along Highway 104 and look over at a stand of trees that would have been clear-cut if the tribe's representation had not been honored. Shawn saved that stream and many others that summer. Wild fish in the tribe's U&A![66]

The S'Klallam Natural World

Port Gamble S'Klallam and Point No Point Treaty Council advocacy for fisheries habitat extended to every corner of the S'Klallam resource use area. A recent example is dramatic: the runs of salmon on the Elwha and Dungeness Rivers were among the most extensive in the Pacific Northwest. Dams built on the Elwha in 1913 and 1927 decimated these runs. Recently, Elwha S'Klallam, supported by Jamestown and Port Gamble, led an effort to breach the dams in what will be a massive restoration of salmon habitat and runs.

Hunting

Bill Jones, at age 73, still takes an elk every year. Like many Port Gamble S'Klallam hunters, Bill learned to hunt from his father:

> My Dad [Foster Jones] was a real deer hunter. Well, he hunted everything too. But as little guys when we was really young we wasn't old enough to carry a gun but he'd take us along for eyes. 'Cause we could spot them animals a long ways away through the woods or whatever. . . . My Grandfather give me a dugout boat, seventeen feet long . . . [He would] give me three shells for the shotgun and he'd tell me "Now don't you shoot until you get at least two ducks lined up." . . . And I'd get anywhere from forty-five to fifty-five ducks with a box of shells.[67]

Bill Jones demonstrates how S'Klallam hunters continued their hunting tradition, despite having their treaty rights severely restricted by the state. Before treaty times, S'Klallam men hunted large and small mammals in the lowland areas all year. They hunted bear, deer, and marmot, among other animals, and joined in communal elk drives in the high mountains during the late summer and early fall. Some hunters took their families into the mountains for weeks at a time, where they camped and dried the meat before packing it home. Hunting and berry picking often occurred during the summer and fall at fishing encampments along Hood Canal.

S'Klallam also hunted waterfowl and marine mammals, including seal and whales, on the saltwater. For example, Chemakum Jim (James Webster Sr.'s father) hunted hair seals on Smith Island in the Strait of

Juan de Fuca.[68]

Few twentieth century Port Gamble S'Klallam elders remember the hunting forays of their ancestors first-hand. The weeks-long trips deep into the Olympic Mountains—to the headwaters of the Elwha or the rivers draining into Hood Canal—receded in memory by the 1900s. Like it did to traditional fisheries, the State of Washington infringed upon S'Klallam hunting places and practices beginning in the early 1900s.

State hunting limitations paralleled restrictions on fishing. Until around 1900, state game laws were rarely enforced on anyone, so there was little interference. But around 1913, conflicts with the state over hunting rights erupted. By this time, courts had ruled that Indians were subject to state law when hunting off the reservation. Skokomish hunters were even being arrested *on* their own reservation. One elder complained that Indians were arrested every time they went out to get a deer![69]

In 1905, the state outlawed all elk hunting, a ban that wasn't lifted until 1933. Even though elk had been plentiful in the Chimacum Valley and around Port Ludlow, they became off limits to S'Klallam hunters. By 1942, all hunting was illegal in Olympic National Park, important S'Klallam hunting grounds. These limitations may help explain comments by Lester Jackson, Con Sullivan, and Dorothy George that in their memory, Port Gamble S'Klallam men rarely hunted elk.[70]

Arrests of Skokomish, Suquamish, and Quinault hunters must have been well known among the Port Gamble S'Klallam, and these incidences no doubt discouraged them from resorting to many of their traditional practices and places. Over time, they lost previous knowledge about species they used to hunt farther up in the mountains, like marmot, because state restrictions forced them to hunt closer to home. The area now known as Driftwood Keys was a favorite deer hunting spot until it became so built up that there were more "No Trespassing" signs than deer. Present day elders mainly hunted on the reservation or in back of Cliffside. Ivan George recalled:

> There was real good blackberry patches all around that big bay in there....We used to shoot deer and everything down there.... Drag them down to the beach and put them in the canoe and got two pullers . . . had two pullers in that big canoe. Oar 'em home....Yeah [that was a lot of work].[71]

With all the waterfowl near Port Gamble Bay, duck hunting was a favorite way to feed S'Klallam families. In earlier times, among other places, Port Gamble S'Klallam ancestors would watch ducks dive for herring and then catch them with nets as they surfaced. The most common duck hunting spots were Discovery Bay and Scow Bay, whose spit meant "duck net." But the state and federal governments began restricting duck hunting in the early twentieth century. For a time, an Indian could not even *possess* a dead duck that had been killed legally by an oyster grower to protect their oyster beds. After strong protest by Indians, certain "fish ducks" were exempted from the ban.[72] Port Gamble S'Klallam elders' memories of duck hunting usually included these "fish ducks," as Bill Jones described:

> [We hunted] what we call coots. There's some with the little white heads, we call them "skunkies." And the big black ones, "bull coots" we call them....Them are all soup ducks; and mallards and widgeons and loon bills are all roasting ducks....Then there's saw bills mergansers and helldivers were flat roasting ducks.... Brandt. Mom used to stuff the Brandt.[73]

Jake Jones described the best time to hunt for ducks:

> You can't get them too early. They come in in the first part of winter, but then they're full of little small pinfeathers. You have to kind of wait until the middle of winter. Then if you wait too long, the herring come in and the ducks . . . eat herring and smelt and they get real big and fat but they get so fishy . . . they're no good to cook anymore for duck soup. Ducks usually eat clams and they dive down and get small clams and then their gizzard grinds up the clams, so they're good eating at that time before they get fishy.[74]

Irene (Jackson) Purser's family did a lot of duck hunting:

> We used to save the feathers for our pillows. We made mattresses
> or whatever we'd put on the floor—we used to have a whole
> pile of them. Somebody would come and just go get a feather
> bed and throw it on the floor and make a bed.[75]

The Jones family was particularly well known for their duck soup. As
Ted George said:

> No one makes duck soup anymore. Every once in awhile, one of
> the Jones got ducks and someone made duck soup, and Indians
> came crawling out of everywhere for it![76]

State arrests of Indian hunters continued unabated through the
twentieth century. For example, Geneva (Jones) Ives, mother of seven
children, was arrested by the State of Washington in April 1972. Her
crime? She had frozen venison for her family in her freezer. The meat
was confiscated and never returned. Port Gamble S'Klallam elders
testified for Geneva at her trial. They painted a picture of their need
for their treaty hunting rights. At that time, they said, three-quarters of
the meat eaten by tribal members came from the reservation: clams,
oysters, deer, quail, rabbit, ducks, pheasant, and fish from the Bay. "We
were brought up to depend upon the wild meats and things off our
own land," said Clara (George) Jones. Martha George added, "When you
hunt and get your game, it don't cost anything but your effort to get out
there. We were brought up that way [preferring wild game over store
meat] and it is passed from one generation to another."[77]

Ted George was arrested in 1988 for elk hunting in the Coyle unit south
of the Dosewallips Bridge. This is an area of checker-boarded National
Forest (where hunting was permitted) and private land (where it was
not) with few landmarks designating the difference. Three cars of
game wardens surrounded George, arrested him, and confiscated his
elk. After a full trial in which George forcefully asserted his treaty right
to hunt, he won. "We cleaned their clocks!" George said of the victory.
Later, the Director of the Department of Fish and Game was invited to

the Port Gamble S'Klallam Tribal Council. The Council warned him that before they would begin any talks with the state, his department would have to begin treating Indian hunters with more respect than they had treated Ted George.[78]

Around the same time as Ted George was defending his treaty right to hunt, Skokomish tribal members had also won some hunting cases in state court. They began writing their own hunting regulations and felt certain their hunters would be safe if they concentrated their hunting on federal lands. Port Gamble S'Klallam quickly followed the lead of their friends at Skokomish, and these tribes were among the earliest to regulate their own treaty hunting. While restricted to fewer locations than many hunters would like, S'Klallam hunters are once again exercising their treaty hunting rights to stock their freezers with deer and elk.

Generations of S'Klallam children went gathering with their grandmas, and many still do to this day. These three grandmas may have been on such an outing, although their baskets and grandchildren are not pictured. One of the women is likely Leda Laurence, Gertrude Adams' mother. Photo courtesy of Gertrude Adams.

Gathering

S'Klallam women would gather berries, roots, plant materials, and medicinal materials during fishing trips to places like Hood Canal, but the women also went on special gathering trips when a particular plant was in season.

Huckleberries, blueberries, wild blackberries, black caps, strawberries, salmonberries, elderberries, service berries, gooseberries, currants:

generations of Port Gamble S'Klallam children could tell stories about berry picking with their grandmothers—memories of huge containers that had to be filled before the children could go home; special, often-secret berry patches; and—best of all—berry desserts and jams that lasted all winter.

Ellen (Sigo) George, like many a S'Klallam grandmother, required discipline and hard work from her grandchildren. Bill Jones, Jake Jones, and Con Sullivan remembered her gathering routine: she took all her dishpans and baskets and would not leave until everything was full. All the grandchildren would go." Fifteen or twenty of us all lined up," William Jones remembered, "and we had a hard time keeping everybody picking berries 'cause every time they'd pick, they'd want to eat 'em." She kept them picking with stories of *slapu?*, the Wild Woman of the Woods, who could make her eyelid look like a berry. Sometimes Grandma George would give them little pieces of an energy-building plant. Whenever the group would pass Jenny Jones' house on the way to her berry patch at Shorewood, Grandma George would say, "Be quiet! Be quiet!" She didn't want anybody to know where they were going to pick.[79]

Irene (Jackson) Purser also had to pick until all Grandma Nancy Jackson's baskets were full. They picked blackberries, huckleberries, and elderberries near Pumpkin Junction. "We never ate a meal when we didn't have dessert after it was done, and we had some kind of berries.[80]

In earlier times, S'Klallam usually preserved their berries by drying them. In the memory of most of today's elders, like Dorothy George, their grandmothers put up berries by canning, sometimes over a fire right on the beach where they were camping.[81]

Jenny Jones (b. 1864) had a very old method of preserving berries, as her granddaughter, Virginia (Jones) Ives, recalled:

> I think the neatest thing was how they kept berries in the old days, when I was about 8 years old. I was so amazed. In June, Grandma [Jenny Jones] would take a half-bucket basket that was waterproof and line it with maple leaves. She'd put a layer of

leaves, then a layer of berries, then a layer of leaves, then more berries and more leaves. She'd put the basket in a hole in the mud and then come Thanksgiving, when there were no fresh berries, she'd dig them out and they were just like fresh—from June 'til November! I said, "My Grandma's a magician!"[82]

Martha John's family used a similar method. She remembered that after the berries were unearthed, they didn't last very long, "So whenever the person that had preserved the berries would open the basket, everyone in the community would get a little bowl of berries."[83]

Picking and preparing *sxʷaʔya'səm*—soapberries—was a specialty of many Port Gamble S'Klallam grandmothers. While today's elders remember Indian ice cream with delight, it is a taste that not all of their descendents share. Irene (Jackson) Purser:

> I remember Sammy Charles and them used to camp down where Hansville is now. There was nothin' there then. And we used to go down there and visit them and Susie used to go get her *sxʷaʔya'səm* she had soaking. And she had a white enamel bucket and, I don't know what kind of limbs they were, and she used to just whip. . . . She didn't have an eggbeater; she just whipped the *sxʷaʔya'səm* up with that. . . . Put sugar in it and that was a treat for us. She was always taking care of kids, because she had a lot of grandchildren.[84]

Jake Jones' family gathered *sxʷaʔya'səm* in Port Townsend. His mother used salal berry leaves to stir it and then they added berry jam for flavoring. It was better to make Indian ice cream with green berries, because the red ones were bitter. Currently, these berry bushes are hard to find because of development.[85] Discovery Bay was home to another patch of squossum, according to Ivan George. Indians from all over used to go there to pick.[86]

Before canning became commonplace, S'Klallam women dried *sxʷaʔya'səm* the same as other berries. Christine Charles' mother, Susie (Dick) Charles, picked *sxʷaʔya'səm* near Jamestown. She spread a sheet under the bushes and shook them to collect the berries. Then they put the berries on a white sheet out in the sun to dry, then sealed them into pint jars. Christine's father, Sammy Charles, made cedar spoons for eating the *sxʷaʔya'səm;* he wouldn't let them use silverware.[87]

BLACKBERRIES AND CHICKENS

One day when she lived at Point Julia, Louise Butler Webster Buttner threw out some spoiled preserved blackberries and her chickens ate it. They all fell down as if dead. One hen she especially liked, so she gave it some painkiller to save it. Later, all the chickens came to, having only been knocked out drunk, while the painkiller killed her favorite hen.[88]

Berries were not the only plants harvested during the lifetime of today's elders. Port Gamble S'Klallam women gathered bear grass, sweet grass, and cattail for making baskets and mats. When Gene Jones was young, Aunt Martha sent him down to Eglon Slough in the spring to gather cattails for her. He waded through the muck and cut it at its base, being careful to watch for snakes.[89]

Irene (Jackson) Purser's grandmother was also a weaver of mats. "My Grandma [Nancy Jackson] used to make cattail mats all the time too. And she made one for each one of us and we'd lay on the floor in front of the stove and do our homework."[90] In addition to Martha John (b. 1895) and Nancy Jackson (b. 1854), other early Port Gamble S'Klallam weavers were Susie Solomon (born around treaty times), Emily Webster (b. 1883), Ellen (Sigo) George (b. 1884) and Clara (George) Jones (b. 1903).[91] According to Cultural Director Marie Hebert, these women passed down their traditional knowledge to younger weavers who continue today to make baskets, cedar bark hats, vests, visors, and other woven materials. Unlike the materials made by S'Klallam ancestors, however, today's woven items are regarded as art rather than the functional tools and clothing they once were.

While cattail and cedar bark are still available today, locations for gathering bear grass and sweet grass have diminished substantially. Either traditional locations have been usurped by development, or they lie in restricted habitats. Despite this, these plants are still entitled to protection in the same way as other treaty resources.

Tribal biologists try to keep track of the locations of native blackberries, squossum, and basketry materials like sweet grass in order to protect them from the waves of development and logging. Biologist Ron Hirschi tried for years to find out where Geneva Ives' favorite squossum gathering spot was in eastern Jefferson County in order to protect it. True to the ways of her grandmothers, Geneva would never tell!

S'Klallam weavers can still find cedar bark today, but the forests of old growth cedar—the huge trees the ancestors used to fell and hollow out for ocean-going canoes—have vanished. The presence of mills throughout S'Klallam territory came at a price: they may have brought S'Klallam people employment, but they also brought the destruction of the old-growth forests. Today, S'Klallam canoe carvers are forced to rely on the Pope Resources timber company or the U.S. Forest Service to donate a log big enough to serve as a future canoe.

Over a century has passed since Irene (Fulton) Purser's childhood journey to the S'Klallam fishing camp on Hood Canal, but her descendants, along with other Port Gamble S'Klallam, have kept their ancestors' memories alive by asserting and protecting their treaty fishing, hunting, and gathering rights. Today, tribal members honor the return of the salmon with a First Salmon Ceremony, just as their ancestors did. Traditional hunters continue the practices of taking a cleansing bath before hunting and thanking the deer for giving its life to the hunter. Children are still taught to demonstrate respect for what is taken and to only take what they need.

Irene Purser's nephew, Ron Charles, reflected on the past thirty years of the treaty rights struggle. Although recent years have seen conflicts between tribes over fishing catch allocation or areas, the effort to enforce treaty fishing rights has resulted in stronger tribes who are united in their effort:

> There were some really difficult times during the first years after the Boldt decision, but one thing always stood out: the tribes were united, spirits were high in the community, and, for the most part, people seemed supportive of each other. When people were successful, most thought that was good. Tribes didn't have too much to fight about; they were so focused on achieving the fifty percent, and the common enemy, the state, provided us with a focus. . . . This was a very special time for tribes, wherein a federal judge was able to erase well over one hundred years of abuse by the state, and make them go back,

and if not, put things right for all those years of wrongdoing, to start anew with guarantees, in the form of a percentage of the catch, so that, from there on, the tribes would be able to say the government is living up to its obligations. I can sleep at night, knowing that I helped protect this tribe's treaty rights, and some measures I helped to bring about will be there even after I am gone.[92]

CHAPTER 4

The Mill

Ron Hirschi

*"All of my uncles worked there and I remember the
smell of their clothes and seeing their big black lunch
boxes and hard hats all the time. I remember after
it closed officially thinking how quiet it seemed and
how dark it was over there at Port Gamble."*

–Kelly (Sullivan) Baze

Long before there was a mill in Port Gamble, S'Klallams harvested cedar, yew, and other trees for house planks, posts, canoes, paddles, herring rakes, and other necessities. The coming of the mill soon became central to the lives of tribal members, as Ron Charles recalled:

> Why does Port Gamble exist as a federally recognized tribe today? I believe a lot of the reason our people stayed together, and weren't scattered to the winds like a lot of other Indian people, was that we had a reason to stay together as a community: the mill. (Not the only reason, for sure). Several generations of my family, the Fultons, not only worked over at the mill, they worked, and were experts, in working the pond and sending logs up to the mill. All seven of my grandpa's sons worked at the mill, and his six daughters' husbands also worked at the mill. So, you can quickly start to see the importance of the mill in our lives.

The Mill

Oliver J. Olson being loaded at dock, Port Gamble.

"My Grandpa Jacob was a longshoreman in these days. He always wore a hat like that guy. That guy might be my Grandpa on the far right" (Jake Jones).

"My Dad, Ed Purser, was a longshoreman then. That might be him there (fourth man from left: Rude Purser).

Lumber was loaded by hand onto ships at the mill well into the 1900s. Rollers, looking like rungs on a ladder, helped bring milled lumber to the edge of the dock. Longshoremen like Ed Purser and Jacob Jones pulled the wood from the rollers and onto the waiting ships after each board was tallied into notebooks. Photo circa 1910, courtesy of Ron Hirschi.

The mill was this noisy, smelly place that many would have thought a nuisance, and probably wouldn't even be permitted under today's laws, but it represented a way of life for us. We all knew what time the whistles blew, and what they meant. Folks would tell their kids to come home when the mill whistle blew, and we would know that was five o'clock. There was an emergency whistle or siren, and if that blew, we all got concerned, because it meant that there had been an accident, and we all had family there. Kids could sometimes go to the store and their dads would charge something for them on his bill (taken out of his check, unfortunately).

So, somewhere we should try to put into words just what that dirty, smelly old mill meant to our people.

As I looked at census numbers for Jefferson County, you can see that there were quite a few Indians back in the old days around there. What happened to them? They moved, or perhaps inter-married to the point where they were not considered Indian anymore. They just are not there any more. The same could have happened to our people.[1]

S'Klallam ancestors spoke about times past, but it is hard to piece together what took place in the early years of the mill. Early accounts of mill history were written by non-Indians with little mention of Indian people. But a long tradition of oral history has provided many stories, and researchers continue to search for new discoveries in print. This chapter hopes to combine the oral histories and published accounts of the mill in Port Gamble. It should be remembered that S'Klallams also worked at other mills. They always moved by water and, even after getting jobs in Port Gamble, continued to move freely in their usual and accustomed areas to fish, hunt, and visit relatives.

One thing is clear: S'Klallam men and women were critical to the success of the mill in Port Gamble. S'Klallam women were especially important in the early days of the mill, marrying white men who came from Maine and supporting those early white workers in the same way other women supported their S'Klallam men. S'Klallam sons, grandsons, and great-grandsons worked in the mill right up to the time it closed.

Among the first S'Klallams to work in the mill was probably Tommy Tom. His wife, Nellie Tom, told a story about the first white men to reach Port Gamble, which could mean she was there when it happened: "There was an ancient cemetery on the slope. After the mill came, the whites gathered the bones of the cemetery, piled them and poured coal oil on so they could raise potatoes. Joe Tom's mother told about this."[2] In a 1953 account of the arrival of the first whites, Pope & Talbot reported that an Indian village sat across the bay. They also suggested that all the remaining area was completely unsettled land, stating that the crew of the first ship to arrive "found wilderness. Dense forests of enormous trees stretched unbroken from the horizon to the water's edge. The whole world seemed covered with a silent, impenetrable blanket of green."[3] These same forests had been the source of S'Klallam canoe logs, homes, and fires for many centuries.

The new people came with a different view of the forests. Andrew J. Pope and Frederic Talbot founded the mill company. These two men were the sons of mill owners who left East Machias, Maine, in 1849, arriving in San Francisco in December of that year. They were in the lightering trade, which involved moving cargo over long distances, and they parlayed their cargo business into the large lumber mills that bear their names.[4]

Originally, these New England loggers and mill owners fell towering eastern white pine that became mast trees for naval vessels, cargo ships, and cod fishing schooners. Pope and Talbot arrived in Port Gamble Bay with a long history of forest exploitation.[5] Their relationship with the forest stood in sharp contrast to the way in which native peoples used the ancient cedar, fir, and hemlock around Port Gamble Bay. Each time a part of the tree was taken for basket material, housing planks, or other uses, the S'Klallam thanked the tree first.[6]

There are no written records of the first encounters, those first conversations between the Popes, Talbots, and mill company men with the S'Klallam ancestors. But oral tradition and S'Klallam cultural ways have been handed down in unbroken form, enough to know the differences between the Easterners and S'Klallams. It is easy to imagine S'Klallams watching as the mill company began to set up their small operations, thinking that these men were going to cut trees for local use—that trees would be felled and treated as had always been done in the making of homes, boats, and other needs. S'Klallams lived in a healthy environment that these new people called wilderness, a land and waterscape the S'Klallams had sustained for countless hundreds of years.

When Nellie Tom witnessed the burning of her S'Klallam ancestors' bones, she and others must have known that a major change had come to the land. One of the big changes came when tribal members moved across the bay; a change remembered by elders, including Martha John. Martha's father was a longshoreman, and she was born only a few short decades after the first mill was built. According to her memory, S'Klallams used to live in Port Gamble where the general store is now, and all around where the cemetery is located. The mill people came along and sent the Indians across the Bay on the spit. They promised to always have jobs for the men and also gave them enough lumber to build a house for each family.[7]

As Martin Charles remembered:

> On the mill side, that's Klallam property. On this side, all the way up to the homes there is Klallam property. Lester [Jackson] had the deed but it was burned after Lester died. . . . Pope & Talbot tried to get rid of the Klallam Indians. They used to live where the mill is. They agreed that this property belongs to the Klallam Tribe. They made that agreement. Tribe should make a claim for that property.[8]

In recalling her family history in East Machias, Maine and the town of Port Gamble, Daisy Cotter Hirschi remembered the same promises made to S'Klallams by mill owners.[9] Her grandfather settled on Hood Canal in 1859, where he logged for the mill in Port Gamble. Daisy's father, Henry Cotter, was a tallyman on the docks at the mill. Her husband, Walter, shared the job of sawyer with Russell Fulton Sr.[10] Daisy was proud of her Port Gamble (town) heritage and enjoyed sharing stories with her contemporaries, including Irene (Fulton) Purser. She told stories about many S'Klallam elders like Mary Jackson, who sold clams to her parents, and Nancy Jackson, a family friend. Like Daisy's own grandparents, both of these women would have passed along many stories about the old days, including times well before the arrival of Pope & Talbot. Daisy's son, LaVerne Hirschi, remembers that the mill company made many promises, saying that "Pope & Talbot would always have jobs for tribal members or if the mill stopped, the land that is Port Gamble would be returned to the tribe."[11]

Not long after it was established, the mill in Port Gamble quickly became one of the largest lumber producers in the Pacific Northwest.[12] As the town and mill grew in size and importance, S'Klallams mostly lived on the spit while the men worked in the mill. They never forgot the promises made by the original mill owners. As Harry Fulton Sr. (b. 1915) recalled:

In the beginning, our people used to live where the mill is now. The Company moved the people over on this side. Our forefathers settled along where the mill is now. The Company moved the Indians on this side, with a promise that they would always give them work and they would always see that they had lumber to build new homes. But that was only verbal; nothing was ever put in writing to that effect. Otherwise we could still be getting lumber, because we owned that at one time.[13]

Oral history recounts that when Pope & Talbot arrived,

Sailing ship being loaded at dock, Port Gamble. Note the peavey on the dock in front of the men, all working by hand to load lumber onto waiting sailing ship. Peaveys were used in the woods by loggers, at the front end of the mill to roll logs, and on the docks to move big timbers like these, cut from old growth trees. Jacob Jones and Foster Jones were both longshoremen who learned to use peaveys and other logging tools long before working on the docks. They, like their sons, also worked in the woods, cutting trees and selling logs to the alder mill on the outskirts of Port Gamble. Photo courtesy of Ron Hirschi.

the group of Indians living amid the tall timbers of their native lands and subsisting off the wealth of the sea had no trouble agreeing to move across the Bay. Having known Port Gamble Bay for centuries, tribal members could have believed that resources like trees, clams, and fish had always been and would always be a part of their landscape. It is unlikely tribal ancestors could have comprehended how quickly the newcomers would transform the land.

Industry meant jobs for tribal members, and S'Klallam tribal members have contributed years of steady and highly skilled labor to Pope & Talbot's mill. These jobs would seem like jobs in a shipyard, grocery store, or any other place of employment today. However, in 1853, when Pope & Talbot arrived in Port Gamble, those jobs had a far different meaning to the lives of S'Klallams. Before the mill, S'Klallams knew work as a part of an ongoing pattern that took from the forest and salt water, but one that never depleted that resource. For the mill company, Indian labor was as vital as it was in places like Seattle, where "Indian labor would facilitate much of Seattle's early development."[14] With a promise of jobs forever, it must have been easy for S'Klallams to facilitate the development of the mill at Port Gamble.

From the early days, S'Klallam men worked in the mill, acquiring money to purchase goods, but they continued to hold to the basic belief and right, just as today, that they could hunt and fish in all their usual and accustomed places. The income from mill jobs allowed them to purchase a new style of clothing and machine-made goods. S'Klallam interviewed in 1905 stressed the importance of their treaty rights even while they adapted to some of the white men's ways:

> The idea that they could seek food where they pleased was the theory the Clallams carried away and clung to from that time on . . . and sought to maintain themselves in the old way, taking up what they wished of new food, clothing and weapons brought among them by the whites.[15]

The mill may have been a new way of working, but tribal members working in the mill used traditional means to travel back and forth to work just as they used traditional means to gather shellfish and catch salmon for meals. Louisa Pulsifer (interviewed at age 94, born 1880) remembered how Tommy Tom and Joe Tom would paddle across the bay from their breaks at the mill for lunch. They would have tea and hardtacks, and then return for work.[16]

Until the road from Little Boston around the bay to Port Gamble was completed in about 1916, tribal mill workers had no other choice than to row or paddle across the channel to their jobs. The idea of commuting by car would come much later, but in those first decades after the mill began, traditional transportation remained by choice and necessity. Even in more modern times, men would row to work, "some from Coontown tying up their boats on the north end of the mill and those of us down on the spit keeping our boats down on the booms at the south end of the mill."[17]

Rowing even came in handy as part of mill work. According to Harry Fulton III:

> My Grandpa would row out and light the lights in the channel. The ships needed to come into the channel to tie up at the docks. I imagine it must have been kerosene, but I'm not sure. It was before there was any electricity to keep those lights on.[18]

Little did the first S'Klallam workers know that the mill owners came with a completely different belief system. As had been the case in Maine, these newcomers came with a basic understanding that land could be bought and sold. While they shared in the bounty of the sea, dining on clams, salmon, and other "free" foods, whites quickly bought up properties. As Beckwith et al. state: "With the treaty signed, the S'Klallam were quickly deprived of their traditional lands with the increasing homesteads, and they had no land to call their own."[19]

The mill company had convinced S'Klallam ancestors to move across the Bay to Point Julia. But, in 1863, the land that eventually would become the reservation actually became Pope & Talbot property. "The newcomers had acquired all of the land bordering Port Gamble Bay by 1872, long before S'Klallam people could obtain land under the Indian

Homestead Acts of 1875 and 1884."[20]

This meant that for the first few decades they worked at the mill, S'Klallam workers could not reinvest their earnings into the very land that had always been theirs. However, by1886, tribal members began to acquire property in the same way the white settlers had. Millwork, including long shoring, was their only reasonable means of acquiring money to buy the land. As Ted George remembers, the mills needed labor and, "So many of us, our Indian people, were able to change very easy from subsistence living to work and cash."[21]

It is not clear from Pope & Talbot records how many and for how long tribal members worked in those earliest days. Letters from Josiah P. Keller during the period of 1853-1855 continually reported a lack of labor in general, citing anything from workers abandoning the mill for new gold strikes in eastern Washington to a lack of understanding of how to work the saws.[22]

The invasion of northern tribes and other "Indian Troubles" affected the mill in the first ten years of operation, and Keller did not consider S'Klallams to be friendly to his causes. As he wrote to Charles Foster on November 1, 1855, "We ourselves are surrounded by these miserable though considered friendly Clalms." All the while, he realized the need for these "miserable Clalms," as seen in a letter written to Foster in August of that same year. Keller made it clear that S'Klallam workers were essential to the mill's success, saying, "We now just about make the mill go with what native help we get."[23]

Keller also wrote to Foster on November 11, 1855, where he noted the impact of the "Indian troubles" on business and mentioned that a blockhouse was under construction. Reflecting on past relationships between whites and natives, he mentioned obtaining firearms and ammunition, adding:

> I had hoped that the necessity of destroying these miserable
> creatures with powder & ball would never occur here but I
> suppose as has been the case in all new countries so it must

be here. So here it goes if need be—There are undoubtedly bad white men in the Territory that should be killed with them—there are always such encouraging the Indians to murder & plunder.[24]

The best-known "Indian Trouble" occurred in November 1856, when northern Indians clashed with the U.S. Navy, as described in Chapter 1. The truth of the time was that native peoples were *troubled,* not trouble. Tribal members throughout the northwest were being devastated by smallpox, so much so that an estimated ninety percent of the native population vanished in the 1800s. To many of the east coast Protestants arriving in the northwest, this was a good thing. The Methodist historian, Gustavus Hine was quoted in 1850 as saying, "The hand of Providence is removing them to give place to a people more worthy of so beautiful and fertile a country."[25]

Today, we might think of the first mill workers and their families as being isolated. But S'Klallams were hardly isolated in ways others might think. Their ancestors were always canoe people, and they continued to use the same water routes they had used to reach hunting and fishing areas. Then too, paddling across to work in the mill was not much of a journey. It is not known how many men worked in the mill at first, but it was certainly more convenient for them to paddle across the channel to the mill than to commute to more distant locations for employment.

People from other tribes were also either working in the mills or supporting millworker husbands. The territorial census of Jefferson County in 1880 lists thirty-six Indian citizens, mostly women and children, in the nearby mill town of Port Ludlow.[26] Both S'Klallam and other Indian people also worked and lived at the mill at Seabeck until it burned down in 1886.

Despite the attraction of jobs in other places, the mill at Port Gamble offered employment close to home. Further, with the mill came a store. Besides Hudson's Bay Company trading posts, nothing even approaching a store had ever been situated in the aboriginal lands of S'Klallam people. Imagine the moment the first shoppers entered to purchase a dress, shoes, or fresh cut pork. No matter the wonder created, it is clear from the following interview in which Darlene Peters talks about her grandmother, Josie (Pulsifer) Anderson, that S'Klallams were adept shoppers early on:

> And so we pulled across for groceries and had to pack it up that big hill, but when she'd go into the store, we would go in there and she would forget English. And then she'd go up and talk to the people at the counter in S'Klallam and make some signs for them so she had everybody in the store following her around the store and watching her. I never could get used to that 'cause she'd go in and she'd only speak S'Klallam. She knew her money; she knew her English and she did it all that way without. . . .And they always helped her 'cause I think it was that they just thought she was ignorant. And what she was doing was speaking two languages, understanding the math and getting what she wanted. So she was good with people too! Yeah. She was really something![27]

The store and the mill were inseparable for many reasons, one of which was that a person might work for wages, but end up owing the store his monthly salary. As a company store from its inception, any charges for groceries, work gloves, clothing, and other purchases were deducted from the worker's paycheck. But the store was far more than a place to simply shop. It was also a social hub for town residents and mill workers.

As Floyd Jones remembers, time spent on the clock at the mill was steady work and:

> The only time we had to visit was at noon when I started working day shift. We'd come up to the store for pop and other snacks and to talk. It was lucky too at that time, I had been working on an electronic lumber grader but they took them away, so we had to be up closer to do a better job of grading and it was more physical and demanding of attention. It probably saved our life. We'd of been chomping all those snacks (at the electronic grader) and would have weighed 300 pounds.[28]

The Mill

Floyd Jones had a long career working at the mill. Here, he is at work in the Carving Shed. "I've always loved to work with wood." Photo courtesy of Port Gamble S'Klallam Archives.

When Floyd first started working in the mill in 1962 he was paid $2.32 per hour and he worked five days, eight hours per day. He had an account at the store as well, but unlike others, he kept up with payments. "There were some who never got paid since they charged so much." [29]

In earlier days, the store also allowed bartering. Store accounting records from 1890-91 show that most payments were in cash, but balances at month's end were sometimes made in other ways. Shoppers paid by work, spuds, and wood, receiving a total of $1.85 on accounts for one and a half cords. Still others paid with fresh crops, as indicated by the fifty cents allowed on an account for "berries." [30]

The original store lay closer to the water, and offered its shoppers a great deal of variety, including furniture. [31] As a result, the store provided groceries and other necessities to mill workers and their families while continuing to supply workers with snacks and gloves until the mill closed in 1995.

In recent times, mill workers mostly lived in Little Boston, but several families moved into the town of Port Gamble as well. Ed and Irene Purser may have been the first to make this move. Their name is penciled in to the very first Port Gamble (temporary) telephone directory. Their number, 2721, was one of fifty-eight listed for residences in that early "phone book."[32] Other families living in town during the 1950s and '60s, either for brief or extended periods, included Fred Wellman, Bud Purser, Claude "Skip" George, Terry Wellman, Reggie Fulton, Jim Fulton, and Delbert Charles.

Like most wives and daughters of mill workers, tribal women usually did not work outside the home, but some did. Rose Purser, for one, recalls working at the Port Gamble Hospital while her father, husband, and brother all worked at the mill.[33]

Young men from Little Boston also enjoyed sneaking over to Port Gamble to date the Wellman girls. As Floyd Jones recalls:

> [My brother Jake, Lloyd Fulton and I came over to town by boat and] took the girls out to Whiskey Spit one evening. On the way back, the outboard wouldn't start. We pulled and pulled on the starting rope, but it still wouldn't start. It took forever to get it going and by the time it did, it was very late. Finally, we got back to the beach on the far side of town near the Wellman's house. We knew we were in big trouble, but didn't know how soon. There was Mr. Wellman standing on the beach shining a flashlight in our young faces, waiting and none too happy. It was a while before we had nerve to come back.[34]

Floyd and others mainly came to town to work. They came by boat and by car, around the bay and up the highway to the mill. Their careers included many of the most skilled and responsible jobs, and S'Klallam men taught those skills to new generations of workers as well. Many tribal members

The Mill

started work in the mill at a young age too. Joe Anderson began his long stint at the age of fifteen. "Mr. Anderson had been steadily employed at Port Gamble mill from 1877 to June 1934 when the mill closed down. During the summertime, the family picked berries, but as the season is closed they are without means of support."[35] Among others who began working in the mill in their teens was Rudy Purser, who started before World War II at the age of sixteen.[36]

Many family members had several men working in the mill at the same time. Often, a large percentage of the work force was made up of S'Klallam men. A listing of Port Gamble S'Klallams working at the mill in 1934 is just one snapshot in time that shows hundreds of years of combined service to the mill.[37]

Clarence Charles	Jas. Webster Jr.	Bennie George
William Charles	Joe George	Richard Purser
Lester Jackson	Louis George	Chester Charles
Peter Jackson	William George	Harry Fulton
Foster Jones	Louis John	Herbert Charles
Jacob Jones	Joe Tom	Frank Sullivan
Henry Lambert	Russell Fulton	William Pulsifer
Frank Lawrence	Ray Garrison	Emore George
Leo Lawrence	Claude George	Frank Napoleon
Henry Napoleon	Carl Sparks	Harold Fulton
Edward Purser	Cecil George	Francis Webster
Cyrus Webster	Ralph George	George Sparks

Many tribal members can remember the names on this list. For some, including members of the Fulton and Purser families, the memories cross several generations. Rudy Purser remembered:

> My Dad, Ed Purser, was a longshoreman. . . . I went to the mill and worked when I was sixteen, but then went in the service. When I came back, I got back on at the mill but was laid off when other guys came back from the war. I worked for a time at Keyport, then got on at the mill again. I worked in the planing mill until I retired in 1964.[38]

Rose Purser added:

> Our son, Rudy, worked in the mill his whole career except when he
> was in the Navy. When he got back from the Navy, he had to get the
> military to send a letter to the mill, letting them know about giving
> jobs back to returning servicemen. He worked in the mill until it
> closed down. My dad, Fred Wellman, also worked in the mill, driving
> a lumber carrier.[39]

Rose also recalled how her Grandpa Harry Fulton "worked in the sawmill
at the pond pushing up logs. Pushing them into, onto the conveyer belt
that took them up into the mill. All sawmill workers, all of our family was
sawmill workers."[40]

Rose's brother, Terry Wellman, also worked in the mill. His wife, Laurel,
recalled that Terry worked for about thirty years as a carrier driver, just
like his dad. The family lived in town, and Rose was even born in the
Port Gamble Hospital.[41]

In Rose's family alone, men contributed more than 145 years of labor to
the mill. A conservative total for all tribal members who worked in the
mill would total more than 500 years. Clearly, the mill benefited from
the S'Klallam, just as S'Klallams benefited from work at the mill. This can
be seen in the family of Ron Charles, who wrote:

> Harry Fulton Senior was my grandfather, and he was born around
> 1879 or 1880. James Fulton (from Maine) was his dad, and I think
> he worked at the Seabeck mill. He had three children with a Klallam
> woman named Susie, and then left his family. We had thought all along
> that he died, but in the last few years we found out that he went over to
> the east side of the Sound, where he started another family. His family
> was left in Seabeck, where my grandfather and his brother, also named
> Jim, became somewhat orphans, and were taken in by Tommy Tom
> and Nellie Tom after their mom died. Nellie was my grandpa's aunt.
>
> Sometime probably in the early 1890s, the Toms moved to Port
> Gamble where Tommy worked at the mill, bringing my grandpa

and his brother with them. … The way the family tells it, Grandpa was a boom man, and he kind of learned it from his father in law, Solomon. Several other Fultons were also boom men, including Harold, Russ Sr., Russ Jr., and Lloyd. So, a few generations of Fultons worked at the same job.

Another interesting anecdote on our family was that Grandpa had two children with his first wife, Alice, and then she died. He then married Angie, a Skokomish, and they had 11 more children. Each of the Fulton

Russ Fulton, Sr., on the right, with an unidentified friend at the Port Gamble mill in the early 1970s. Salmon were so plentiful in those days they could be caught by casting off the dock. Photo courtesy of Lloyd Fulton.

men, and each of the Fulton women's husbands, worked at one time or another at the mill. That just shows how important the mill was to life around here. That was because, outside of shellfish harvesting, it was the only place to work, especially before there were cars to drive around the Bay.[42]

Harry Fulton III also remembers the mill with a sense no other tribal member or mill worker can truly relate to. Like many who grew up in Little Boston, Harry listened to the sound of the mill whistle as a child. He would go over to the mill dock and dive off the north end into the cold waters of the channel that divided Port Gamble from the Little Boston community. He knew how hard his dad worked, lining up for the big edger, a job that was very physically demanding.

Harry was the third generation of Fultons to go to work for Pope & Talbot when he began his career there in 1967. In those days, ships still came into the docks after turning around in the shallow waters of the bay. Not wanting to get tied down in one job at the mill, especially those jobs that might find him in his later years still pulling lumber, Harry quickly began learning how to operate mill machinery. By the time he left the mill in 1994, he could operate all the machines with great skill. He'd operated the head rig, ran the quad band saws, and even worked the gang saws that ran on a carriage—saws that had been operated in earlier years by Russell Fulton Sr.

Harry's experiences reflect times when the mill was not so efficient. He recalled that anyone within earshot of the mill could always hear the whistles blowing. But closer to the mill, the sound of saws and sawdust flying were ever present. The first gang saws Harry operated were a quarter of an inch thick. Those saws buzzed huge chunks of wood, creating sawdust that filled the barges at the north end of the mill. These barges would then be towed away by tugs. Despite this system, the mill grew more efficient as time passed.

During Harry's later years at the mill, thinner saws greatly reduced the amount of wasted wood that had plagued the mill's earlier days. It was at this time that Harry learned to work in quality control. He would measure lumber with a precision tool, then feed the information into computers that could alter the saws if they were not cutting precisely. As the mill became more high tech, Harry adapted and learned, helping to guide the daily operations into more modern times.

But the mill did not keep up with many needed changes, especially with regard to safety and training. No one knows that truth in the way

The Mill

Harry saw it with his own eyes. Harry's son, Tracy, also worked in the mill, the fourth generation of Fultons to do so. After having served in the army, Tracy went to work for Pope & Talbot in 1991. In 1993, Tracy was killed after having fallen into a conveyor improperly equipped for worker safety. Harry was right there when his son was killed and it was not long after this time that he left the mill for work at the tribe. Soon after this, the mill in Port Gamble closed, leaving only the memories of the countless tribal members who had worked there.

All hearts, thoughts, and memories of the mill will always be with Tracy and his mom and dad, Alice and Harry Fulton III.[43]

The mill brought hardship along with steady employment and income, and it also left indelible memories in the minds of today's younger generation of Port Gamble S'Klallam. Kelly Baze remembered the mill in a way everyone can relate to, even if they never stepped foot inside the mill gate. Her father, Daryl Sullivan, got his first job at the mill and stayed there for ten years. Like many tribal members, Daryl rowed across the channel to work. Like many children of mill workers, Kelly has vivid memories of the days, when the mill was still a dominant part of everyone's life:

> All of my uncles worked there and I remember the smell of their clothes and seeing their big black lunch boxes and hard hats all the time. I thought it was so cool one time when my uncle Roger was able to get a bunch of scraps of lumber and made a whole box of blocks for his house. I remember being a kid and my mom used the five o'clock whistle to remind us to come check in with her. You could hear the whistle all throughout the rez. We used to camp out under the stars at the Point in the summer and I remember us being woke up by the sounds of the mill starting up for the day. Foghorns would always go off and the sounds of trucks and machines seemed constant. Until it closed, we didn't realize how much noise it made, or how much light it gave off. I remember after it closed officially thinking how quiet it seemed and how dark it was over there at Port Gamble.[44]

CHAPTER 5

"We Have to Stay Here With Our Fathers, With Our Dead"
Port Gamble S'Klallam Land

Emily Mansfield

"Many, many times they have asked us to move.
They ask us to move to Port Angeles, or they say,
'you can all be together at Neah Bay.' We can't move
and they don't understand it. We have to stay here
with our fathers, with our dead."

–Sammy Charles[1]

As a young man at Tulalip Boarding School in 1886, Sammy Charles became motivated to lead the fight for Port Gamble S'Klallam land. He wrote of his awakening to the injustice of his tribe's situation during his last year at Tulalip:

> On my last year in Tulalip School I ask[ed] some of my schoolmates pertaining [to] their people's homes. I was advised that they own a Reservation and houses with the aid of the Government Agency. There are Lummis, Suquamish, Skokomish, Makahs all have good houses. Us, the Noosclime [*nexʷsX̣áyəm*] Tribe, largest tribe, have nothing that we might call our home. Most of our people are squatting on beaches; few have small

Page 89

Port Gamble S'Klallam Land

purchased ground for homes.[2]

Fortunately, others in the community were fired up with the same desire as Charles, because the Port Gamble S'Klallam struggle for land would require the energy, political know-how, and persistence of many people over the next fifty years.

After the S'Klallam signed the Treaty of Point No Point, it quickly became clear that the white newcomers' relationship to land was radically different than the S'Klallam's. In the new view, land was a commodity that could be owned by individuals. When the Indian people relinquished their territory through treaties, the federal government became the owner of all of the land, now referred to as "the public domain." To encourage settlement and development, the government devised a variety of means through which eager settlers, timber companies, miners, and other newcomers could acquire their own share of the land. Native people throughout Washington Territory watched as surveyors drew their lines, and the shorelines, watersheds, forests and prairies that once shaped their territorial concepts were carved up into squares that could be bought and sold. By 1872, three years before Native people were legally permitted to hold land outside of reservations, all of the neatly surveyed parcels on the Bay were taken.

Date	Land Law	Land	Conditions	Available to Indians?
1847 -	Military Patents (Statutes at Large Vol. IX:125)	160 acres	War veterans received "script" for acreage anywhere. Script could be sold to a third party who used it to get free title to a particular parcel	No
1850 -	Donation Land Law (Shackleford 1940:402)	320 acres free (640 acres to a couple)	4 years on the land	No
1854 -	University Land Grant (Gates 1961:56. Puget Mill Company (or its associates)	72 square miles	Territory reserved 72 sections to be selected by UW and sold to raise money	No

obtained 7,000 acres on Port
Gamble Bay by selecting
sections for the University
of Washington and then
purchasing the land from
UW (Ficken 1987:41))

1862 -	Homestead Act	160 acres	Actual settlement and cultivation.	No
	(Homestead Act of May 20, 1862.	(or 80 in an	Reside 5 years prior to taking title	
	A General Land Office Circular	"organized district")		
	of August 23, 1870 extended the			
	General Homestead Act to Indians			
	but it was apparently not widely			
	utilized by the S'Klallam)			
1875 -	Indian Homestead Act	160 acres	Act of 1862 applies to Indians.	Yes, if tribal
	(Act of March 3, 1875. 43 USC 189)		5 year trust restriction	ties are abandoned.
1884 -	Indian Homestead Act	160 acres	25 year trust restriction	Yes, if tribal
	(Act of July 4, 1884. 43 USC 190))			ties are abandoned.
1887 -	General Allotment (Dawes) Act	160 acres	25 year trust restriction	Yes

When the S'Klallam people moved across Port Gamble Bay and built homes on the sandy spit, they were determined to stay. Here on the Bay, shellfish filled the tidelands and people had access to fishing, hunting and gathering areas, and employment at the mill. No matter where they had come from, the Bay was now their home. They refused to move to the Skokomish Reservation at the head of Hood Canal, as envisioned in Article III of the Treaty of Point No Point. Throughout the late 1800s and early 1900s, they still refused to leave, even when Indian agents tried to entice them with the promise of allotments on other reservations.

Indian agents wrung their hands over how and where to locate these S'Klallam on their own lands.[3] But the S'Klallam already knew how to stay on Port Gamble Bay: they would take matters into their own hands and become landowners themselves. Joseph Anderson led the way.

Indian Homesteads Near Port Gamble Bay

Joseph Anderson (b. 1865) grew up on the spit at Point Julia[4] and became the first and only S'Klallam from Port Gamble to take advantage of the Indian Homestead Acts. How did this young man learn that Indian people were no longer cut off from legally acquiring their own land? How did he negotiate the maze of incomprehensible federal land laws? Perhaps Anderson developed knowledge of the new land system during his year at Tulalip Boarding School,[5] or, more likely, he learned of the laws from his dealings with the white men at the mill where he started working as soon as his age permitted.

However he managed to decipher the new system, in 1885 Anderson staked a claim to an 80-acre parcel inland from the Bay—the land closest to Point Julia that had not already been claimed by whites.

The Andersons began building their house in November 1885. By the time his family had "proved up" their claim in 1891, they had cleared seven acres and built a 15′ x 23′ two-room home. They had constructed a chicken house and hog shed and had planted twenty-four fruit trees, an acre of strawberries, and had about two acres in cultivation.[6]

Homestead land was free from the federal government, but for Indians, it came with restrictions. First, the claimants had to state that they had "abandoned relations" with their tribe.[7] The Andersons, like other Indians anxious to gain a foothold on their native lands, repeated the words required by the federal law, but continued their full participation in the S'Klallam community. In fact, Joseph Anderson remained a respected leader among his people and he received a document from agent Edwin Eells in 1889, certifying that he was recognized as "Head Chief of the Port Gamble Band" by the federal government.[8] When Anderson stated on his patent application that the character of the land would be "Good for a town," he had his Port Gamble S'Klallam relatives and friends in mind. As events unfolded, his land became central to the S'Klallam community that lived both on the bluff and further inland. After Anderson staked his claim, others bought land shortly after in an area that was later called "Coontown," which earned its name for its many raccoons.

The second restriction on Indian homestead land was a twenty-five year trust period during which time the owner could not sell the land. Trust land could not be taxed by the state, a feature that enabled many Indian homesteaders to hang on to their land through hard times.

The Andersons petitioned the government in 1909 to remove the trust restrictions on their land. According to the Indian agent who recommended the change, there were a few Indians in the village who wanted to buy an acre or two for homes of their own. Also, the Shakers wanted to build a church on the Anderson property and, since the church would be built by donations, they wanted the church to have title to the land on which it would stand.[9]

Once their land was cleared of its trust restrictions, Joe and Josie sold five acres to Newton M. Pulsifer, Josie's brother in 1913. They sold another five acres to Cyrus Webster in 1915 and six acres to Henry Lambert in 1916.[10] They also set two acres aside for a cemetery and the Shaker Church that Joe Anderson had helped establish.[11]

James Henry (b. 1852) also attempted to take an Indian Homestead near Port Gamble. In 1886, he chose an eighty-four acre parcel on the east side of Hood Canal at Vinland and began the homesteading process.[12] It is unclear why Henry and his wife, Emma (Sly), chose land at that location instead of closer to Port Gamble Bay. Joe Sly, a S'Klallam/Makah who lived at Port Gamble and owned land in Quilcene,[13] might have been closely related to Emma; perhaps the Henrys tried to take land across from Quilcene to be close to Joe. Regardless, the Henrys built a home on the property but sold the acreage to a Norwegian settler before 1890.[14] They never "proved up" and owned the property.[15]

James Henry finally bought land in Coontown in 1903.[16] Here, he and Emma built a house and dug a well that also served neighboring S'Klallam families.[17] James and Emma's son, William Henry, and his wife, Louise Sigo, did not stay in Coontown with the Henrys, but lived in the

Chico area, on Dye's Inlet near present-day Silverdale, where the Sigo family made their home.[18] William and Louise Henry were the parents of Ruth Martinez (b. 1915), called "Grandma Ruth" by everyone who knew her.

Land Purchased by Port Gamble S'Klallam Families

On the heels of Joe Anderson's claim, three other S'Klallam men purchased a block of land between the Andersons' parcel and the Bay. They would have undoubtedly preferred to take advantage of free land under the Indian Homestead Act, but by 1886 there remained no public domain land on the Bay open to homesteading. In the very short thirty years since the treaties, these men must have come to understand the inevitable need to adapt to the white man's ways, at least as far as land was concerned. If they wanted a permanent land base, they would have to purchase it.

Solomon, Chief Cookhouse Charley, and Charley Jones each bought eleven acres from James Mead, a laborer in Port Gamble. The men probably knew Mead from working together at the mill. Each paid Mead fifty dollars, no small sum in 1886, but well worth establishing an official S'Klallam foothold on the bluff overlooking the Bay.[19]

Solomon

Solomon, also known as King Solomon and Old Solomon, chose the middle third of Mead's thirty-three acres. Solomon sold the north half of his land to Eddie George in 1911.[20] Eddie held onto the land through the 1930s when many of the Coontown residents lost their homes in tax foreclosures. The property was still recorded in his name in 1955. The George family farm was either located on this property or on Eddie George's portion of the Cookhouse Charley parcel, described below.

Meanwhile, Solomon's daughter, Alice (b. 1883), married Harry Fulton Sr. (b. 1878). After the birth of their third child, Alice died at the young age of twenty-three. Harry Fulton later married Angie Peterson (b. 1889) from Skokomish. The couple stayed on Solomon's land (now only the south half of the original eleven acres) and raised their eleven children.[21] The Fulton's "Old Place," along with the George and Anderson farms, formed the center of Coontown. After Harry Fulton Sr. died in 1954, the family sold their home and moved down to the new reservation.[22]

Cookhouse Charley

Chief Cookhouse Charley bought the eleven acres that lay immediately north of Solomon's land, and between the Andersons' claim and the Bay. Cookhouse Charley was born around 1850. Chief Charley had little time to make a home on his new land, however. He died in 1888, leaving the property to his wife Annie and sons Sammy (b. 1869) and Tommy Charles (b. 1871). In 1902, they divided the land in equal thirds, with Sammy's portion on the north, Tommy's in the middle, and Annie's to the south.[23]

It does not appear that either of the Charles brothers ever lived on the property. Tommy and his wife, Susie Littleman (b. 1881, San Juan Island), lived at Little Boston when they weren't traveling, and Tommy sold his property in 1930.[24]

Angie Peterson caught the eye of Harry Fulton, Sr., when she came to Point Julia with her father, Thomas Peterson (Skokomish), teacher at the Port Gamble Day School. Harry's father-in-law, Old Solomon, knew Harry needed a wife, so he contacted Angie's father and arranged the marriage. Photo courtesy of Rose Purser.

Sammy Charles and his wife, Susie Dick, from the Jamestown S'Klallam, also continued to live on the Spit. They sold their Coontown parcel in 1917 to the United States as a site for a new day school. The U.S. never built a school on the property, but it did lease the land in 1940 to the S'Klallam Shaker Church.[25]

Annie, Chief Cookhouse Charley's widow, married Eddie George (b. 1863), who considered owning his own land to be particularly important. George had watched in 1871 when the U.S. government had tried to force Indians in Port Townsend to move by burning their houses to the ground.[26] As Eddie told his great-grandson, Claude "Skip" George, "We were standing on the beach on Indian Island. They burned down our beach in Port Townsend. We all stood there and cried. White people burning our village down."[27] In light of witnessing this tragedy, it is not surprising that Eddie George eventually owned three parcels of land at Coontown.

When Annie George died in 1926, William George (b. 1882), Eddie's oldest son, moved into Annie's home with his wife Ellen Sigo (Suquamish, from Chico), where they raised their ten children.[28] At least one more home was added to the land after William and Ellen's daughter, Cyrene "Dolly" George, married Frank Sullivan. The Sullivans' nine children were born and raised on the Coontown property.[29] Claude "Skip" George Jr. also spent the first twelve years of his life here.

Charley Jones
Charley Jones (b. 1864) bought the third parcel on the bluff above Port Gamble Bay, south of Solomon's land and adjoining Anderson's. Around the same time Charley Jones bought his property, he and his wife, Lucy, had their first child, Louisa, who was born on the Skokomish flats and later married Tom Pulsifer, a Skokomish man.[30]

Within two years, Charley sold the south half of his property to Jim Williams and his wife Mary Ann (b. 1858).[31] After Williams died, Mary Ann married George Adams (b. 1857). Remaining in their home on the Spit, the couple sold their Coontown parcel to Annie George in 1905. Since the Georges already owned the southern third of the Cookhouse Charley land, Annie and Eddie gave their half of the Charley Jones land to Eddie's son, William, in 1905.[32]

As noted earlier, James Henry purchased the north half of Charley Jones' land and built a home there. Charley Jones himself apparently never lived on his land. His daughter, Louisa, split her childhood with her mother and granduncle in a longhouse on the Skokomish Reservation and with her father and his people at Port Gamble.[33] The next generation of Joneses grew up visiting their Aunt Louisa at Skokomish.

Jacob and Jenny Jones
As the century turned, more families moved to the bluff at Coontown. In 1903, Jacob (b. 1869) and Jenny Jones (b. 1864) bought seventeen acres about one half mile north of the other S'Klallam parcels on the bluff, likely the closest available for sale. The land also fronted on the Bay. On this farm, three generations of Jones flourished.[34]

Ed and Irene Purser
After Jacob and Jenny Jones had developed their farm north of Coontown, Ed Purser bought the adjoining forty acres in 1919.[35] The same year, Ed married Irene Fulton, daughter of Harry Fulton and Alice Solomon, and the two turned their acreage into a farm for their family of nine children, eight of whom survived childhood. Later they made room for their returning adult children, including their oldest son, Stan, and his new wife, Irene Jackson.[36]

George and Nancy Howell
While Coontown grew, George Howell bought forty acres from the State of Washington in 1897 and an adjoining forty acres a few years later.[37] The land lay inland about a half mile south of the Spit. After his wife, Nancy, died around 1924, George moved to Lummi.[38]

Louie and Martha John (b. 1891) bought twenty acres from Nancy's son George Howell Jr. in 1927, where the Johns built a home on what later became known as "Martha John Creek."[39] Louie John was sometimes called "Dr. John" after his Makah father. When Louie passed away in 1940, Martha continued to live alone in her house on the creek. In her elder years, she sold the property to Pearl Warren, a Makah relative of Louie John, and moved onto the reservation.[40]

Bennie and Martha George
Bennie George Sr. (b. 1887, son of Eddie George and Lucy Emore) bought five acres from the Howells in 1916. Bennie and Martha (Purser) George

ultimately found that the crossroads now known as "George's Corner" was a better place for their livelihood. Halfway between Port Gamble and Martha's home in Suquamish, they bought land and ran a store and gas station.

Martha's sister, Josephine (Purser) Sparks, lived at George's Corner when Josephine's triplets, Cubby, Delores, and Maxine were born in 1930. The Sparks family eventually moved

Bill and Lizzie Pulsifer. Bill (b. 1879) was the brother of Josie (Pulsifer) Anderson. Lizzie (b. 1880) was the sister of Harry Fulton, Sr. Photo courtesy of Port Gamble S'Klallam Archives.

to Point Julia, where the children grew up.[41] Martha and Bennie later built a home on Martha's property on the Suquamish Reservation.[42]

George's Corner also attracted Bill and Lizzie Pulsifer, who built a home on twenty acres a little south of the intersection. After houses were built on the new reservation in 1940, the couple moved to another home they had built on the bluff that ultimately passed down through Josie (Pulsifer) Anderson into the Anderson family.[43]

Jackson Family

Tyee Jack (b. 1838) bought twenty-two acres on Hood Canal near Lofall, but it is not known when.[44] By the time Irene (Jackson) Purser was born at Lofall in 1922, her grandfather, Tyee Jack, had died. Irene's parents, Peter and Ellen (Moses) Jackson, had built a home there large enough to accommodate Peter's mother, Nancy, Ellen's brother and family, and Peter and Ellen's own twelve children. Irene remembered that every time more children or relatives arrived, Peter would add another room to the house. The farm had a barn on the beach, fruit trees, vegetables, chickens, cows, and a strawberry field.[45] From the timber on his property, Peter supplied wood for the schoolhouse at Little Boston.[46]

There are several possible reasons why this location, miles from Little Boston, was chosen by a man who was a leader at Port Gamble. Maybe, like the James Henry homestead on Hood Canal, it was at or near a site that was important to the S'Klallam in earlier times. The Lofall area was known in the S'Klallam language as "a canoe-making place" because of its many large cedars.[47] Or maybe it was a matter of land available at an affordable price. Whatever drew the Jacksons out to Lofall, Irene and her brother were the only Indian children in the Breidablik School. They visited the Spit and Coontown by boat. Irene remembered rowing from Lofall to Port Gamble with her grandmother and stopping at the store in town to buy fruit for their visits with Susie Charles and the Jones family.[48] The family sold the land after Peter Jackson's untimely death in the 1930s.

Littleman Homestead

At the same time that S'Klallam families were acquiring land on Port Gamble Bay, Susie Littleman Charles' parents, George and Mary Littleman, filed an Indian Homestead claim on the south end of San Juan Island on Kanaka Bay. The San Juan Islands were important fishing grounds to both the S'Klallam and other tribes, and the Salmon Banks off Kanaka Bay were one of the most productive fisheries in Washington Territory.[49]

Mary Littleman (born around 1850) was S'Klallam from Victoria, B.C.; George was also S'Klallam, a cousin of Henry Lambert. The Littlemans filed their Indian Homestead application in 1884. They dedicated twenty acres to farming and grazing, and built a log house with a fireplace, a chicken house, and a woodshed. Under their care, the land also had fruit trees, fences, and a well.[50]

In April 1889, George Littleman set out in a canoe for Victoria. As a fisherman, he must have been adept at navigating the waters of the San Juan Islands, but this trip was different, and he never reached Victoria. Mary searched for him in vain and asked about him in Victoria where he was well known, but his body was never found.

Port Gamble S'Klallam Land

Mary carried on without her husband, and in 1892 she received the final patent on the homestead. By this time two of her four children had also died. Mary only lived four more years, dying of consumption on her hard-earned land. The family held the Littleman homestead until 1946, when Mary's heirs took it out of trust so that it could be sold.[51]

WHERE DID ALL THE OTHER S'KLALLAM GO?

Following the treaties, during the period of white settlement and Native dislocation, S'Klallam people tried to stay in their traditional territories, grouping themselves in clusters along the Strait of Juan de Fuca and Hood Canal. Several families bought 160 acres of land on Clallam Bay around 1880, but sold out a decade later when the land became desirable to whites.[52] Lord Jim Balch and people from the villages at Dungeness, Port Discovery, and Washington Harbor bought 210 acres north of Sequim, establishing the Jamestown community in 1874. Ten S'Klallam families pushed from their traditional home sites in the Port Angeles and Elwha River areas became landowners, under the 1884 Indian Homestead Act, in the lower Elwha Valley. Others, unable to buy land, did their best to stay together on the shores west of Port Angeles, Ediz Hook, and Washington Harbor.[53] Some S'Klallam and the few remaining Chemakum were burned out of their Port Townsend homes in 1871 and forcibly removed to the Skokomish Reservation, from which they quickly dispersed to other S'Klallam groups or back to the Port Townsend outskirts. For example, *Chits-a-mah-han* (the treaty signer also known as Duke of York), his son Lach Ka Nim (Prince of Wales), and James Webster returned to Indian Island, where they lived at the north end of Scow Bay.[54] By 1911, the Indian Office identified S'Klallam "settlements" in Bremerton, Chico, Port Gamble, Port Ludlow, Quilcene, Hadlock, Langley, Port Townsend, Oak Harbor, Port Discovery, Blyn, Port William, Jamestown, Dungeness, Elwha, Crescent Beach, Pysht, and Clallam Bay.[55]

Port Gamble S'Klallam Land

1910–1925: The S'Klallam Refuse to Move, The Mill Company Refuses to Sell

While Coontown was growing, most Little Boston families continued to live on the Spit. The community persisted, however, at the pleasure of Puget Mill Co. The mill company owned the land and could evict the families at a moment's notice.[56] Government agents concerned about this arrangement agreed with the S'Klallam that a more permanent land base was needed.

Between 1910 and 1925, Peter Jackson and other S'Klallam leaders worked on three different strategies to obtain a land base for the tribe. The first strategy involved federal government attempts to purchase land on the Bay from the mill company; the second entailed the government giving the S'Klallam people allotments on the Quinault Reservation; and the third concerned a cash settlement for broken treaty promises.

The government's first land strategy was the most obvious solution: buy land from Puget Mill Co., preferably Point Julia and the adjoining uplands where the people already lived. However, the mill company adamantly refused to sell any of its land for a little town site. The request was scaled down to a small parcel for a school. Still, the company positively refused.[57] Exasperated with the mill company, the Port Gamble Day School teacher wrote, "They should *give* it to them as they secured so much land fifty years ago under false pretenses."[58]

The Indian Office's second strategy imagined that the S'Klallam might take advantage of surplus allotments on the Quinault Reservation, hundreds of miles across the Olympic Peninsula, on the Pacific Ocean.[59] The surplus land was supposed to go to the Quinault's immediate neighbors on the coast, the Hoh, Ozette, and Quileute peoples. But since the Reservation was originally set aside to include "other fish-eating Indians on the Pacific Coast," the Indian Office saw no problem adding the S'Klallam and other landless tribes to the mix.[60]

Individual S'Klallam would have to be adopted by the Quinaults, enroll in that tribe, and move to allotments far out on the coast. Worse still, the

The Port Gamble S'Klallam refused to leave their cherished homes on Point Julia to move to logged-off allotments on the Quinault Reservation in the 1910s. Even though Puget Mill Company could evict them from their village at any moment, they saw their future linked to the Port Gamble Bay area. Photo courtesy of Port Gamble S'Klallam archives.

federal government envisioned logging the land first, leaving the new arrivals with nothing but stumps.[61]

The S'Klallam saw other problems with the arrangement. The government would treat them as individuals, abandoning their status as a tribe.[62] And they worried that allotment to the S'Klallam and others would take money and land from the Quinaults, causing trouble among the tribes.[63]

Peter Jackson, the primary spokesman for the Port Gamble people, stated the position of all the S'Klallam at a Council meeting of the whole tribe in 1914:

Although these homes were small, they were dear to the owners; and that to leave such homes and go to a wilderness of stumps and begin over would put them back 50 years....They wanted to advance and have something to live on.... [T]he government had not kept its part of the treaty with them.[64]

Resolution of May 11, 1914

... WHEREAS ... We are not asking for lands merely because we have never received any allotments from the Government. We are asking for a settlement of our treaty right signed by our forefathers ...

RESOLVED, that we will accept allotments on the Quinault Reservation including all the timber growing thereon on such allotments, on condition we shall be allowed to live wherever we can make an honorable living, that we as a tribe shall benefit through any sale of timber that may be on such allotments we may hold, the same as any other party may benefit who enrolled before the suspension of allotments on that Reservation, and be it further

RESOLVED, that such allotments be made to the Clallam Indians as Clallams and not as adopted Quinaults ...

RESOLVED, that in the event the Government does not approve of the wishes of the tribe at large, that the Indian Office shall approve a bill if presented to them for a cash settlement to aid the Clallam tribe in purchasing additional lands at home thereby enlarging their lands, this would also assist those that are still homeless to purchase a few acres for home sites ...

Signed by: . . . Peter Jackson, Tommy Tom, Joe Tom, Leo Sam, Cy Webster, James Webster, George Howell, Ed George, Sammy Charles, William George, Joe Anderson, Henry Lambert, Tommy Charles and William Pulsifer.[65]

Port Gamble S'Klallam Land

Peter Jackson also appealed to President Woodrow Wilson, urging him to appoint a commission to enter a new treaty with the S'Klallam, one in which the tribe would have an equal voice. He wrote, "Today the State of Washington stands amazed at the treatment of its Indian inhabitants, which remains a national disgrace."[66]

National disgrace notwithstanding, the Indian Office made its position very clear: the U.S. government owed nothing to the S'Klallam.[67]

Through these years, the tenacity of the S'Klallam leaders was remarkable. They carried out a seemingly endless campaign of letter writing, petitions, and meetings with government officials. Peter Jackson, Sammy Charles, and the other leaders continually emphasized the unfulfilled rights the Treaty promised to the tribe. They always held their status as a *tribe* firmly in mind.[68]

Also, throughout these years the S'Klallam leaders were guided by elders who had been alive in 1855 at the time the Treaty of Point No Point was negotiated: Tyee Jack, Mary Jack, George (Eddie George's father), Skookum John (Louisa Sparks' father), *La-Hash*, Tommy Tom, and others.[69] For example, during one of the many meetings with federal government officials, when an official explained his belief that the government had fulfilled all treaty promises, the elders grilled him with questions that must have left him squirming in his seat. They demanded proof as to which S'Klallam chiefs and bands had left their villages and moved to Skokomish. (There were none!) Which half of the S'Klallam Tribe was allotted at Skokomish? (Only one man!) Who was paid the money due under the treaty and where were the receipts? (No one; none!)[70]

The S'Klallam campaign also involved an extraordinary lobbying effort to garner support from influential groups and individuals, including the Board of Indian Commissioners, the Northwest Federation of American Indians, and the Washington Congressional delegation.[71]

The Board of Indian Commissioners visited Little Boston and reported that removal to the Quinault Reservation would be a "grim joke." There was no livelihood there for the Port Gamble S'Klallam men who had a strong work ethic laboring in the mill. Instead, the Board recommended a reservation should be purchased on Hood Canal.[72]

In the end, Frank Law, Susie (Dick) Charles' half-brother, was the only S'Klallam to get an allotment at Quinault.[73]

By 1915, the S'Klallam had decided that their best likelihood for fulfillment of broken Treaty promises would be a cash settlement of $10,000 for each person for the lands ceded in the Treaty as well as a guarantee of treaty fishing, hunting, and gathering rights. Once again, they presented their request in a petition.[74]

1915 Petition Signers

For the first time, the Port Gamble signers of the 1915 petition included many women: Sammy Charles, Philip Howell, George Howell, Harry Fulton, George Sparks, Cy Webster, John Solomon (by his X), Skookum John (X), James Henry (X), Tyee Jack (X), Tommy Tom (X), Anna Garrison, Peter Jackson, Rosaline Webster, Nancy Jack (X), Susie Solomon (X), Ellen Jackson, William Garrison, Willie Pulsifer, Bill George, James Webster, Joe Anderson, Eddie George, Louis George, Jacob Jones, George Adams, Joe Tom and George Pulsifer.

At the same time, the Northwest Federation of American Indians, led by Snohomish tribal member Thomas Bishop, took up the cause of unallotted Indians in western Washington. Since the S'Klallam had already organized around the issue and had presented their story so eloquently, Bishop used the S'Klallam as the foremost example of unfulfilled treaty promises of land. The S'Klallam figured prominently in Bishop's *Sacred Promises*, a booklet that was distributed widely to politicians and others in the non-Indian world.[75]

Bishop's efforts, in which the S'Klallam case had initially played such a pivotal role, led the Indian Office to appoint Charles Roblin to investigate the plight of landless Indians in western Washington. Roblin reported that the S'Klallam deserved the government's attention and should get a reservation:

> [They] live as squatters on lands belonging to the [mill] compan[y]. These lands may be needed by the compan[y] at any time, however, and then the Indians will be told to move on. Where can they go?[76]

Cash for Broken Treaty Promises

In 1919, Congress introduced legislation that allowed certain tribes, including those in western Washington, to bring their treaty claims to the U. S. Court of Claims. The S'Klallam could have joined in this approach. But by now they had generated enough support for their own cause that over the next five years, they were able to proceed toward their own settlement.[77]

True to their words of support, the Washington congressional delegation introduced a bill in Congress to appropriate one million dollars to purchase lands for the S'Klallam. The Indian Office, however, favored a direct appropriation of money for individual S'Klallam.[78]

The S'Klallam enlisted the help of the Clallam County prosecuting attorney, William Ritchie, to submit their statement of claims based on the government's failure to provide land, a physician, education, and expenditures for their benefit as promised in the Treaty of Point No Point. The committee working with Ritchie included Sammy Charles, Peter Jackson, and Bennie George Sr., as well as men from Elwha and Jamestown. They reasoned that because the government had offered allotments at Quinault as satisfaction of the tribe's claims and each allotment was worth $10,000, each of the estimated 400 S'Klallam were entitled to $10,000.[79]

In his negotiations with Congress, Ritchie fought for the full $10,000 for each individual, but when the Act of March 3, 1925 finally passed, it authorized only $400,000 for the entire S'Klallam Tribe.[80]

Although this appropriation was drastically less than the S'Klallam believed was due, the tribe fared better than if they had joined the others who sued the U.S. in the Court of Claims: those tribes received nothing.[81]

Enrolling all S'Klallam

After Congress passed the S'Klallam appropriation, the government's timeline for distributing payments to rightful recipients was practically overnight. In April 1926, Agent Dickens received instructions for preparing the S'Klallam payment roll only one month before the final roll was due to the Indian Office. The funds would revert to the federal treasury if they were not spent by June 30th. In less than two months, all S'Klallam were notified to apply for enrollment, a committee of S'Klallam was convened to make recommendations about each application, and the official roll was prepared.

Although there were differences of opinion as to who should receive compensation, ultimately Agent Dickens announced that the test for enrollment was S'Klallam blood (of no particular quantum) *plus* recognition by the tribe.[82]

On April 15, 1926, over 300 people attended a meeting at Jamestown to request enrollment. S'Klallam census rolls were consulted to help prove S'Klallam blood, but "recognition by the tribe" was more subjective. An Enrollment Committee had been formed with members from Elwha,

The 1925 S'Klallam Council, also known as the Claims (or Enrollment) Committee. Photo courtesy of the Jamestown S'Klallam Tribe.

Jamestown, and Port Gamble. In addition, Pysht Tim, Joe Johnson, Johnny Cook, and *pačwi'ləs* (Prince of Wales)—all old men—advised the Committee. As each hopeful S'Klallam came forward to be enrolled, *pačwi'ləs*, on behalf of the Committee, either nodded approval, or did not.[83]

Four-hundred and fifty (450) applicants proved S'Klallam blood and received the Committee's recognition. However, the Committee refused to recognize nearly twice as many others because they lacked current affiliation with any of the existing S'Kallam communities—people who lived near Clallam Bay, Pysht, Port Angeles, Jamestown, Dungeness, Discovery Bay, Port Townsend, and Port Gamble.[84] The Committee was determined that the already-reduced claims dollars should not be divided among so many people that the amount per person would be meaningless. All the S'Klallam communities, who had struggled hard to stay together for so long, agreed. In the end, the Indian Office approved another eighty-three applicants, bypassing the Committee's disapproval.

Port Gamble S'Klallam Land

The old Shaker cemetery on the former Anderson homestead was exempted from tax foreclosures of the 1930s. It is the only S'Klallam land remaining in the former Coontown community. In recent years, the tribe has taken over the maintenance of the cemetery and today it is a sacred haven, a testament to the families who lived here. Photo courtesy of Laura Price.

Port Gamble S'Klallam people received their $722 checks on September 14, 1926.[85] According to the terms of the Claims Act, this amount compensated the people for all the government's broken promises and they, as a tribe, relinquished any further claim against the United States.

Coontown Land Is Lost
The Great Depression of the 1930s weighed heavily on the Port Gamble land holdings at Coontown. The land was taxable since it was not held in trust by the U.S., as land is on most reservations. By the 1930s, even the Anderson's Indian homestead had been taken out of trust status and could now be taxed. With cutbacks at the Port Gamble mill, some S'Klallam men lost their jobs. While most families ate well and got by thanks to their farms and their fishing, hunting, and gathering abilities, the Kitsap County treasurer accepted nothing but cash for payment of taxes.

The loss of the Anderson homestead is a poignant example of what likely happened to other families. Joe Anderson was a thrifty, responsible, hard-working man who was determined to save money. For example, speaking of his children's claims checks he wrote: "I want their money to last long ... you can depend on that. Anything I say, it's a go ... you can ask anybody around here."[86]

Seventy-three years old in the mid-1930s, Joe Anderson was supporting four minor children, an older child in ill health, and a divorced daughter with three children. Ever since their land was taken out of trust, the Andersons had paid their taxes every year. But losing his job at the mill cut off Anderson's cash income. He died in 1936 and Josie was no longer able to withstand the County's threats of foreclosure. In 1938, Kitsap County took the property.[87]

Other S'Klallam families also lost land in tax foreclosures, one due to a tax debt of $8.69. William George's parcel on the former Charley Jones property was taken in 1936, and Newton Pulsifer's piece of the Anderson homestead was foreclosed on in 1938. By 1936, the County owned two of the George Howell parcels, as well as the land belonging to Phillip Howell, Bennie George, and Cy Webster, undoubtedly through tax foreclosures.[88] Tommy Charles sold his Coontown land in 1930, early enough to avoid the heartbreak of foreclosure.[89]

The claims payments of 1926 were an important achievement of justice for the S'Klallam Tribe. The legislation came about as a result of the S'Klallams' intense and sophisticated lobbying campaign and it vindicated, to an extent, broken treaty promises. But neither the legislation nor the payments to individuals secured a permanent homeland for the Port Gamble S'Klallam people. In spite of having acquired a number of parcels of their own land and in spite of decades of lobbying for a land base, the majority of the Port Gamble S'Klallam still lived on Puget Mill Co. land. Because of the tax foreclosures of the 1930s, many of the families with land in Coontown also became landless once again. It would not be until 1938 that the Port Gamble S'Klallam people would finally have a reservation established on Port Gamble Bay that they could permanently call home. The story of the reservation's creation is told in Chapter 7.

Meanwhile, the Port Gamble S'Klallam community at Little Boston was staunchly surviving the enormous cultural changes that were occurring all around it. Just as families adapted to the new cash economy by holding jobs at the Port Gamble mill and just as some adopted the new system of land tenure by purchasing their own property, the Little Boston community would survive by adapting some new ways to suit its needs while retaining the heart and soul of its S'Klallam culture.

CHAPTER 6

"If Someone Was In Need, You Helped Them"[1]
The Little Boston Community

Emily Mansfield

"Things were so simple a long time ago . . . what you didn't have, you didn't miss."

–Mildred Fulton DeCoteau[2]

Little Boston on the Spit, 1850s – early 1900s

1896: Five-year-old Martha (Charles) John watched the two large ocean-going canoes as they floated, waiting off the beach next to her home on the Spit on Port Gamble Bay. Like the rest of the village, she had come out when she heard the approaching drums and singing, and she was excited to see the young girl her age who stood on the platform created by planks between the two canoes. Martha could see that her cousin wore a traditional woven cedar-bark dress and regalia and that she perched atop a high pile of blankets—gifts the girl's father and his Cowitchan people had brought all the way across the Straits for their S'Klallam relatives. Martha knew that the girl's mother, her father Sammy Charles' sister, had died in childbirth and that her cousin was being raised by her Cowitchen family who periodically brought her to Little Boston so that she could know her S'Klallam relatives. After the singing subsided, Martha's family welcomed the Canadians ashore for several days of visiting and celebration. This visit was the last time

The Little Boston Community

Martha (Charles) John kept alive S'Klallam stories, histories, and culture which she passed along to younger generations. Among her stories were memories of welcoming family members from Cowitchen, British Columbia. She was a treasure house of S'Klallam culture, as when she shared S'Klallam songs with Loral Wellman in this photograph. Photo courtesy of Port Gamble S'Klallam Archives.

Martha's cousin was brought over; but as an adult, Martha made certain that her niece, Monica Charles, knew the story of these visits and knew that the family had relatives among the Cowitchan.[3]

The scene Martha John remembered—the old way of remembering and honoring relatives from distant villages—could have taken place during any of the preceding centuries. But the backdrop of the scene in 1896 suggested that many things had changed. Frame houses with flowers next to some front doors replaced traditional plank longhouses. A neat one-room schoolhouse and a similarly styled Catholic church stood where once open fires blazed. Men in overalls returned home from their work at the mill and women wore cotton dresses rather than the water-resistant cedar bark clothing of their ancestors.[4] In the waning years of the 1800s, the ceremony, regalia, and ocean-going canoes of the past were quickly giving way to more "modern" ways of life, a constantly evolving transition that had been taking place since white newcomers first arrived.

Native people, including the S'Klallam, had always been vibrantly flexible in adopting the useful new technologies and innovations that came their way. For example, in earlier times the S'Klallam would trade with other Native groups for otherwise unavailable goods like buffalo robes, dentalia, and mountain sheep horn dishes. Blankets, steel, and guns were readily snapped up from the Hudson's Bay Company and other traders. Even new spiritual practices were adopted from the whites when their power seemed so evident.[5]

It is no surprise, then, that the Port Gamble S'Klallam adopted the newcomers' houses and clothing, cash employment, and material accessories that made life easier when given the opportunity. In the mid-1880s, Missionary Myron Eells noted: "In fishing they use many of the old style articles, as they see no advantage in giving them up; but when they see something that is an improvement and they can obtain it, they are not slow to do so."[6]

"People adapted quickly but kept the things that were really important," according to former chairman Ron Charles. The things that mattered were the core values that guided their survival as a people: family and community, traditional food gathering and preparation, and the central importance of spirituality.[7]

The first obvious change occurred sometime after 1862, when villages with old style multi-family plank houses were gradually replaced by New England-style houses that were built with material from the mill.[8] One or more old style longhouses, or potlatch houses, continued to stand at Little Boston until at least 1887, apparently still housing families

The Little Boston Community

The village on the Spit became known as "Little Boston" because its New England-style houses were fashioned after those of the "Bostons"— the white American newcomers. The schoolhouse and Catholic church sat in the center of the village. A raised trough running the length of the village carried water to each home. Photo ca. 1930, courtesy of National Archives Records of the Rehabilitation Division.

and ceremonies.[9]

Although the village site was convenient to the mill and the resource-rich Bay and its clam beds, the Spit flooded at high tide. When the people built the new frame houses, they raised them on blocks so that the high tides would wash underneath them.[10] The frame houses were modern construction, and it took awhile for families to adapt their ways of living to suit life in a house that was so different from their large multi-family longhouses. The Tom family was the last to give up the old way. This late 1800s description of the way the Toms adapted their new home to incorporate their traditional way of living likely applied to most homes during the decades after they were built. Louisa Pulsifer said:

All the people in Little Boston had stoves except Tommy Tom. They were the only ones that tried to live the true Indian life, even after we were trying to be modern. They smoked their salmon in the ceiling of their house because they kept a place in the middle of the floor for a fire, with a square hole in the middle of the roof.[11]

Harry Fulton Jr. (b. 1915) recalled that the Toms cooked over an open fire and used mats for beds.[12] The Port Gamble S'Klallam may have proudly built new style houses, but the families in them lived by the S'Klallam value that encouraged caring for several generations under one roof. In the larger longhouses, children had been able to freely and safely wander from their parents' fire circle to their aunties' and grandparents'. It must have been harder to raise extra children in the new houses designed for one little "nuclear" family. But helping relatives with child rearing was so important that the practice continued. Through the 1900s, as Rose Purser recalled, "Lots of family, lots of people lived in a house. There wasn't very much housing then, so it could be two or three families in one house."[13]

The Tom family was a good example, as Vic Tom Jr. explained: "Our whole family all lived together: my aunts, my uncles, my dad [Victor Joseph Tom Sr.] and Barn and I and Laverne and Janalee and Arlene and Saul, they was in one house but that was years ago—but we made it, we made it through the hard times."[14]

The new houses were permanent structures, not to be dismantled to carry on canoe trips and resource expeditions. Along with work at the mill, this lent a year-round permanency to the community. However, the Port Gamble S'Klallam continued their tradition of traveling by canoe for resources, visiting, ceremonies, and marriage as much as possible. Living in such a key location on the route between the Straits and Hood Canal, they were visited quite a bit as well. There are a few remaining descriptions of these gatherings from S'Klallam eyes: for example, Frank and Henry Allen's memories of an 1875 secret society initiation at Port Gamble, and an account of a gathering at Quilcene in the 1850s.[15]

The Little Boston Community

Missionary Myron Eells' limited perspective provides a picture of how earlier gatherings, potlatches, and visiting continued at Little Boston through the turn of the nineteenth century. In February 1878, sixty people in five canoes from Port Gamble attended a potlatch at Jamestown for a week.[16] On their return, Twana, who had also been at the potlatch, stopped at Little Boston for a small feast of potatoes and rice. They ate during the afternoon and three times through the night. "After dark the women assembled in one house and sat down in two rows, opposite each other, where they sang for an hour or more, accompanied by drumming and pounding on sticks."[17] Then the Port Gamble women made presents of yards of calico to each of the Twana women. Later, gambling went on most of the night. The next morning after a breakfast of bread, crackers, and coffee, the Twana continued on their journey home, fortified with breakfast leftovers.[18]

By 1887, Catholic missionaries had built a church in the village on the Spit.[19] This church did not see use for very long. Although Catholics were the first Christians to offer their religion, the Port Gamble S'Klallam were open to other religious persuasions, including the visits of protestant missionary Myron Eells.[20] By the early 1900s, the Catholic Church on the Spit sat empty after everyone became Shakers. Kate (Anderson) Moran remembered peering through the holes in the walls with her friends to see the "ghosts"—statues—standing inside.[21] By Harry Fulton Jr.'s childhood in the 1920s, the church was just an open building for kids to play in. Later, it was torn down to make room for a baseball field.[22]

A schoolhouse was also added to the village about the same time as the Catholic church. The buildings were of similar construction, but the school had a flag pole, a swing, and "merry-go-round."[23]

Around the turn of the century, Sammy Charles and Bennie George constructed a gravity-fed water system from Little Boston Creek above the Spit. The square trough ran the length of the Spit. At each home, there was a loose square board with a hole and a plug where the home's residents could fill their buckets.[24]

Another feature of the village on the Spit that is still recalled with fondness by today's elders was Sammy Charles' woodshop at the base of the hill. Using driftwood to keep his wood stove burning, Charles carved and shared S'Klallam stories and history with youngsters who came to his shop.[25] Sammy's daughter, Christine, remembered him in his shop making his own tools and trolling gear that he either sold or gave away.[26]

Into the 1900s, people continued to speak the old languages in Little Boston, although S'Klallam remained the predominant language. With marriages among the S'Klallam and the Makah, Chemakum, Twana and other groups, many languages could be heard at Little Boston. For example, Clara (George) Jones, whose mother was Suquamish, spoke S'Klallam, Suquamish, Makah, and Chinook Jargon.[27] In the old

Sammy Charles' daughter Christine remembered him in his shop on the Spit, making tools and trolling gear that he sold or gave away. Christine is pictured in 1935 at Emily Webster's home on the Spit. Photo courtesy of Gertrude Adams.

days, when a couple spoke different languages, each would speak his or her own language in the family.[28] As Harry Fulton Jr., remembered: "My father was Clallam and mother was Twana. So they didn't speak or understand each other's language."[29] Con Sullivan remembered hearing his grandmother, Ellen (Sigo) George, speaking Clallam and Suquamish with her father-in-law, Eddie George. They would laugh and look at

The Little Boston Community

young Con as if they were talking about him.[30]

Most of today's elders grew up hearing their grandparents speaking Indian languages, although few learned to speak the languages themselves. Darlene Peters remembered the lilt of her Grandma Josie Anderson's language: "I heard the language all the time and often responded to it. Like when *kaya* would always pray over the meals it was always done in S'Klallam. Always. Up at the Shaker church much of that was in S'Klallam. The women spoke in S'Klallam."[31]

Kate (Anderson) Moran, Irene (Fulton) Purser, and Bill Sparks were the last ones at Little Boston to speak S'Klallam.[32]

By the late 1880s, Christian marriage had become

Nancy Jackson (b. 1854), photographed in Port Gamble with the child of friends, the Hirschis. As was common in earlier times, Tyee Jack was married to two sisters at the same time – Nancy and her older sister Mary. Photo courtesy of Ron Hirschi.

common, while polygamy had nearly died out.[33] Irene (Jackson) Purser's grandfather, Tyee Jack, who married sisters, Mary and Nancy, was the last man at Little Boston to have two wives at the same time. Arranged marriages continued into the 1900s. Harry and Angie Fulton's 1906 marriage was arranged, as was the 1908 marriage of Bennie George Sr., to Martha Purser. The couple married when Martha was seventeen and Benny was twenty-one. When Martha's mother told her, "You're marrying Benny," she responded, "I thought we were just friends!"[34]

Nettie (Charles) Purser (b. 1904) with son, Jelmer, (b. 1923) at their home on the Spit. Although Tommy and Susie Charles, Nettie's parents, owned land in Coontown, three generations of the family continued to live on the Spit. Photo courtesy of Ron Charles.

Even when a young couple chose a marriage, their parents and family had to consent. Irene (Jackson) Purser described how her father, Peter Jackson, had to ask permission from his father to marry Irene's mother, Ellen Moses. After his father agreed, the family got together to approach Ellen's family. When all permissions were secured, Ellen's relatives, the Patsys from Hadlock, came to Little Boston for the wedding. Following the wedding, "they all jumped in their canoes and headed back to Hadlock. Had a dance at Chimacum."[35]

Little Boston: the Spit and Coontown, 1900 – 1940

In the early 1900s, as the Andersons, Georges, Fultons, Pursers, Jones, and Sullivans built homes and farms on the land they had bought in Coontown, the Little Boston community had two branches. Although about one and a half miles separated the homes on the Spit from the Coontown farms on the bluff north of the present reservation, they formed one community. They were united by family, S'Klallam tradition, the Shaker Church, the school on the Spit, and contemporary twentieth century activities like music and sports. As Ted George recalled, "There was always a community spirit that was around and that was one of the good things we had going on."[36]

The best impression we have of Little Boston life in the early 1900s was from the S'Klallam who grew up there. Interviewed as elders, they still had strong memories of their childhoods on the Spit and the Coontown farms. Life at Little Boston—seen through the eyes of children—centered on the beach, especially in the summertime. Christine Charles voiced the experience of many other S'Klallam children:

> Oh, we used to play, on the beach, play with shells and we used to play ball on the beach. We used to build houses and all kinds of furniture out of small shells and make furniture out of the wet sand. We used to play some game—we used to throw the ball over the house. We used to call it Anti-I-over. And another game we used to play was something called stink-base. . . . We'd play just simple things but we used to have a lot of fun, though. Nowadays, everything's just hurrying, rush, rush, rush, all the time.[37]

Jake and Floyd Jones lived in Coontown, but spent their summer days on the beach on the Spit. They fished for bullhead and cooked them in a coffee can on the beach. They had a place called "the hot sands" where they would lay down to get warm after swimming in the cold water. The boys made rafts out of driftwood and hunted birds with homemade slingshots and bows.

> And then we always made hoops out of bike rims and made sticks to steer 'em along with and followed them around all the time. Then we made wheelbarrows. I remember Floyd makin' one . . . put a bike tire on it and made it real fast—called it Red Skeleton—painted it red. . . . But we always kinda done our own thing.[38]

For Rose Purser, staying on the Spit while visiting her Auntie Lina and Uncle Martin Charles was so fun it was almost like camping.[39]

In the winter after a snow, the children would slide down the trail that climbed the hill to the Shaker church in Coontown. Their sleds packed the snow to ice. Skip George remembers hiding in the woods waiting for the churchgoers to come out from a Shaker meeting. As he peeked out to watch them descend the icy trail, shaking, singing and ringing bells, he could hardly wait to see them slip down the ice:

> Sitting there laughing—old people go sliding down. I was never so disappointed: they all come walking, just walk right down on that ice like that. All the way down, never even fell down or nothing. "Wow, how'd they do that?" Used to think that those people got a little more power than I know about![40]

All year 'round, children created their own games. Boston competed against Coontown in football, baseball, and hockey, which was played with sticks with an evaporated milk can as the puck. The two groups even competed at rock throwing! One football game was designated "The Clam Bowl."[41]

SCENES FROM THE SPIT

Josie Anderson walked all the way from her farm in Coontown to the Spit, packing a bucket under each arm. The buckets were full of fresh eggs from her chickens, which she sold for twenty-five cents a dozen. If children playing on the Spit were lucky, this would be one of the days when she also made big cookies to sell for 5 cents each.[42]

Josie Anderson was a frequent visitor to the Spit, walking the mile from her homestead in Coontown. Photo courtesy of the Anderson family.

Old Jacob Jones, fondly known as "Bomp," could often be found sitting on a beach log, flanked by several children—some grandchildren and some just admirers—as he told stories, mainly about "how we should live." While he talked, he whittled a piece of driftwood or sanded the handle of one of his tools with his dogfish skin sandpaper. Once he told how he and George Sparks were spotting deer at night and accidentally shot somebody's horse. Old Bomp laughed at his story as hard as the children.[43]

Young Ivan George and his pals hit their baseball over the Adams' high fence, which had been built to contain their mean dog. Since George Adams was hard of hearing, the boys had to holler loudly to him to retrieve their ball. "Nice old guy!"[44]

Dorothy George and other girls were frequent visitors at the Webster's house, where they baked cookies with Emily.[45]

Many days during the school year, brothers Jake and Floyd Jones raced back with Fred Fulton to the Little Boston schoolhouse—forty-five minutes late from noon recess—after fishing in the creek and losing track of the time.[46]

The Little Boston Community

But the reality of life on the Spit in the late 1800s and early 1900s was undoubtedly more difficult than childhood memories—tempered by time—suggest. The Spit only flooded during extreme high tide, but when it did "everything would be under water," according to Harry Fulton Jr. "We had planks and would put something on them to hold them together, get a pail and get on the planks and then we would push our way to the school."[47]

Carl and Josephine Sparks' family lived by a creek on the Spit. As a child, Barbara Sparks would awaken in the winter to see her shoes floating by; there was so much water in the house. Not surprisingly, she got sick with pneumonia.[48]

Families suffered illness and death from having to constantly battle the elements. Jenny Jones' brother lost twelve children to the cold and flooding. (One daughter, Julia, survived childhood to marry George Sparks, but died during the birth of their first child.)[49] The damp conditions, harsh winds, and relentless tides must have weakened people and left them more susceptible to disease. For example, the flu epidemic of 1918 hit Little Boston at least as hard as it hit the rest of the world.[50] During the years people lived on the Spit, tuberculosis touched almost every family.

Flooding on the Spit was not the only hazard. While everyone traveled by boat, rowing across the Bay in the wind-whipped winter waters to buy groceries at the Port Gamble Company store was dangerous. The icy waves took several lives.[51]

People toughed it out during hard times, especially during the Depression. Even so, malnutrition was generally not a problem: most families kept themselves well-fed through their hunting for deer and duck, fishing, and digging clams and oysters, some of which they would sell. Some of the less able-bodied had to rely on government rations. In general, however, people considered the welfare officials to be too intrusive and judgmental to be worth the pittance in return. In 1917, the local rations list included a very few of the elders in the direst need—

Pastor Foster Jones, (far left), with members of the United Full Gospel Church about to be baptized in Port Gamble Bay, July 1946. Jones started the new church to involve young people. Jones and James Webster, Jr. managed to raise money to buy the former Assembly of God building even though, until then, most of the donations had been in the form of pies baked by "the five old grandmas" who were members (Jake and Floyd Jones, 2005). Photo courtesy of Port Gamble S'Klallam Archives.

and specifically those without relatives to help them. One young mother and her children were hospitalized at Cushman for eighteen months for malnutrition.[52] Thankfully, these situations were unusual.

Throughout this time, the Port Gamble S'Klallam's thriving spiritual life helped people get through hard times. Whether it was the traditional practices, the Shaker Church, Foster Jones' United Full Gospel Church, or more recent denominations, the S'Klallam people have always been sustained and enriched by their faith, and the church has always been a cornerstone of the community. As Rose Purser said, "Religion was real important with all the families."

Shaker Church Memories

"The old Shaker cemetery was up on a high hill from where Grandma George used to live. When it was icy and snowy us kids used to slide down on a sled. It was up there where they had the Shaker meetings. Joe Anderson was the minister of that church and they'd have really good services with their singing and bells. And then they shook when the spirit moved them." **–Dorothy (Garrison) George (b. 1922)**

"[There were] wood benches and the stations. . . . When I walked in, there's the old wood stove at the far left hand side and I think the strongest memory I had was of the old women singing. It was usually the women who took the sick and sang over people and they did it in Indian. They did it all in S'Klallam." **–Darlene (Anderson) Peters**

"Some of the fondest memories that I have when I was young are of the old Shaker Church in Coontown. I can remember that people came from all the different reservations. The younger guys used to play marbles and have a lot of fun. Some of the older guys used to make a fire outside and sit around and talk. I can remember when they had a 20' x 40' dining hall and would ring a bell for the meal. We would run and try to get the best place. Before we could eat someone would speak, sing, and do shake practice." **–Orville "Bud" Purser (b. 1931)**

In the early 1900s, daily life in Coontown may have been easier than on the Spit—at least it was drier and less weather-dependant—but children were expected to work hard on the farms. The Andersons had a big pigpen, so Kate Moran's job as a youngster was to slop the pigs.[53] The Jones kids had to weed their Grandpa Jacob's two big vegetable fields when all they really wanted to do was go fishing in the creek. They had to trudge up the hill to the cement water tank and clean the leaves out of the wooden troughs so the drinking water that flowed to the Jones and Purser homes wouldn't turn orange. They also arose at four in the morning to milk the cows before school. With no electricity and with gas for the gaslights in short supply, everyone went to bed when it got dark.[54]

Ivan George carried water from the Fulton's farm to his parent's house. His sisters helped with the wash, which in the early days meant using a scrub board and wringing the clothes by hand.[55] As Martha John remarked, "Children of long ago were not wild and carefree."[56]

The farms at Coontown supplemented traditional S'Klallam foods harvested from the sea and woods. Ivan George's parents' farm was typical:

> We had a couple of cows we bought from the Japanese. [We] had one of them outside coolers at the time and bought big blocks of ice. Mom [Ellen Sigo George] used to make homemade bread. . . . Dad [William George] made our own shingles. . . . We had a great garden there in Coontown. . . . Had a whole acre of strawberries. . . . Apples was growing right along the road. . . . Mom canned deer meat and salmon, wild blackberries, huckleberries, grew our own beans, potatoes, apples. . . . We grew our own onions and potatoes.[57]

The Anderson, Jones, and Fulton farms, like the George's, had fruit trees, vegetable gardens, and domestic animals. With cows, families had milk and homemade butter. After growing up on the Fulton farm, when Inez (Fulton) Wellman had her own family, she made a rule for herself that she would put up one-hundred cans of peas, carrots, and string beans every year. She made apple butter and traded with people who had an orchard.[58]

The Little Boston Community

While most of Little Boston's men worked at the mill, other means of livelihood were necessary to keep Port Gamble S'Klallam families afloat during the first half of the twentieth century. Foster Jones, Peter Jackson, and others sold firewood. Nearly everyone harvested clams and got good market prices for them. Frank Sullivan worked on tugs out of Neah Bay, hitchhiking home only on weekends since he had no car.[59]

Women contributed to families' livelihoods in a variety of ways. For example, Josie Anderson sold hand-woven baskets during the Depression. Kate (Anderson) Moran canned for a woman in Kingston. Martha John, like most S'Klallam women, was skilled with her hands, and was always busy embroidering, knitting, crocheting, making rugs, weaving baskets from bear grass, and spinning yarn using a treadle sewing machine she had re-configured for that purpose. She also cut and hauled wood and cared for cattle. It is likely one or more of these endeavors earned some money on the side. When they didn't, she sold pop bottles back to the store in Port Gamble. Dorothy George, Thelma Fulton, Millie DeCoteau, and others worked in the Bainbridge Island strawberry cannery. Shirley Loeffler hired out to pick berries in Bainbridge fields. Many women took in laundry from non-Indian neighbors.[60]

After the Depression, more cash employment became available to women, although the jobs often involved enduring long commutes, learning new skills, and juggling the needs of large families with work schedules. For example, while raising ten children and a number of nieces and nephews, Irene (Jackson) Purser sold goods at Sears and Roebuck in Seattle, pumped gas and changed spark plugs at a gas station in Suquamish, worked at the torpedo station in Keyport, and shucked at an oyster plant.[61]

The most tragic circumstance to confront the Little Boston community during the twentieth century wasn't a disease, bad weather, or hard times. The government policy of removing children from Indian homes that white social workers considered "unfit" split many families apart.

At Little Boston, as elsewhere in Indian Country, these decisions often had less to do with a family's actual ability to care for its children than it did with non-Indian perceptions of "proper homes." The outside system generally did not recognize that relatives were always willing to step in and help raise a child if parents were unable to do so.

It is not known how many children were removed from Port Gamble S'Klallam families before the 1970s when the federal Indian Child Welfare Act (ICWA) effectively ended the misguided policy. The removal of Indian children from their families and reservations created a strong incentive among the Port Gamble S'Klallam to strengthen their tribal court system in order to handle these cases themselves. As Ted George said, "The pre-ICW era reminded us that we've got to take care of our own!" That motivation paid off: in 2012, the Port Gamble S'Klallam Tribe became the first in the country to completely take over all child welfare cases.

The George Family Store

Martha and Bennie George owned a store and gas station at George's Corner from 1928 to 1942, and the family lived in the back half of the store. In the winter, farmers and S'Klallam elders took refuge beside the store's woodstove. The store was a bridge between the Indian and white communities, as well as between the Suquamish and S'Klallam. For several years, Martha ran the store while Bennie worked as a pipefitter at Keyport. Their son, Ted, remembered: "I think her biggest problem is that it was Depression time and she had too many relatives with hungry kids and she was always giving credit. . . . I'm sure she went the extra mile to try and help, but she was kind of notorious for that."[62]

Martha and Bennie sold the store in 1941 when two of their sons were drafted into World War II. Martha went to work at the Naval Ammunition Depot "to make sure the boys got ammunition."[63]

Music and Entertainment

Like rural communities across the globe, Little Boston residents provided their own entertainment. One popular source of entertainment, music, had been bringing communities together for centuries. In 1878, missionary Myron Eells described S'Klallam people singing and dancing at a Skokomish potlatch. The S'Klallam, he wrote, were "about the best musicians and performers on the Sound."[64]

This musical talent was passed down through the generations. In the 1930s and '40s, an unusually large number of talented musicians occupied Little Boston—fully enough to make up a dance band. Harry Fulton Sr. played the violin while Emore George manned the banjo. The pair of Bennie George on banjo and Lyle George on saxophone played quadrilles at the dances, some of which were held in Harry Fulton's big living room.[65] Peter Jackson played the piano, sometimes to accompany his daughter Irene's singing. Russ Fulton played the violin.

Rose (Wellman) Purser remembers singing around bonfires while her aunts and sister-in-law played guitar. Joe Tom enjoyed playing harmonica on the family's porch.[66] No one had the benefit of music lessons; they just picked up their instruments and learned to play. Musical talent continues to characterize the Little Boston community to this day.

In the 1930s and '40s, the Fulton's entire family would fill the farm after church for a grand meal together.[67] Other families sometimes got together to play cards. Martha John and Foster Jones came out to the Jackson place on Hood Canal twice a week to play cards with Peter and Ellen.[68]

Camp Meetings

Elders today remember the church's week-long camp meeting as a highlight of their summers. In the early years, the meetings were held at Lower Elwha and Skokomish. Everyone camped in tents, and some people brought deer, fish, and clams for the whole encampment. During the era of Foster Jones' church, a different preacher would speak every night. Rose Purser remembers the beautiful singing, guitars, and accordions. "We could rock that great big tent!" Friendships made at camp meetings with people from neighboring tribes have endured to this day.[69] Camp meetings were a continuation of the traditional seasonal gatherings that brought people together from different communities.

Basket socials in the old community hall brought families together, both during the Depression and after. People brought baskets of food, which others bid upon. The winner and the person who brought the basket then shared the meal together. At pie socials, people donated pies to be sold by the slice. Marie Hebert still remembers longing to be old enough to drink the good strong coffee, whose aroma filled the air at each social.[70]

As self-sufficient as the Little Boston community was when it came to entertainment, they were not cut off from the modern world. In recent years, an interviewer asked elder Martin Charles about his memories of dancing expecting to hear about traditional smokehouse dancing, but Charles answered that the dancehall dances were all his generation wanted to do! That, and go to silent movies in Port Gamble.[71] In 1922, an Indian newspaper reported that Harry Fulton Jr. and Ed Purser saw Ethel Barrymore in person at the opening performance of *Delcasse* at the Metropolitan, and that Cy Webster went to Seattle to see *Foolish Wives* and attend a lecture on psychology and metaphysics.[72]

Some people kept the traditional S'Klallam songs and dances alive. Eddie George used to sing the old Indian songs, and he taught them to his great-grandson, Claude "Skip" George. A S'Klallam love song—"loving each other and needing each other"—was particularly meaningful to him. Skip recalled Grandpa Eddie once showing him a S'Klallam dance. When Ellen George, Eddie's daughter-in-law, saw them from her vantage by the window, she yelled out, "What is the matter with you people out there, dancing like Indians!" Eddie said to Claude, "We're going to stop so we don't get in trouble here."[73] During the first half of the 1900s, with pressure from the outside to assimilate to the non-Indian world, not everyone recognized the value in preserving these expressions of S'Klallam culture.

Chico Indian Community

After the treaties, Indian people who did not live on the new reservations searched for safe, available places to sink roots, usually in areas close to former settlement sites. One such place was Chico and Erland's Point on Dye's Inlet, near present-day Bremerton. A small band of Indian families worked in William Renton's nearby sawmill and took up land on the Inlet. Other Indian families in the area grew from marriages between early settlers and Indian women, including the Sigo, Garrison, and Sackman families.[74]

Present-day Port Gamble S'Klallam families trace their ancestry to the Sigos and Garrisons. George (aka Joseph) Garrison, the son of settler John Garrison and his Native wife, Jane, lived at Little Boston after George married Lizzie Pulcifer. They were the grandparents of Dorothy (Garrison Day) George.

Ellen (Sigo) George, a matriarch of the William and Bennie George families as well as the Clara (George) and Foster Jones family, hailed from Chico. So did Louise (Sigo) Henry, Ruth Martinez' mother. William and Louise Henry moved their family from Little Boston to Chico in the early 1900s to live with other Sigos. Martha George's mother, Julia Purser, was also a Sigo.

The Sigos were an important bridge between the Port Gamble S'Klallam and Suquamish communities. Contemporary Port Gamble S'Klallam families continue to honor their ancestral ties with the Sigos into the twenty-first century.

Of all the themes that run through the stories told by today's elders about life in Little Boston, the most prevalent is the way people helped each other and shared what they had. As Rose (Wellman) Purser recalled, "Anybody who was hungry and didn't have someplace to go, they'd stop in at mealtime. And there was always extra space. Even if we had to have another little table for the kids."[75] Irene (Jackson) Purser added to the story: "Susie [Charles] used to cook down on the beach for everybody. And if you went anyplace, you had to sit and eat with them, you couldn't just go there, you had to eat. We had to eat a meal with them."[76]

When the village on the Spit needed sprucing up in 1915, families worked together to clean up both the school and the houses, rake the street and side yards, and burn rubbish. Children cleaned yards, washed windows, and scrubbed floors. When the Anderson's house and everything in it burned down in 1914, the community raised fifty-two dollars for Joseph and Josie to re-build. In later years, when elders needed firewood, everyone put baskets of food together and brought their saws and pickup trucks for a community wood cutting day. When an expectant mother was close to delivery, the women's *Chi-i-chee* club made baby clothes, diapers, and blankets for her baby. *Chi-i-chee* means "the workers/those who get the work done" in the S'Klallam language.[77]

In short, the Port Gamble S'Klallam community at Little Boston survived because people actively cared about one another. As Ted George put it:

> Helping, taking care of one another. That was a common thing among everybody. If someone was in need of something you helped them. If someone needed to build a house, several came in and helped build it. If you had extra stuff you gave it away to someone else who may not have had something. And so I think that's probably the singular thing where you're really part of a clan or a family, a tribe where we help each other out. If someone grieved, you were there. If someone was hurt, you were there.[78]

The Little Boston Community

Port Gamble S'Klallam Veterans' Day celebration, November 2010.
Photo courtesy of Port Gamble S'Klallam Tribe.

Veterans

The men and women who serve in the Armed Forces are an important and honored segment of the Port Gamble S'Klallam community. Each and every one has a valued story of his or her own, but several stand as examples. Ed Purser volunteered to serve in World War I, where he was gassed and shot during combat in France. He had returned to Little Boston and was working in the mill when World War II broke out. With eight children, the World War I veteran that everyone described as "a very gentle soul" nevertheless volunteered for the army. This time he served in the South Pacific, where he survived jungle rot and combat. Although he didn't need to go to war a second time, Purser did anyway, and now he stands as a true hero in the S'Klallam community.[79]

Ivan George also served in the army in World War II, as a member of the invading forces that landed on the beaches of France on D-Day in 1944. Aaron Purser, a navy man, served on a ship in the Pacific that was attacked by Japanese airplanes.[80]

Veterans are honored at Port Gamble S'Klallam every year in an annual Veterans' Day celebration. The first Veterans' Day honoring was held for the men returning from World War II, seen here at the 1947 event. Photo courtesy of Port Gamble S'Klallam Archives.

Following in his grandfather Ed's footsteps, Rudy Purser Jr. signed up for the Navy during the Vietnam War. He was proud to serve his country for three tours of duty, but when the time came for his dispatch home, he gladly allowed himself to be whisked off the deck of his ship by a helicopter, leaving in such a hurry that all of his clothes remained behind at the laundry.[81]

In 1947, Bennie George Sr. created a Veterans' Day event at Little Boston to honor the veterans of World War II. Veterans are highly respected by the S'Klallam, as they are in other Native communities, and the Veterans' Day celebration became an annual event to honor all veterans that is still celebrated today.[82]

The Little Boston Community

The evolution of the Little Boston community from treaty times to the mid-1900s demonstrated how resourcefully the Port Gamble S'Klallam melded new ways with their own core cultural values. Although they embraced Christianity through the Indian Shaker Church, for example, the Shaker religion embodied elements of traditional spirituality like spiritual healing, and it helped keep the S'Klallam language alive. Some families took up non-Indian agriculture, developing thriving farms, while traditional resource harvesting continued to sustain everyone, especially during hard times when cash was low. The foundation of survival for the traditional Strong People was the strength of family ties—helping relatives and caring for children and elders—and this is what held the Little Boston community together as its people navigated through the changes around them.

Survival as a People is more difficult with no land base. In addition to living their daily lives in the rapidly changing world, the Port Gamble S'Klallam people continued to struggle to gain a homeland of their own.

CHAPTER 7

The New Reservation

Emily Mansfield

"The old timers around when our Reservation was created were some of the smartest, most visionary people I've ever met."

–Ted George, 1994

"We have a reservation because our people just kept after them!"

–Ron Charles, 2008

Throughout the 1930s, as families dealt with the Depression's mill closure, the Coontown tax foreclosures, and the insecurity of living on land owned by the mill company, the Port Gamble S'Klallam people continued their tenacious fight for a permanent homeland. The old school house on the Spit and the Shaker church in Coontown were frequently alive with discussions about land during meetings of Little Boston community members.[1] It would seem that every available strategy had been exhausted. It would seem that the land problem could never be solved in the midst of a Depression. But times were changing in federal Indian policy and the era marked a potential turning point for all tribes around the United States. The Little Boston community had successfully held itself together for long enough to

Page 143

seize the opportunity these changes brought.

Federal lawmakers—motivated by John Collier, the reform-minded Commissioner of Indian Affairs—were beginning to understand the folly of the allotment policy, which, since 1887, had led to the loss of about ninety-one million acres of Indian land around the country.[2] Indian agents had assumed an iron grip over every aspect of Indian people's lives and land so that by the 1930s, tribal sovereignty had been almost completely overtaken by bureaucratic meddling on every level. A major change in policy was in the wind.

The Port Gamble S'Klallam had been less affected than many other tribes by the allotment and agency policies of the 1800s. Their land had already been taken at the time of the Treaty of Point No Point, they had no reservation to carve up, and no agent lived in their midst.[3] They would, however, be among the first to gain some land back under the new federal policy promoted by Collier—the Indian Reorganization Act of 1934 (IRA).[4]

The centerpiece of the IRA consisted of a nationwide land acquisition program that accompanied the end of the allotment era, and provisions for consenting tribes to organize formally under tribal constitutions. Many tribes across the country viewed the IRA with suspicion. In fact, its tribal organization provisions generate controversy to this day. For the Port Gamble S'Klallam, however, the IRA brought a reservation and a constitutional form of organized tribal government. It also led to the construction of the first houses on the bluff on the new reservation.

A New Reservation

When Congress began appropriating funds to carry out the IRA's land acquisition program, the Port Gamble S'Klallam Tribe was at the top of the priority list of all tribes in the United States.[5] Peter Jackson, Sammy Charles, and the other leaders throughout the early 1900s had successfully brought the Port Gamble S'Klallam's need for a secure homeland to the attention of officials at the highest level. When Congress appropriated $1 million for nationwide land purchases under the IRA, the Tulalip Agency received $28,000 to buy a reservation on

Port Gamble Bay.[6]

This time, the mill company was ready to sell. Photographs taken in the 1930s of the uplands above Point Julia indicate that the second growth timber on the land had been recently logged. With the mill closure and other economic downturns during the Depression, and with the timber removed from some of the land, it appears that the Indian Office's purchase offer came at an opportune moment.

While land acquisition was central to carrying out the IRA, the act also required that, in order to be eligible for land purchase, a tribe must become organized under a tribal constitution that would establish a tribal council as its governing body. Indian Office policy also required that to receive land, a tribe had to show good prospects for taking advantage of the "rehabilitation" credit provisions of the Act.[7]

Fortunately, at the outset, the Port Gamble S'Klallam appeared to be an exceptionally good candidate on all three counts. First, its acute need for land had long been known. Second, the tribe was eager to organize a tribal government under an IRA constitution. And third, reports on the tentative land purchase touted the economic prospects of the new reservation's location: the site was close to the mill where Port Gamble S'Klallam men had labored for nearly a century; there were rich tidelands with valuable shellfish beds that provided sustenance as well as a good commercial livelihood; fishing in the Bay was excellent; and the reservation land could potentially be used for gardens, fruit and nut trees, and cattle grazing.[8]

One Indian Office official noted that the S'Klallam had waived any further claims against the federal government when they accepted payment under the 1925 legislation; but he believed that the $400,000 payment for the whole of S'Klallam territory was so obviously inadequate that the government could afford to ignore this "so-called settlement."[9] The claims payment was never mentioned again as a barrier to land acquisition.

On September 30, 1935, the United States offered to purchase 1,234 acres and forty acres of tidelands from McCormick Lumber Company

The New Reservation

The Port Gamble S'Klallam Reservation, established June 16, 1938, included 1,234 acres, with Point Julia and 40 acres of the tidelands that had sustained the Port Gamble S'Klallam people for so long. This photo shows the 1988 reservation boundaries. Photo courtesy of the Port Gamble S'Klallam Natural Resources Department.

(formerly Puget Mill Co.) for $15,000.[10] Due to setbacks and regulatory snafus, however, it would be three years before the land would become a reservation. Finally, the Port Gamble S'Klallam Reservation was established by order of the Secretary of Interior on June 16, 1938.[11]

Organizing Under an IRA Constitution

Although the Port Gamble S'Klallam agreed among themselves that they would form a constitutional tribal government under the IRA, the matter of S'Klallam organization was not so clear-cut to the Indian Agency. Because the S'Klallam had no reservation, the Indian Office did not conduct a tribal vote on acceptance of the IRA.[12] For a time, it appeared that the Office might become forever stuck in its own circular reasoning: the S'Klallam can't organize without a reservation, and they can't get a reservation until they organize.[13]

For two years, memos flew back and forth in the Indian Office debating the S'Klallam organizational issue. Early in the process, the Office considered having all the S'Klallam organize together.[14] None of the three bands favored that cumbersome task, given the geographic distance between them.[15] The Elwha and Jamestown tribes ultimately declined to organize under the IRA during the 1930s, although the Elwha acquired 353 acres of trust land under the Act.[16]

In the end, the Office decided that the Port Gamble S'Klallam could organize as a separate "band," but legal quandaries delayed the tribe in adopting a constitution until after the new reservation was established.[17]

Housing and "Rehabilitation"

While the S'Klallam land purchase was being considered, the "rehabilitation" plan, also launched in 1935, became mired in red tape and "catch-22s." The near failure of this aspect of the S'Klallam plan could have derailed the reservation establishment, since Indian Office policy linked the two so closely.[18] The rehabilitation plan was particularly important to many Port Gamble S'Klallam because it was through this program that they hoped to see twenty new homes built on the bluff, giving them an alternative to the winter flooding of their decaying homes on the Spit.

Three years dragged by as federal agencies argued among themselves over the roadblocks they saw to the "Port Gamble Community Project." First, insufficient funds were available for the houses and development plan that officials thought would lead to S'Klallam self-sufficiency. The plan entailed building a dike around the Spit to dry it for hay production, constructing a water system, clearing land, and fencing land for farms and dairy cattle.[19]

The solution to their lack of money, officials decided, was to enlist the help of the Works Progress Administration (WPA), which would provide the labor. The WPA, instituted during the Depression to put people to work, required that Indian laborers must be used for Indian projects. These laborers, it insisted, had to have been on public relief (welfare) from May to November of the previous year. At Little Boston, however, no men could be found who had received welfare during those months. According to one official, they had all "managed to keep clear from a regular federal relief agency."[20]

During these May to November months, Port Gamble S'Klallam families were fishing, shellfishing, and gathering their subsistence for the upcoming year rather than receiving relief. For example, Ivan George remembered that to get through the Depression, his family moved up to Foulweather Bluff and Skunk Bay where they lived on fish, clams, oysters, and berries while his mother baked potatoes and bread in the sand.[21] Most other families followed similar strategies. Ironically, federal regulations dictated that S'Klallam self-reliance might now prevent them from receiving assistance toward "self-sufficiency."

The Port Gamble Plan also worked its way through another Depression era program, the Civilian Conservation Corps (CCC). Although the CCC initially denied the plan, it ultimately approved five projects. Diking the Spit for hay production was notably absent from the list after the Port Gamble Council had its say![22]

While the Indian Agency awaited a waiver of the WPA labor regulations, it also worried about whether the new reservation was practical for agriculture after all, and whether the Port Gamble S'Klallam people themselves were well-suited for farming.[23] In addition, the Tulalip Agency and the Rehabilitation Division wrangled over the details of house construction. When bathrooms cost too much and latrines were substituted to save money, the Rehabilitation Division questioned why a water system was needed.[24]

The Port Gamble S'Klallam CCC Projects

- Boundary Survey

- Clear old logging railroad for a "truck trail" to headwaters of a spring to be developed for community and school

- Clear five acres for schoolhouse, church, teacher's cottage and playground

- Fence around reservation boundary to protect water supply from outside stock

- Cattle guards at existing roads[25]

After new homes were built on the newly-established reservation, the village at Point Julia was burned to the ground in October, 1940. Although happy to have the homes on the bluff, many elders grieved the burning of their old village. Photo courtesy of Port Gamble S'Klallam Archives.

The housing portion of the Port Gamble Community Project might have sunk under the weight of bureaucratic hand-wringing had it not been for the political savvy of S'Klallam leaders, who by now knew the value of a good public relations campaign. S'Klallam leaders enlisted the help of Reverend Karl Leonard of the Assembly of God Church, members of neighboring communities, the Kitsap County Board of Commissioners, both of Washington's senators, and even First Lady Eleanor Roosevelt, all of whom pressed the Indian Agency to go forward with the new housing.[26] Former Little Boston school teacher, Lucille Weisenburger, recalled:

> Eleanor Roosevelt came over, 'cause President Roosevelt had polio and he wasn't able to do much traveling. He sent her all over the country to check up and see how everything was. And she told him that people up here were really dying of

tuberculosis. . . . Eleanor Roosevelt went back and said they really need some money to build some houses up on the banks, so they don't have to live up on the water. That's when they built all the houses.[27]

Finally, the Kitsap County Health Board provoked the Indian Agency into action when it warned that strict measures would be taken if the housing project was not completed *immediately*. It intended to condemn the houses on the Spit.[28]

The Indian Agency and the Port Gamble S'Klallam Council approved establishing a Rehabilitation Trust Fund of $33,000 to build twenty homes, latrines, and a water system.[29] The bluff was cleared and construction began in June 1940.[30] Except for four homes built for elders, each family who received a home agreed to repay the Trust Fund the cost of construction at a rate of five dollars a month.[31]

The S'Klallam held a grand gathering on October 26, 1940 to celebrate the completion of the new houses. To the music of the Port Gamble Band and the aroma of baking clams and roasting salmon, the tribal community hosted agency officials, Congressman Warren Magnuson, and the Kitsap County Commissioners. Then, by order of the Kitsap County Board of Health, the houses on the Spit were doused with gasoline and burned to the ground.[32]

Christine Charles remembered that white officials had come to talk to the old-timers living on the beach to try to convince them to move. "They said they were building new houses and oh, they promised them everything."[33] While many people were relieved that the government had finally loaned them the money for new homes, the elders were heartbroken to see the only homes they had ever known go up in smoke.[34] Harry Fulton Jr. (b. 1915) and his sister, Mildred (Fulton) DeCoteau (b. 1925), watched with the rest of the community. Harry described the occasion:

> Some of the older people didn't want to leave the Spit because it was the only home they knew. They lived there practically all

of their lives. They were forced to move. They moved all of Mrs. George Adam's furniture out, she didn't want to move. They had to make her come out of her old home. She was sitting in an old chair, while they were packing her stuff out. She was sitting there crying and talking to herself and singing in Indian. It was pitiful to watch them. There were a lot of hard feelings because the people didn't want to leave the only home they knew. But they had to comply with the health laws, so we burned everything down to the ground.[35]

Owners of the New Houses, 1940

Two-room houses for elders: Louise Butler, Julia Purser, George and Mary Ann Adams, and one unassigned. (Grants with no payback)

Three-room houses: Henry Lambert, James Webster Sr., Richard Purser, Cy Webster, William George Jr., Harry Fulton Jr., George Sparks. ($573.43 payback)

Four-room houses: Clarence Charles, Frank Sullivan, Nettie Purser Long, Claude George, Russell Fulton, Joe Tom, Ralph George, Carl Sparks ($688.12 payback)[36]

The New Reservation

The 1940s on the New Reservation

Life in the new homes on the bluff evoked mixed feelings in contemporary elders who remembered their families' moves. For Russell Fulton Jr. (b. 1932), whose parents Daisy (Garrison) Fulton and Russell Fulton Sr. had lived at the end of the Spit, it was a great improvement:

> I was seven years old when my family moved to a house the government built on the banks at Little Boston. Life was easier in the new house because we had electricity [later, after World War II] and water, and our home didn't flood like it did every winter at Point Julia.[37]

On the other hand, Betty (Wellman) George (b.1939) remembered the difficulties of living on the edge of the woods:

> When we first moved here in 1941, we didn't have any electricity or indoor plumbing. There were a lot of cougars and bears around; it was scary when you went to the outhouse. The roads were just like a washboard—and all gravel. We also had a wood cook stove. To get the wood to the house we had to wheel wood in on

Daisy (Garrison) Fulton, pictured here, and her husband Russell Fulton, Sr., were among the former Spit residents who moved to a new four-room house on the bluff. Their son, Russell Fulton, Jr., liked the new homes with electricity and no winter flooding. Photo courtesy of Port Gamble S'Klallam Archives.

wheelbarrows. We did all the cutting of wood by hand.[38]

Children from the Jones and Sparks families pose in front of the new Port Gamble S'Klallam school, 1942. Once the reservation was established, a new school, a church, and a community center joined the new homes on the bluff. Finally, the Port Gamble S'Klallam people had the security to build on land they knew the tribe would always own. Photo courtesy of Port Gamble S'Klallam Archives.

The former Little Boston village on the Spit was being recreated on the bluff. In addition to the new homes, a new school had been built in 1938 (with a second classroom added in the early 1940s), and members of the Assembly of God had erected a new church alongside the school.[39] Foster Jones bought this church a few years later for the newly organized United Full Gospel Church. The Assembly of God re-built on Harry Fulton's property in Coontown.[40]

Next came a community center. After the new homes were completed, the tribe was pleased to find that the Port Gamble Rehabilitation Trust Fund had roughly $6,000 remaining, money saved during the construction. The schoolhouse on the Spit and the Shaker Church in Coontown had always served as the community's gathering place. Now an actual community center could be built. The Council persuaded the Agency to permit its construction, promising to be responsible for the upkeep of the building. The Agency committed to equipping the center with a range, steam cookers, sewing machines, a loom, tables, and chairs.[41]

The tribal women's club, *Chi-i-chee*—"the workers"—maintained and operated the hall. They also cooked noontime meals there for children in the new Little Boston School.[42] Church camp meetings were often held in the center. The hall's basement included showers—men on one side and women on the other.[43]

By the advent of World War II, the new village still lacked electricity, indoor plumbing, and an actual road. Families continued to use kerosene or carbide lamps for light. "It's a wonder we didn't have more fires in those days when they used so many candles and gas lights," recalled Rose (Wellman) Purser. "Some of our older people would fill their gas lights in the house instead of taking it outside and they'd spill gas on the floors."[44]

Despite multiple requests, the Indian Agency would not allocate money for electrification, insisting that since the S'Klallam men had jobs at the mill, they should pay for electricity themselves. The reservation was not electrified until after World War II.[45] Dorothy (Garrison) George rejoiced when she no longer had to bake bread in her old woodstove:

> I was already married when electricity came here. I forget what year it was, but we used kerosene lamps down on the beach. It must have been around 1948 or so. I learned how to keep heat at a certain temperature to bake bread in the wood stove. It was hard because if you got wet wood it was too cold, and dry wood got too hot.[46]

Families continued to make their way to outdoor latrines into the 1960s when septic systems and plumbing finally reached all homes. Rose (Wellman) Purser remembered that the new Council had much to negotiate with the Bureau of Indian Affairs (BIA) about infrastructure during the first decade of the new reservation:

> We didn't have lights. One thing we were working on was a road through here. . . . Seems like we were always mad at the

BIA for something. They just kept puttin' us off on everything.
. . . And I believe it was [after the 1950s] when Indian Health
finally started putting in septic tanks. . . . So wonderful to have
a toilet and septic tank and lights.[47]

A road between Eglon and Coontown was built to replace the old
railroad bed that had previously been used. Aaron Purser remembered
that people had to cross a high railroad bridge with only one foot
on either side of the tracks. Once again the tribe enlisted the help of
Reverend Leonard to pressure the Kitsap County Commissioners to
improve the road.[48]

The new Port Gamble S'Klallam Reservation was unique in Indian
Country. The entire reservation, including the housing lots, was held
in trust by the United States for the tribe. The individuals who would
own title to the houses after repaying their loans would not own the
land itself. Bennie George and other members of the Tribal Council
foresaw that private land holdings on the new reservation could
create divisiveness among the people.[49] To this day, every acre of the
reservation belongs to each and every member of the Port Gamble
S'Klallam Tribe. Ted George, Bennie George's son, summed up the
benefit of this way of creating the new reservation:

> The Port Gamble S'Klallam . . . may have the best opportunity to
> create a new sense of tribe and community because they're not
> divided by boundary lines—no one owns the land. My dad, and
> Foster Jones, Cy Webster, and Lester Jackson were some of the
> old timers around when our reservation was created. They were
> some of the smartest, most visionary people I've ever met.[50]

The establishment of the Port Gamble S'Klallam Reservation—a
permanent land base for the tribe—was the culmination of three

quarters of a century of sustained effort. The Port Gamble S'Klallam were among the first tribes in the nation to take advantage of the new federal Indian policy in order to finance the reservation's purchase. In this, the people followed in the footsteps of their parents and grandparents, who were among the first Indian people in the area to turn the new jobs in the mills to their advantage. In past decades, Port Gamble S'Klallam leaders had learned how to lobby Congress; in the 1930s, they learned how to work through the Indian Office bureaucracy to achieve gains for their people.

With the new reservation came new responsibilities. The Little Boston community had to work together to develop and maintain the reservation's infrastructure and make decisions about the future. Almost overnight, the tribe was in the position of a government that needed to exercise powers over its territory.

CHAPTER 8

Early Tribal Government: A New Sense of "Tribe"

Emily Mansfield

"No matter what, we never let go of each other
as a People."

–Gina Stevens, 2009

The S'Klallam Way of Leadership

The traditional S'Klallam form of leadership had served the Port Gamble people well through the challenges of the 1800s and early 1900s. Under the S'Klallam Way, leaders were heads of families who conferred together when decisions needed to be made.[1] Irene (Jackson) Purser described this way of leadership and decision-making as it occurred in the early 1900s when her father, Peter Jackson, was a leader:

> The old guys used to sit around and talk about whatever they talked about. Some of the times the stories were funny, and some of the times it was business, trying to get this reservation started down here. There used to be a bunch of them, they were good together.[2]

Leadership passed down through a family provided that each new leader had personal qualities and wisdom that inspired people's respect. For example, the first Port Gamble S'Klallam census (1877) listed Tyee Jack and Skookum John as "sub chiefs." Cookhouse Charley was also called a "chief."[3] Peter Jackson and Sammy Charles, the sons of Tyee Jack and Chief Charley, were important leaders at the turn of the century: Jackson led the political fight for land and Charles was the tribe's main history-keeper.[4]

Joseph Anderson was given a certificate in 1889 by the Indian Agent showing he was recognized by U.S. officials as "Head Chief of the Port Gamble Band."[5] After the deaths of Anderson and Peter Jackson in the early 1930s, Bennie George Jr., William George, Lester Jackson, Cy Webster, and Foster Jones stepped into leadership roles.[6]

Port Gamble S'Klallam leaders had the backing and respect of the people because of their capabilities, charisma, and wisdom, and had no need for elections or formal offices. The old way worked well, but in the mid-1930s, the Port Gamble S'Klallam people understood that organizing a formal council-style government was linked to land purchase under the

Sammy Charles, pictured in 1958, exemplified the traditional S'Klallam way of leadership. The son of Chief Cookhouse Charley, Sammy was a skilled fisherman who took on the role of tribal historian, and the community looked to him as a leader. He was a strong figure in the tribe's fight for land in the early 1900s. Later, he advised the younger leaders. Photo courtesy of Port Gamble S'Klallam Archives.

Indian Reorganization Act (IRA). With the reservation purchase at stake, their decision to organize formally under an IRA constitution came easily. A Constitution Committee—chaired by Lester Jackson, with Bennie George, Frank Sullivan, and Ed Purser[7]—represented the tribe in cooperation with the Indian Office, but the going was difficult.

Early Tribal Government: A New Sense of "Tribe"

It seemed impossible to get information from the federal government. Sometimes the agent would cancel a meeting, then show up unannounced.[8] The leaders struggled to have their voices heard by the Indian Office, which was mired in its own legal questions about S'Klallam organization. During this time, Lester Jackson wrote: "It is our impression that we were to organize as self-government but for some reason or another we are kept in the dark. As soon as we lift our voices we are shut up."[9]

Still, the committee pressed for certain topics that it deemed important: a bill of rights, appointment of guardians for minors and incompetents, and a method for holding and exchanging land assignments. Of these, the last was the only one actually addressed in the constitution the Indian Office offered.[10]

Lester Jackson (above) followed his father, Peter Jackson, as a tribal leader after the tribe organized under a constitution and by-laws. Peter Jackson had followed his father, Tyee Jack, as a tribal leader when he headed the lobbying efforts for land in the early 1900s, prior to an elected form of tribal government. Photo courtesy of Gertrude Adams.

Once the Indian Office decided that the Port Gamble S'Klallam could legally organize as a separate band, the Office held up the process while they worked out a "simple" boiler-plate constitution for all small Indian communities around the country.[11] But the two most important issues to the Port Gamble people's new government were specific to their own situation: 1) The territorial jurisdiction of the tribe would cover the reservation and any lands added to it; and, 2) tribal voting membership would encompass members of the band, not all residents of the reservation. The latter possibility would have been permissible according to the Indian Office, but would have included non-members among those who could vote. The Constitution Committee, no doubt guided by elders in the community, chose band membership over residence as the basis for the new Port Gamble S'Klallam government.[12]

The new constitution and by- laws were adopted on August 5, 1939, with thirty-two voting for and seven against, certified by Harry Fulton Jr., chair, and Cyrus Webster, secretary of the Port Gamble S'Klallam Election Board.[13]

The Transition to Elections, Councils and Membership Rolls

Centuries of independence without bureaucratic oversight undoubtedly made it difficult for the Port Gamble S'Klallam people to move to a Council/Business Committee form of government. This community of mill workers, fishermen, artisans, and subsistence gatherers were a self-sufficient group. As a tribe, they had never seen a need for meeting quorums or delegating powers. It was little wonder, then, that for the first two decades after adopting the constitution, governance was an informal affair.

Harry Fulton Jr. (b. 1915) saw ways in which the new format of electing a chair was similar to the former practice of leadership by the person best suited for a particular undertaking:

> When we got the Reservation organized, Bennie George [Jr.] was the first Chairman. Also Lester Jackson. They would just choose the man that they thought would be the best Chairman and vote him in. They didn't fight over being Chairman in those days. They just went along with whoever they thought would make a good Chairman. Bennie George was a good man. He was very firm with what he thought. The people never pulled anything over on him.[14]

Early Tribal Government: A New Sense of "Tribe"

But compared to governance today, Ron Charles noted the informality:

> Early Councils seemed to change regularly, there was little continuity to things and there were no funds to do much.... Little attention was paid to quorums, whether or not those elected were even tribal members, and certain Chairmen seemed to "do their own thing" and didn't have specific authorization from the Community Council. . . . There was much apathy about tribal governance from the forties through the sixties, and, with no resources and no help from the BIA [Bureau of Indian Affairs], why would anyone want to be on the Council?[15]

For example, the early 1960s saw no election for three years, despite being required annually in the constitution.[16]

Still, tribal leaders tried to carry on. In the 1950s, housing loan repayment and lot issues were two of the main responsibilities of the new Council officers.[17] This probably discouraged many from serving, as Ron Charles noted:

> Debt collection was very likely not a fun job. . . . Some of the homeowners were apparently very steady and paid their monthly payments, but some fell behind. . . . There is no evidence that there were evictions for not paying, so when others learned that, they would stop paying too. I could see where a Council member who got involved in debt collection would soon prove to be quite unpopular in the community.[18]

Floyd Jones recalled the reality of the early years of tribal government:

> When they voted me in to be chairman [1965], we had nothing. We had three thousand dollars over at the BIA and that's all the money the tribe had. Our budget was a hundred dollars a year for a couple of years. And then we went to two hundred dollars. . . . I don't know how many years I was chairman. Nobody wanted the job. No pay and no thanks![19]

Early Tribal Government: A New Sense of "Tribe"

As the leaders struggled to carry out tribal business in the new format prescribed by the federal government, the drawbacks of the BIA's one-size-fits-all constitution became apparent. Under the new constitution, all powers of the government rested with the Community Council—the entire voting membership of the tribe. In order to transact the simplest business, a majority of all members over the age of eighteen had to vote and agree. This difficulty was compounded by another provision that required annual meetings in January and July. July was a time when many families were traveling either for fishing and gathering or for seasonal work. Con Sullivan recalled that during this time, they rarely achieved a quorum at the monthly meetings: "[T]he tribe was at a standstill."[20]

In a major step to make their new form of government more workable, the tribe delegated the Community Council's powers to a Business Committee made up of the officers and two members. Twice between 1947 and 1955, leaders tried unsuccessfully to hold meetings with enough voters to approve this delegation of authority. Finally, on April 22, 1956, a quorum of 68 people met and passed the necessary resolution. After that, the six-member Business Committee did the official work of the tribe.[21]

1958 Port Gamble S'Klallam Tribe's Budget[22]

Rentals--- $229.19
Revolving Fund ---$55.00
Water System Fees-- $4.50
Cash in Bank ---$229.19

Early Tribal Government: A New Sense of "Tribe"

The new constitution also raised questions that took the Indian Agency years to sort out. For example, in 1953, a Jamestown representative complained that Bennie George Jr. was ineligible to serve as Port Gamble's Community Council chair—and thereby as their representative on the S'Klallam Claims Committee—because he lived off the reservation. The issue did not bother the Port Gamble S'Klallam, who had every confidence that George was entitled to represent them. But once the question was raised with the BIA, the Agency spent the next seven years considering it. The tribe's view that there was no residential requirement for officers in the Port Gamble S'Klallam Constitution finally won the BIA's agreement.[23]

The advent of elections and officers brought another change from the old ways of leadership: the need to determine who was a "member" of the Port Gamble S'Klallam Tribe. In earlier times, if people were part of the community, they participated in community affairs regardless of where they were born. When decisions were called for, the leaders sought advice from elders and others based on their wisdom and experience; no "membership rolls" needed to be consulted. The constitution based Port Gamble S'Klallam membership on the "official census roll of January 1, 1939" and it required that a base roll be prepared within two years of approving the constitution. There was, however, no Port Gamble S'Klallam census roll of 1939. Censuses existed, but they covered all bands of S'Klallam. The task of creating a membership roll in the two years allowed was clearly impossible. The tribe developed a list of eligible voters in 1947, but it did not pass muster with the Indian Agency. Constitutional amendments were required to extend the deadline for creating an official roll.[24]

Until the 1960s, the Indian Agency may have been more concerned about constitutionally correct rolls than the Port Gamble people were. As Ted George pointed out, "They didn't have much to fight over then," so early on there was little controversy over who was or was not on a membership roll. But people recognized the need for clarity about membership and sometime between 1960 and 1968, an Enrollment Committee was formed to oversee establishing an official membership roll. With Dorothy (Garrison) George, Virginia (Jones) Ives, Jennarose

(Charles) Fulton, Helen (Jones) Nicholson and Clara (George) Jones on the committee, and with Geraldine Purser overseeing the roll preparation, the tribe furthered its tradition of involving representatives of different families as a way to prevent conflict.[25]

The Committee's job was daunting. For the base roll, they had to verify birth dates and blood quantum of all Port Gamble S'Klallam people who were alive on January 1, 1939, as well as their parents' blood quantum. And they had to review applications from potential members born after 1939 in order to make the membership roll current. With virtually no financial backing for this task and with little help from the BIA until Pat Rudd (enrollment specialist) came to their aid in the 1970s, it was not until 1974—twenty-seven years after the first voters' list—that the Port Gamble S'Klallam Base Roll of [1939] 1974 was finally approved.[26]

Dorothy (Garrison Day) George (right) with Mary Lou Salter. "Auntie Dorothy" served on the tribal council in the 1950s when she lobbied Congress and helped establish the first tribal budget. She was also a member of the first Enrollment Committee. These positions marked the beginning of a long career of service to the tribe. In 1995, George was named "Community Woman of the Year" and "Woman of Achievement" by the Puget Sound Chapter of the YWCA. Photo courtesy of Port Gamble S'Klallam Archives.

Building Reservation Infrastructure Helps Create Governance Infrastructure

From the time the reservation was established through the 1960s, the reservation's infrastructure was one of the leaders' primary concerns. There was no shortage of needs. People still lacked septic systems, and there were no fire hydrants. No one on the reservation had a telephone. The nearest fire department was in Kingston. Two houses

Early Tribal Government: A New Sense of "Tribe"

burned down because the fire department couldn't get there on time.[27] As Con Sullivan recalled: "[E]verything was deteriorating around here. . . . [T]he cemetery—no one even wanted to be buried there, it was so bad. The Scotchbroom was higher than the ceiling right here, so we had that cleared off."[28]

The water system installed when the reservation was created did not meet public health standards. Due to leaks, very little water reached the homes, and the old system frequently failed completely.[29] Floyd Jones recalled that even with volunteer labor, the system often did not deliver clean water:

> At that time, our water supply was from a dam. They dammed up the creek up here about a mile. And so in the winter time when the leaves would fall our water would all turn real dark brown like tea. And so we'd have to go up there and we'd open up the dam and let the water out. Fred Wellman made some scrapers and we'd scrape all the mud—it'd be about a foot deep in there. We'd scrape it all out and put it into the creek. And after we'd got that all out, the leaves in there, we'd plug it back up and we'd have muddy water for I don't know how long, until it flushed out of the system. We had a chlorinating house that worked part of the time, so we had bugs and worms and dirty water. I still have a hard time drinking water to this day.[30]

To the tribe's request for help, the BIA answered that it had no money; the tribe would have to ask Congress. This was something tribal leaders knew how to do. Dorothy George called upon Senator Warren Magnuson. The senator, who had supported their earlier housing efforts, quickly submitted a bill to Congress seeking funding. The bill initially failed to pass, but by 1959, the tribe had its new water system. A water commission under Daniel Jones was appointed to oversee the system and collect the one dollar per month fee.[31] Ray Ives and Carol DeCoteau also worked on the system for a few years before Eugene Purser was hired to maintain it.

Dorothy George enlisted the BIA's help in documenting the tribe's budget

Page 168

When Rose Purser served as Community Heath Representative in the 1970s, the job of "water technician" fell to her since she had environmental health training. Photo courtesy of John Stamets.

so that the Business Committee could effectively collect rent and water fees. If the tribe had a budget, she believed, people would be more likely to pay their share.[32]

Community volunteers performed the infrastructure work. Others saw their efforts and were inspired to become involved as well. Floyd Jones described how work on the old community center became a springboard for others' commitment to tribal government and programs:

> All we had was an old community building over there. The windows were all knocked out and it had the little nine-by-twelve windows. I mean they were ALL knocked out. So Con [Sullivan] and I, we got some money from somewhere and went

and bought a whole bunch of them little windows.

Every night after work at the sawmill, we'd come and gather over here. Dicky Doyle was married to Patty Sparks at that time. He learned how to take the old putty off. We found out if we used those little torches we could heat the old putty up and it would come off easy. So we all got torches and putty knives and every evenin' for, I don't know a couple years I guess, we was up there putting windows in there.

We had no electricity and no heat, so Con and I went together and we charged a little airtight stove. I said, "Put half on me, half on Con." So they done that. We had a little airtight heater and some stovepipes and we put it in there and that was our heat for the whole building. . . .

[W]e didn't get too warm, but we held our meetings and the people started seeing what we were doing. A lot of them older people, Carl Sparks and Fred Wellman and a lot of the older people, they saw we was really trying to do something. Then almost the whole community started backing us.[33]

Even some of the bills were paid through volunteer efforts. Rose Purser remembered that after electrification of the community hall, she and her husband Rudy would often pay the two dollar monthly electric bill themselves. They would be reimbursed later after Reverend Foster Jones held a church camp meeting in the building and contributed money for the lights.[34]

Little by little, the leaders and the people were building the reservation's infrastructure and forging workable systems of governance and service programs. In 1960, the Business Committee passed the tribe's first official tribal law, the Lot Assignment Ordinance. An Adoption Ordinance followed. 1964 marked the creation of a summer youth program with Ted George employed as counselor. By 1972, the tribe had three employees: Ron Charles, tribal manager; Virginia (Jones) Ives, community aide; and Warren DeCoteau, chair of the Housing Authority.

Early Tribal Government: A New Sense of "Tribe"

Their offices were in the old community center, which was heated by the wood stove Con Sullivan and Floyd Jones had purchased and installed.[35]

When the houses that had been built in 1940 needed enlarging, Port Gamble leaders identified outsiders who could help. Floyd Jones and several others went to meetings of the Kitsap Community Action Agency in Bremerton:

> Kitsap Community Action Club was starting in Bremerton and they invited us over and they said, "Maybe we can help you out." And so we went over to a few of their meetings with their doctors and lawyers and teachers and they're talking way over our heads but we sat in there and listened. And then the people from the Kitsap Community Action come up here to see what was going on and they said, "If you can find the lumber, we'll furnish the money to pay for the workers." That's how we got additions put on our old houses. They paid the money to hire the people to work on them. Fred Wellman got lumber from the mill to do the work on the houses and get them additions on. . . .

> [W]e finally got people in there that knew some people that wrote grants. They started surrounding themselves with educated people. That's how we got started building up the community. And all the buildings we have now were just a dream that Jake and I had years ago.[36]

During the 1950s "termination era," federal Indian policy took a turn that deeply affected some tribes. The BIA pressed tribes across the country to legally end their sovereign tribal status. Thanks to the foresight of Aaron Purser, chairman in 1960, the Port Gamble S'Klallam did not succumb to the pressure. Purser wisely refused to sign a "termination" document that would have ended Port Gamble S'Klallam existence as a sovereign tribe just as it was on the threshold of becoming a modern tribal government.[37]

1973 marked a turning point for tribal government when the tribe tried out a new election system. As Bennie George Jr. and Ron Charles vied for the position of chairman, the tribe offered voting through secret and absentee ballots, increasing voter participation.

Even as tribes organized their tribal governments during the 1970s, small tribes like the Port Gamble S'Klallam found they had little chance of competing with larger tribes for federal attention and dollars. To address this problem, the Port Gamble S'Klallam joined the newly formed Small Tribes of Western Washington (STOWW). STOWW pooled the political capital of the area's many small tribes and helped Port Gamble and others address the "feds" with a stronger, louder voice.

Aaron Purser, pictured here while in the Navy, became chairman in 1960 when the BIA tried to persuade all tribes to "terminate" their sovereign status. Purser wisely declined to sign the agreement, saving the Port Gamble S'Klallam Tribe from federal "termination." Photo courtesy of Port Gamble S'Klallam Tribe.

By the mid-1970s, with the transition to formal tribal governance behind them and with hard-earned improvements in tribal infrastructure, the Port Gamble S'Klallam people had established a solid foundation upon which to build the thriving sovereign tribe that emerged during the last decades of the twentieth century. Chapter 13 continues the story of the tribe's transition to the modern government we know today.

Meanwhile, one challenge the Port Gamble S'Klallam faced in the 1950s was to sue the federal government for failure to adequately compensate the S'Klallam for the land ceded in the Treaty of Point No Point. In another example of S'Klallam tenacity, the tribe—joined by the Jamestown and Lower Elwha—pursued the case in litigation for over twenty years.

Port Gamble S'Klallam Business Committee, 1940–1973

Unfortunately, many early Business Committee members' identities are lost in time. Their service is appreciated, nonetheless.[38]

1940–1954   Lester Jackson, chair

1947   James Webster, chair; Mrs. James, secretary

1948–1949   Foster Jones, Chair; Bennie George Jr., vice chair

1949–1950   Lester Jackson, Chair; Harry Fulton Jr., vice-chair; Josephine Sparks, secretary; Carl Sparks and Jewel Makris, council members

1953–1954   Rose Purser, secretary

1954–1960   Bennie George Jr., chair

1955–1956   Bennie George, Sr., chair; Foster Jones, secretary

1958   Bennie George, Jr., chair; Aaron Purser, vice chair; Theodore George, treasurer

1959– 1960   Dorothy George, secretary

1960   Aaron Purser, chair; Russell Fulton Jr., vice-chair; Dorothy George, secretary/treasurer; Clara Jones, Claude George Jr., Russell Fulton Sr., council members

1961	Lester Jackson, chair
1962–1963	Aaron Purser, chair
1965–1969	Floyd Jones, chair
1965-1968	Barbara Sullivan, secretary
1968-1969	Conrad Sullivan, vice-chair; Dorothy George, treasurer; Joyce Bowechop, secretary
1970–1971	Bennie George Jr. [or Floyd Jones?], chair; Conrad Sullivan, vice-chair; Gerald Jones, treasurer; Barbara Sullivan, secretary
1971–1973	Floyd Jones, chair; Gerald Jones, treasurer
1971–1972	Jewel Makris, secretary
1972–1973	Craig Purser, vice-chair; Carol DeCoteau, secretary
1973	Ron Charles and Betty Roberts, chairs
1975–1986	Ron Charles, chair
1987–1991 and **1993-1998**	Jake Jones, chair
1992	Marie (Sullivan) Stiner (Hebert)
1999–2008	Ron Charles, chair
2009–present	Jeromy Sullivan, chair

CHAPTER 9

S'Klallam Take Their Treaty Claims to the Indian Claims Commission

Ted George and Emily Mansfield

"I don't know how you folks got the idea the federal government set up this process to give you equity. They set up this process to extinguish your claims!"

–ICC Attorney Fred Nolan, according to Ron Charles

One hundred forty five years after the Treaty of Point No Point was signed, tribal attorney Gina Stevens walked the beach at Mats Mats, near Port Ludlow, within the area traditionally used by S'Klallam people. Gina's S'Klallam great-grandmother, Jenny Jones was born in 1864, so it is quite possible that Jenny's father (Gina's great-great grandfather) was present at the treaty negotiations. When Gina passed a property for sale, the sales price stopped her cold: $400,000. The price of a one-acre lot with a small house was the amount the S'Klallam Tribe as a whole received from the United States as payment for half of the Olympic Peninsula ceded under the Treaty of Point No Point. Inflation notwithstanding, it was a harsh realization.

The $400,000 award from the Indian Claims Commission (ICC) was supposed to represent fair compensation. It was supposed to right the injustice of the $60,000 "steal" price stated in the Treaty. From the twenty-first century perspective, $400,000—the price of a waterfront

S'Klallam Take Their Treaty Claims to the Indian Claims Commission

lot near Port Ludlow—is hardly just compensation. Still, the S'Klallam fought hard before the ICC for twenty-five years to get the United States to acknowledge that the Treaty had unfairly undervalued their land. This acknowledgment may have been worth more in the long run than the cash award.

The story of lost and uncompensated Indian lands was the same across the country. Lands ceded by treaties between the U.S. government and Indian tribes amounted to roughly two billion acres. Lands retained by Indians—reservation lands—were approximately 150 million acres before the General Allotment Act of 1887. By the mid-1930s, reservation lands had been reduced by about two-thirds through the policy of allotment of "surplus" land.[1]

In 1946, Congress enacted the Indian Claims Commission Act, which established a commission to determine compensation for lands lost by tribes since treaty-making times.[2] Tribes could now sue the U.S. for claims like the S'Klallams', where the U.S. had paid an unprincipled, unreasonably small amount for the lands taken under the treaty.

After the Indian Claims Commission was established, one of the Commissioners, Brantely Blue, a Lumbee Indian from North Carolina, met with Northwest tribes, including S'Klallam, to explain the compensation process. Each tribe selected an attorney on a contingency fee arrangement, which meant the attorneys would not get paid until all the hearings were completed and settlements had been reached.

The S'Klallam had been through a similar process in the 1920s, when they retained an attorney to assist them in lobbying for the S'Klallam claims settlement legislation of 1925. (See Chapter 5, Land) The legislation had resulted in per capita payments of $722, giving each S'Klallam member a small compensation for broken treaty promises of individual land allotments. (The 1925 claims settlement did not address the government's failure to adequately pay for the land the S'Klallam ceded under the Treaty.)

S'Klallam Take Their Treaty Claims to the Indian Claims Commission

To press their claims in the 1920s, S'Klallam leaders had formed a work group from each band. Bennie George Sr. convened one of the early sessions in Jamestown. He described the anger of an "Old Timer" who spoke in S'Klallam. Bennie interpreted his words: "They have never lived up to what they said they would do and they never will. The only way to get their attention would be for us to go over to Dungeness and kill a few settlers." The crowd burst out laughing. The elder was enraged that they thought he was joking!

Since that time, there were changes in leadership and representatives of each of the three S'Klallam groups, but the format chosen in the 1920s—representatives of the three bands working together as a central S'Klallam council—was followed to direct the ICC case. The S'Klallam Tribe filed the case in 1951.

Like other tribes' ICC cases, the S'Klallam case consisted of three phases. In the first trial, the Commission determined the extent of land the S'Klallam had ceded under the Treaty. In the second trial—the "valuation" phase—the Commission decided what the land was worth in 1859, the year the Treaty was ratified, and whether the U.S. had paid the actual value or not. In the third phase—the "offset" phase—the U.S. was permitted to whittle down the amount due to the tribe by subtracting monies it had spent for the benefit of the tribe. (Money spent for the benefit of individuals was not allowed to be offset.)

While the first phase may have appeared to be a fair approach, ICC policy proved otherwise. Under ICC rulings, the only land that counted toward a tribe's ceded area were lands that the tribe occupied *exclusively*. In the S'Klallam case, this meant that mountain hunting areas the tribe jointly used with other groups were not counted. Likewise, lands around Foulweather Bluff, Port Gamble Bay, Port Ludlow, and the mouth of Hood Canal were not counted because those areas were also used by the Skokomish and/or Suquamish. Although the tribe claimed a far greater area, including tidelands, the ICC ruled in 1957 that the "Klallam Tract" amounted to 438,430 acres with no tidelands.[3]

S'Klallam Take Their Treaty Claims to the Indian Claims Commission

Even the area identified in the case's petition by the Tribe's attorney was smaller than the acreage the S'Klallam believed to be theirs. The attorney, it turned out, had reduced the acreage without consulting tribal leaders so that there would be no conflicts with neighboring tribes' claims.

After the disappointing ruling in the first phase, and as the case dragged on with no action and no word from the attorneys, the S'Klallam Council's morale fell. In the mid-sixties, at a meeting and election at the old Dungeness school, many frustrations and criticisms were expressed, including personal attacks on the characters of those seeking the leadership. No consensus seemed possible. Then, someone suggested that Ted George lead the group, and soon after, Mickey Judson and Elaine Grinnel were elected as vice-chair and treasurer, respectively.

In his thirties at the time, Ted George was possibly the youngest person to be elected as leader of the S'Klallam General Council. Involvement in the Indian Claims Commission case launched George's career of national leadership in Indian affairs. George reflected, "I was blessed to have had the experiences of leadership at that juncture. It was the starting point for my own future work and involvement with all Indian people in a severalty of roles. It's been a great ride!" Photo courtesy of Ted George.

Each S'Klallam group selected two representatives to serve in the work and planning. Virginia Ives and Bill Robb were the Port Gamble representatives selected, joined by Gerald Charles and Lorraine Daebler from Lower Elwha, and Harriet

Adams and Ron Allen from Jamestown.

To get the S'Klallam case back on track, a call went out for all documents each group had on file, so everyone would have the same information and history of the work to date.

The first attorney retained by the S'Klallam was Frederick Post. Post had not visited the Tribe in months, and he had provided little information and few updates on the case's progress. When the Council contacted him requesting monthly reports, Post was angry. He soon resigned.

S'Klallam suspicions that they had been misrepresented were later confirmed by attorneys Fred Nolan and E.L. Crawford. Nolan had been recommended to the S'Klallam by University of Washington professor Ralph Johnson, one of the foremost scholars and leaders in the development of Indian law and programs. Nolan agreed to represent the tribe, and ultimately brought the case to closure in the 1970s.

Nolan reported that between 1959 and 1967, the S'Klallam case was ignored by both the U.S. and the tribe's own attorney. Post had failed to present evidence on the 1859 value of the S'Klallam land, as required by the Commission. Additionally, Crawford wrote that the case as handled by Post left so much to be desired that the ICC made a rare ruling allowing the case to be reopened to gather more testimony on valuation. Crawford went on record before the ICC to state the S'Klallam's dissatisfaction with the area designated as the "Klallam Tract," even though he knew it was too late to change the ruling.[4]

At this point in the proceedings, the U.S. offered a settlement of a few cents per acre. Many of the elderly S'Klallam wanted to take the offer, reasoning that they should be paid before they died. Younger leaders recognized that this was simply a negotiating tactic of the U.S. attorney, and they felt they needed to oppose the elders' desires, although it pained them to do so.

Finally, under the leadership of the S'Klallam Council, and with the help of a new lawyer, the "valuation" phase of the S'Klallam ICC case took place in 1970—nineteen years after the case had been filed! Although the tribe's expert showed that timber on the land was worth $3.47/acre in 1859, the ICC found its value to be $1/acre. The total worth of the "Klallam Tract" of 438,430 acres was $440,000. Under the Treaty, the U.S. had paid $60,000 for all lands ceded under the Point No Point Treaty. This, the Commission ruled, was clearly an unreasonably paltry sum for so much land and the tribe was entitled to the actual value.[5]

During the "offset" phase of the case, the U.S. tried to convince the Commission to subtract from the award the $400,000 paid through the 1925 claims appropriation. However, since that payment had been to individuals for individual treaty claims, the Commission disallowed the offset. The federal attorneys also identified many funds expended for blankets, food, medicine, etc. that they claimed should be deducted from the award, but again the Commission declined to subtract those expenses. The Commission did allow the price the U.S. paid to purchase the Port Gamble S'Klallam Reservation— $15,000—as an offset, and it was subtracted from the total amount owed to the S'Klallam Tribe. The final decision awarded roughly $400,000 to the S'Klallam Tribe as a whole in 1976.[6]

After the Indian Claims Commission award was finalized, the S'Klallam had to decide how the money would be divided up among the three tribes. When Gerald Charles of Lower Elwha suggested that the monies be shared equally, fortunately, all agreed.

The Port Gamble S'Klallam share of the $400,000 ICC judgment enabled the tribe to purchase a large tract of timbered land. After the ICC claim was awarded, the Port Gamble S'Klallam left their share in the federal treasury, where it gathered interest for many years. When, in 2004, the tribe had the opportunity to purchase 390 acres of land adjoining the reservation, enough money had built up in the ICC account to pay for the tract. Once this land is taken into trust, the tribe's ICC claim will be converted into an economic development project for housing and the many other needs of a rapidly growing tribe in the twenty-first century.

A tract of 390 acres adjoining the reservation was bought in 2004 with the Port Gamble S'Klallam share of the S'Klallam Tribe's Indian Claims Commission judgment money. The parcel will serve future economic development or housing needs. Photo courtesy of Port Gamble S'Klallam Tribe.

The twenty-four year saga of the Indian Claims Commission case required all three S'Klallam tribes to come together and work toward a common goal. Persevering over a long time period to achieve justice was not new to the Port Gamble S'Klallam: consider the years-long lobbying campaign that led to the 1925 S'Klallam Claims legislation and the decades-long struggle for a reservation.

Neither the ICC case nor the 1925 legislation resulted in a sufficient monetary outcome. But each was, to a certain extent, a victory in justice served, because each brought into focus the promises of the Treaty of Point No Point. The case and the legislation both forced the

S'Klallam Take Their Treaty Claims to the Indian Claims Commission

federal government to acknowledge it had not dealt honorably with the S'Klallam people in regards to land. The cases upholding treaty fishing and shellfishing rights, described in Chapter 3, gave even more substance to the Treaty of Point No Point in contemporary times.

Other treaty promises for schools and physician services highlight the importance of education and health to the S'Klallam people. Each of these aspects of S'Klallam life evolved uniquely from traditional ways to modern times, stories told in Chapters 10 and 11.

CHAPTER 10

Education

Sharon Purser

*"Education is life-long. You've always got to improve
the way you think, act and behave. I think that the
Port Gamble S'Klallam Tribe is going to be on the
cutting edge of dealing with public school issues
as well as higher education."*

–Ted George, 1994

For S'Klallam children, traditional education began at infancy
and continued on into adulthood, when a person had gained the
knowledge they would need to sustain them throughout life.

S'Klallam children learned from all community members by watching,
listening, and experiencing as they went about their daily lives,
hunting, fishing, gathering plants and berries, and harvesting shellfish.
They were taught which plants were edible, which could be used
for medicine, and which ones were poisonous. They learned about
the tides, the seasons, and the natural signs that indicated things
like weather changes and seasonal severity. As people came to have
more knowledge in the world to supplement the teachings of other
community members, they began to instruct the next generation of
S'Klallam youth.

Education

Children who wandered off to the beach or into the forest without their parents might be snatched by slapuʔ, a mean and ugly old woman who would capture children and carry them in a sack on her back to her home where she would make soup out of them.
Illustration by Jeffrey Veregge.

S'Klallam parents and elders were patient and nurturing in their teachings, but also thorough, because they knew both the lives of their children and the future of the tribe depended upon the knowledge they would instill in their children.

Storytelling, besides being a means for passing on the history of the tribe, was also used as a teaching tool. Stories told of the evil and doom that befell children who ignored their parents' warnings, strayed off on their own, or acted in a way that was unacceptable. Characters such as *slapuʔ*, Coyote, and Raven played intricate roles in development and behavior. Children who wandered off to the beach or into the forest without their parents might be snatched by *slapuʔ*, a mean and ugly old woman who would capture children and carry them in a sack on her back to her home where she would make soup out of them.

The arrival of whites brought the beginning of the kind of academic education we know today. This system of education was vastly different from the traditional S'Klallam knowledge ways, under which people had thrived for centuries.

Although the Treaty of Point No Point provided that agricultural and industrial schools would be established for a period of twenty years, there is no evidence that S'Klallam children went to such schools in the decades after the treaty was signed.[1]

From 1869 to 1882, federal Indian policy changed in response to widespread fraud and corruption by Indian Agents. President Grant's "Peace Policy" was instituted to remove the power to nominate Indian agents from politicians. Indian agencies throughout the United States were now divided up among the various religious denominations' missionary boards.[2] (This, despite the constitutional separation of church and state.)

Indian boarding schools operating under these new policies sought to reorient the students' entire system of values, replace their Indian culture with Western values and skills, and indoctrinate them into the particular religious denomination of the school they attended. Sadly, this policy often only produced Indians no longer rooted in their own tribal traditions, but still uncomfortable acting as assimilated members of American society.

S'Klallam parents were virtually forced to send their children away to the various boarding schools, where vocational skills were emphasized. This subtle aspect of the boarding school experience suggested that Indians were incapable of learning anything more than the skills necessary to work at menial labor, automatically relegating them to second-class citizenship.

Education

Around 1890, a day school was started in the village on the Spit, under the supervision of the superintendent of Cushman Indian School, and operated by the Roman Catholic Church.

As the S'Klallam village at Port Gamble began to grow through the late 1800s, the parents remained skeptical about the necessity of reading, writing, and arithmetic; however, feeling they had no choice in the matter, most began to send their children to both the day school at the Spit, and to the boarding schools. From the accounts of Port Gamble S'Klallam elders, the Tulalip Indian Boarding School may have accepted grade school children, but the Cushman Boarding School's criteria for enrollment required the child to be fourteen, mentally sound, in good health, and enroll for a period of three years. Initial travel costs to the school were paid, but transporting children back and forth between home and school during holidays and vacations was the parents' responsibility. Home visits were only allowed when school was not in session.[3] Needless to say, many parents would never have the means to travel those long distances, thus they would be separated from their children for long periods of time, losing a great deal of control over their child's upbringing.

Eddie George (b. 1863) refused, at least initially, to have his children sent away. When Eddie was faced with the prospect of turning his sons over to an agent to go to boarding school, he took them to Hood Canal and hid out until they could safely return and remain in Little Boston.[4]

On the other hand, during interviews conducted with Port Gamble elders, few indicated much displeasure with their boarding school experiences. Harry (Jum) Fulton (b.1915) said, "When I got to Tulalip Boarding School in the late 1920s, I was supposed to be in eighth grade, but I was only doing fifth grade work. I was glad I went to boarding school, because I wouldn't have learned anything in the Little Boston School."[5]

Ruth (Henry) Martinez (b.1915) said, "Silverdale and Poulsbo were areas with a lot of prejudice. I went to Chemawa Indian School in Oregon because of that."[6]

J.H. Bratley and students in front on the steps of the dilapidated school at Point Julia, 1894. Photo courtesy of Port Gamble S'Klallam Archives.

Actually, more Port Gamble S'Klallam elders would complain about the poor quality of the schools on the reservation than about boarding schools. However, the elders who shared their school experiences lived through an era of very poor economic times, and were not, as a rule, ones to complain. It is possible that conditions in both schools were worse than they indicated all these many years later.

Annual reports by various Indian agents to the Commissioner of Indian Affairs between 1892 and 1905 described the Indian day school at Port Gamble several times.[7] In August of 1892, the agent reported: "There is a day school here of about 25 scholars." In 1893: "The school at Port Gamble has been maintained for nearly three years." In 1894: "Hard times this year—scarcity of work and scarcity of food have kept Indians from 'many excesses' and gotten more children to school." (The mill, during that period of time, may have been experiencing an economic downturn.) In 1895: "Pt. Gamble day school, taught by J.H. Bratley, is successful from every standpoint." Two years later: "The day schools at Port Gamble and Jamestown have done good work, the attendance throughout the year being good." In 1900: "The pupils have done well in their studies. Pupils enrolled at Port Gamble Day School: 11 males, 9 females." And in 1901:

> At Port Gamble the teacher, Mr. Clauson, and his wife have lived among them, devoting their time and energy, besides generous help in food for the sick, material for teaching industries, and the results are evident in the changed character of houses and people. Drunkenness, carousing, and debauchery are rare. A quiet, peaceable, thrifty community is slowly developing as a natural result of honest, conscientious work of the day school, in cooperation with the Department of Indian Affairs. The present outlook assures the future if bad elements can be kept out.

In 1913, Leonidas Swain, the Port Gamble Indian day school teacher, was evidently sent by a very paternalistic Indian Agency to do their bidding, as he offered opinions on how the Indians should conduct themselves, and he reported back what he learned to his superiors.[8]

Mr. Swain's replacement, in 1915, was August Harman, who conducted monthly meetings covering such topics as gardening and farming, roads, bridges, clearing new land, war savings, and thrift stamps. The meetings were not well attended, and often competed with Shaker meetings. In 1918, he reported, "These Indians are industrious and do the best they can to make a living and be self-supporting. When they travel they go in their boats or launches. They have very little use for bridges or roads as they don't use them." By 1917, the Little Boston School was in such poor condition that the government purchased a small piece of property in Coontown—part of the former Cookhouse Charley land—from tribal members Sammy and Susie Charles with the intention of building a new school, but nothing was ever built on the site.[10]

In 1918, the Indian day school teacher, Mr. Harman, left and, with the advent of World War I, the tribe endured a shortage of replacement prospects. For a short period of time, the school closed. The absence of a teacher at the day school left the community in a desperate situation. The law required children to attend school regularly, or the parents faced fines and compulsory actions. The fathers of school-age children sent a petition to E.H. Hammond, the superintendent at Cushman School, requesting that a teacher be sent for their children. They felt their children were too young to be sent to boarding school for such a long time.

Geneva (Jones) Ives was the first tribal member to graduate from North Kitsap High School in 1943. Photo courtesy of Port Gamble S'Klallam Archives.

When it was suggested that one option might be for the Indian students to attend school in the town of Port Gamble, Hammond responded that "local conditions" would make that impossible: that is, the white parents of Port Gamble did not want the Indian children mingling with theirs. Ultimately, the Little Boston school was able to find a teacher and resume operations, although the school temporarily closed again in 1922 due to the building's poor conditions. A new school for the Indian community would not be built until 1938.[11]

Education

The Port Gamble Indian day school faced many obstacles, including difficulty attracting good teachers—and who could blame them when they saw the poor condition of the Indian school building, their inadequate budget, and the difficulty of simply getting to work each day on the Spit? Dorothy George (b. 1922) said, about one of her teachers, "He used to come out from Silverdale. He used to come across to the mill side and then they'd bring him over in the boat. Do that every day. Some days it was too rough or too stormy—we'd get the day off."[12] Ivan George (b.1921) recalled the difficulty of simply getting to school at times, "Tommy Charles would pick us up in his skiff and take us to school when the point would be flooded."[13]

When federal funds were allocated for the Indian day school, they were channeled through the Port Gamble District School Board, an elected body always made up of non-Indians who blatantly shortchanged the Indian school. As an angry Tulalip Indian Agency Superintendent wrote in 1938:

> The County authorities in the Port Gamble District have for many years continuously practiced damaging discrimination against the Indian children of the district and Mr. Morrison [Superintendent of Indian Schools] is seeking to correct this by giving the Indian children as favorable advantages as possible. . . . We are attempting to do what the County and State authorities have selfishly refused to do; that is, give the Indian children of the district as favorable advantages as the white children have. They have been segregated for years in a little shack school house while the white children of the Port Gamble District have been amply cared for with modern buildings and equipment. I trust the County will not be impatient with our efforts to correct their neglect.[14]

In 1928, the Indian Office published the Merriam Report, prepared by The Institute for Government Research. The report detailed the deplorable state of Indian affairs nationally, and included plenty of criticism of the Indian boarding schools. There were complaints about poor diets, overcrowding, poor medical care, student labor issues, and the quality of the teaching staff.[15] If significant changes were made as a result of these findings, there is little evidence that remote communities such as Little Boston saw any benefit.

On September 23, 1940, Little Boston School Board members Foster Jones, Frank Sullivan, and Russell Fulton Sr. voiced their frustrations in a letter to the Governor of the state. The board detailed the history of the Little Boston school, the appalling discrimination their people faced from the Port Gamble, Kingston, and Poulsbo school boards, and the community's efforts to improve the quality of education for their children. The board asked only $2,500 for an additional room on their existing school building.[16]

Dear Governor Martin:

About ninety years ago the Clallam Indians were living a primitive life on Hoods Canal, in the location which is now the site of the Pope & Talbot Lumber Company at Port Gamble, Washington. The lumber company moved in and took possession of their homes and the surrounding timber. The Indians moved across the inlet and built the settlement known as Little Boston. A school was first started in a home at Little Boston. Later, a schoolhouse was built. A board in Port Gamble controlled this. This school together with the Port Gamble School was designated as District Number One. As a general rule old men were hired as teachers, the textbooks were those that the Port Gamble School had discarded. The equipment was poor. As late as five years ago the children had to gather beach wood for fuel and take turns sawing wood for the school, during school hours. The last teacher, a very old man, often fell asleep at his desk. From all investigation it seems that most of the grades were studying out of the same text and receiving instruction as one group. There were eight grades.

The attendance law was not enforced. Attendance was counted however, and the Port Gamble District received money from the federal government for pupil attendance. This was spent on the school at Port Gamble.

The Indian people had no voice in the school business. In 1938 we petitioned Supt. D. H. Wolfle, asking him that a new district be set up. This was granted and an Indian School Board was appointed.

Under Mr. Morrison and our county superintendent we have put forth every effort to make a better school for our children. For the past three years the average enrollment has been thirty-six, all eight grades included. Five pupils who graduated from this school in the past two years are going to High School. No pupils had graduated from the eighth grade for ten years preceding 1938.

Knowing that eight grades with an average attendance of thirty-six was not giving our children a fair educational opportunity, the board, with Mr. Morrison, signed an agreement with the Kingston School board to transport the pupils of the sixth, seventh, and eighth grades to Kingston school.

The day school started some people in Kingston objected to Indian children coming to their school. The Kingston board asked us to release them from the contract that we had signed.

We tried to send the same grades to Poulsbo. There we met with the same insulting, undemocratic refusal. They refused on the mere pretense that we did not have enough in our budget to give them cash for tuition. Not giving us a chance to correspond with Mr. Morrison concerning federal aid.

If we cannot send our children elsewhere, we must have better educational facilities here. Our school valuation is $5,918. We are enclosing a copy of our budget so that you can see that with the funds now available, it is impossible to build an addition to our school building.

We have a growing community. Twenty new homes are almost completed. The rehabilitation project was financed by the Tulalip Indian Agency. The homes are not gifts. Each family will pay for their own home.

It is impossible to get funds from the Indian agency to build an addition to our schoolhouse.

We have two teachers. The grades from four to eight with an enrollment of twenty are at the schoolhouse. The grades from one to three, with an enrollment of nineteen, are at the church.

Since the present school building is inadequate for the education of our children and we haven't enough money available by our budget to build an additional room, we are earnestly petitioning you as our Governor to aid us in this endeavor, which would not cost more than twenty-five hundred dollars.

Thanking you.

Most sincerely,

Members of the Little Boston School Board

Little Boston school teacher, Lucille Weisenberger, takes students on a field trip to the beach at Point Julia. Photo courtesy of Port Gamble S'Klallam Archives.

Tiring of blatantly unfair treatment, and unsure but resolute about using an unfamiliar electoral process for the first time, one year the S'Klallams attempted to elect one of their own members, Frank Sullivan Sr. (b. 1905), to a position on the Port Gamble District School Board. They reasoned that, if elected, he could advocate for a more equitable share of funds to be directed toward the Indian school's needs. The S'Klallams turned out in record numbers, but when the poll workers realized what was afoot, they mobilized one of their own to go into the streets of the town, with all the urgency of Paul Revere, to alert the citizens. Their voters responded, also in record numbers, and the tribal effort was defeated.[17]

Although Sullivan was rejected at the polls, nearly a half-century later, the North Kitsap School Board invited his granddaughter, Marie Hebert, to sit on the school board. Hebert served for two years, contributing a S'Klallam voice and presence to their deliberations.

There were other occasional educational bright spots over the years, and in 1941, Geneva Jones, daughter of Foster and Clara Jones, became the first S'Klallam to graduate from North Kitsap High School. Considering the poor schooling she received at the Little Boston school, and despite the fact that all her friends and relatives had dropped out along the way, it was remarkable that she accomplished what seemed an impossible task. Speaking on the problems S'Klallam children experienced at North Kitsap High School, Mildred (Fulton) DeCoteau (b. 1925) said, "We were hassled so much by the white kids. They made fun of us, for our hairdo and clothes and manners. That is why a lot of kids never went through high school."[18]

Ted George followed in Geneva's footsteps with a diploma in 1947.

There were some exceptions to the poor quality of the teachers at the Little Boston schools, and one was Lucille Jalousie Weisenberger. As a child, she got to know the Indian folks as she accompanied her father in a horse and buggy filled with vegetables from his nearby farm to sell to the Indians at Point Julia. When she graduated from college in the early 1940s, her first job was at the Little Boston school, and one of her first students, Floyd Jones, remembered that "All the boys had a crush on Lucille."[19] The students adored Lucille, and years later, to this day, she and many of her former students warmly greet each other when they meet. She amazes them with her total recall of the names of the students she taught all those many years ago at Little Boston.

By 1951, it was decided that the Little Boston School would be consolidated with Port Gamble, Eglon, and Hansville schools, and all students, grade 1 through 6, would attend the brand new David Wolfle Elementary. This move was something of a culture shock for the Indian children, as Ron Charles recalls, "The reservation kids found out right away when we moved in 1951 that we were far behind the other kids, and it took me a whole school year to catch up."[20]

Despite Geneva Jones' success in graduating from high school in the early 1940s, many Indian parents remained quite skeptical of the need for the white man's education. Most young S'Klallam men could find work at the mill when they were old enough, and many of the young ladies would end up getting married, so, they thought, what good was education? Sometimes going to work was a necessity for the young S'Klallam men, as Jake Jones recalled, "My older brother and I went to

Early Childhood Education Program teacher, Chad Sullivan, gathering berries with preschoolers. Photo courtesy of Port Gamble S'Klallam Tribe.

work at the mill when I was 17 because my dad couldn't work anymore."[21]

It was twenty years later, 1961, before another Little Boston student, Ron Charles, would graduate from North Kitsap High School. Ron reflected, "One by one, over the years, my friends dropped out, or were kicked out. It was discouraging, but my dad wouldn't let me quit."[22]

There was a law requiring all children to attend school until age 16, and that would be enough to persuade most students to remain in school, but those who didn't comply had to deal with a fearsome truant officer named Mr. Webster. Webster had the authority to put violators in juvenile detention, which he was known to do at times.

Lloyd Fulton (b.1935) talked about his troubles with non-Indian students at North Kitsap, "They used to pick on me because I was small. We used

Education

to fight with them. I got kicked out of school and I never went back."[23] There were few, if any, advocates in the school system to encourage Indian students to stay and graduate.

In 1951, Ted George became the first Port Gamble S'Klallam college graduate when he completed his degree in education at Western Washington University in Bellingham. In those days, jobs were hard to come by even for educated Indians such as Ted, but he eventually landed a teaching job at nearby Wolfle Elementary in 1957. Ted would later spend some time helping develop programs for the Small Tribes Organization of Western Washington, and for three years he served as Director of Indian Education for the North Kitsap Schools. He ultimately held an important post on the National Council on Indian Education, a presidential appointment.

In 1969, a U.S. Senate committee detailed the continuing problems with Indian education, and reported that after almost a half century since the Merriam Report, the state of Indian education was as bad as ever. In the tenure of President Lyndon Johnson, and his "Great Society" programs, Indian advocates began to be heard regarding the continuing sad state of Indian education. Gains continued for the tribes into President Nixon's term, and in 1972, the Indian Education Act was passed. These funds would enable schools to hire Indian aides and tutors for Indian children, and to fund special projects.

In January of 1975, the Indian Self-Determination and Education Assistance Act was signed into law, which officially made self-determination, rather than termination, the focus of the federal government.[24] In Title I of the act, procedures were established by which tribes could negotiate contracts with the Bureau of Indian Affairs to administer their own education and social service programs, and they were also able to obtain grants to begin planning to contract directly with the federal government. Title II of the act provided the means for increasing tribal parental involvement by guaranteeing them a voice in the education of their children.

Gradually, the Port Gamble S'Klallam Tribe was able to direct funds toward scholarships for their students, and the number of college graduates started to rise. Northwest Indian College and Evergreen State College were also instrumental with programs that reached out to the reservation community.

The advances made over the past few decades have had a significant impact on the success of S'Klallam children within the North Kitsap School District. Parent/teacher conferences and family reading nights including both Indian and non-Indian attendees are held at the tribal center and are well attended. A number of local teachers are reaching out and embracing the tribe's culture by participating in cultural programs including the annual Stan Purser Memorial Pow Wow, S'Klallam Singers group, and the annual canoe journey. Increased knowledge and understanding of the S'Klallam people improves relationships between students and teachers, elevating the Indian students' chances for academic success.

Today, the S'Klallam have reached milestones that many thought impossible only a few years ago. Over the past twenty years, many tribal members received their B.A. degrees; others have master's and teaching degrees. Gina Stevens graduated from the Seattle University School of Law and is now employed as the tribal attorney. Anthony Jones graduated from the prestigious Massachusetts Institute of Technology and Washington University School of Law in St. Louis. Darlene Peters holds a Ph.D, and is currently the tribe's Education Director.

It is apparent, however, that generations of S'Klallam children have been shortchanged by an educational system that was, at best, misguided, and at times clearly biased against them. S'Klallam students continue to underachieve in the public schools, making it essential that school officials, tribal staff, and Tribal Council do what they can to assist S'Klallam parents. S'Klallam parents are, after all, the ones with the greatest responsibility to see that S'Klallam children can compete successfully in this increasingly technological world.

CHAPTER 11

Health and Healing

Ron Charles, Laurie Mattson, with Rose Purser

Jacob Jones "never did go to the doctor or nothing. . . .
He didn't believe in doctors. . . . He always had Indian
remedies to use all the time for his colds and anytime
he got sick . . . and they always knew where to get it,
so that's what they used most of the time."

–Jake Jones[1]

Varied interpretations address how and when the North American continent was settled by Native Americans. Western scientific explanations emphasize migrations from Northern Asia. Historic S'Klallam traditions talk about how the S'Klallam have always lived here. S'Klallam oral traditions and western science may tell different stories, but they need not be viewed as contradictory. While scientific stories discuss the arrival of people on the North American continent, S'Klallam oral traditions emphasize how people came to have connections to the landscape and the development of and changes in the relationships between people and animals. Archeological evidence demonstrates that Native ancestors have existed on these lands for more than 11,500 years, while S'Klallam oral traditions establish and describe the connections between S'Klallam people and the lands they occupy.

Page 201

Health and Healing

Over those many thousands of years, S'Klallam ancestors developed some innovative remedies for their ailments, and those trained in the use of these natural medicines played an important role in village life. The S'Klallam medicine men also believed that their *tamanous* power could be used to cure some ailments.

At the age of 94, Louisa Pulsifer (b. 1880) recalled a time as a young girl when she was playing with some other children. The play got rough, and she injured her knee so badly that Charley Jones, her father, didn't think she would live. The white doctor wanted to amputate her leg, and her father thought this would save her life. Her mother, Lucy Jones, disagreed and took Louisa back to the Skokomish Reservation.

> Louisa's mother used barnacles to heal her broken knee. The barnacles were scraped off the rock and then ground, real fine. A flour sack was then put on her knee, and then the barnacles put on. Skunk cabbage leaves were then put on top of the barnacles, and wrapped with strips of cedar bark. When the bandage got too dry, salt water was sprinkled on, to keep it moist. The barnacles were left on the leg, until they got stink, then they were changed.[2]

The barnacles drew the infection out. Louisa lived and kept her leg. Skunk cabbage leaves were also used to draw out infections.

Floyd Jones remembers his mother, Clara Jones, using Prince's Pine and other medicinal plants for healing.

Jacob Jones used traditional remedies when he got sick, rather than going to the doctor. Photo courtesy of Floyd Jones.

> Mom used to use, I think it was, Prince's Pine[3] for kidney illness. And there's a little plant with round leaves. Mom used to dig them up and clean the roots off, wash it, put it in a rag and mash

it. Then she'd put that on a boil. You can find them around springtime. Then sometimes for a bruise she would use a squirrel tail and dogwood. I know Grandma Jones and Grandpa would kill a crane and she would render the fat out to warm it up for an earache.[4]

Floyd Jones remembers his mother, Clara Jones, using Prince's Pine and other medicinal plants for healing. Photo courtesy of Port Gamble S'Klallam Archives.

Squirrel tail was another commonly used plant, as Dorothy George noted:

I think Mom [Daisy Fulton] and them used to pick it but I never did until I fell and sprained my leg. . . . Oh, I could hardly walk and Uncle Bill [Garrison] said "I'm gonna get some squirrel tail and boil it up and we'll put hot packs on it." . . . That helped real good.[5]

Traditional Medicines Used by S'Klallam

The S'Klallam ancestors were very knowledgeable about what plants and practices would help to heal injuries and sickness. Anthropologist Erna Gunther interviewed many informants from Northwest tribes during the 1930s and documented how native plants were used.[6] She documented 61 plants that were used by S'Klallams.

Some known S'Klallam medicines include:

Wild choke cherry – boil top bark in water, drain and drink when cool. Used for upset stomachs and chest colds.

Devils Club – boil outer bark, drain and drink when cool. Used as a "strengthening" medicine.

Crabapple Bark – same as above. Helped blood. One woman used it recently and her blood pressure went down.

Seaweed – was used to make birth easier and relieve labor pains. The father would gather it fresh when the mother told him it was time, and she chewed it.

Cascara Bark – Used as a catharsis.

Foxglove – Used for heart medicine. (May contain digitalis.)

Vetch Vine – Prickly clinging weed, soaked in water. Girls rinsed their hair in this to make it soft and sweet smelling.

Alder leaves – dried and mixed with water to form a paste. This was used in the spring to cure impetigo or sores from winter. Some people can remember giving some to sailors in sailing ships for the same ailment.[7]

In addition to medicinal plants and traditional healing practices, spiritual healing practices were common. In historic S'Klallam society, sickness was often connected to spiritual matters. Spirituality was not viewed as separate from physical health and healing. The role of spiritual healing had a prominent place in living healthy. One of the purposes of developing spiritual power (through the obtaining of personal helping spirits) was to aid in curing sickness. People might seek out places of power to help them acquire helping spirits. One named-place on the west side of Puget Sound provides an example of this aspect of healing:

> . . . A spring near the shore-line. *Tuxdada'balt*, "home of spirits." The reference is to the "power" which enables one to go to the underworld for the soul of a sick person . . ."[8]

Many diseases that were prevalent in other parts of the world simply did not exist on this continent. So, when smallpox and other diseases were introduced, it was discovered that the Natives had no immunity to these strange new diseases, and the results were disastrous: Natives who contacted these diseases perished in great numbers.

Variola major (smallpox) was perhaps the most deadly of the diseases the Europeans introduced to this continent. Some of the tribes called it "rotting face." After contracting the disease, the victims almost always died a horrible death, and it was reported that some Indian parents killed their sick children to spare them the suffering.

Smallpox was particularly deadly because the virus could stay active for up to two years, and the Natives had no idea that a healthy persons should not come in contact with an ill person or their belongings.

GHOST SHIP

One story passed down by our ancestors tells of a "ghost ship" that sailed up the coast of Washington in the 1830s, with its sailors perishing, one by one, from smallpox. As they died, they and their belongings were tossed overboard, and as the coastal Indians retrieved some of the items, they contracted the disease. The ship ultimately made it to Port Townsend, but by then, all the crew had perished. Reportedly, an entire coastal Makah village was wiped out from the resulting epidemic caused by the "ghost ship." It could be argued that smallpox ultimately killed more native people, and did more damage to the political and social structure of Indian nations, than warfare with the whites. Photo courtesy of Port Gamble S'Klallam Archives.

When Captain George Vancouver came to explore Puget Sound in 1792 he traded with S'Klallam at Discovery Bay and reported seeing people with pockmarked faces. He wrote:

> . . . One or two had visited us on the preceding Thursday morning [at Port Discovery]; particularly one man who had suffered very much from the small pox. This deplorable disease is not only common but it is greatly to be apprehended is very fatal among them, as its indelible marks were seen on many; and several had lost the site of one eye . . . owing lost likely to the virulent effect of this baneful disorder.[9]

Boyd 1990:30 writes that smallpox was most likely introduced to the region during the 1775 voyage of Bodega y Quadra and Bruno Hezeta who made land falls at Trinidad Bay in Northern California and Quinault near the mouth of the Columbia River on the Washington coast. Over the next several decades, disease epidemics would sweep through the Northwest native villages, wreaking devastation on their populations. When in 1855 the Indians of the Northwest were induced to sign the Stevens treaties, it may well have been they were so weakened by disease epidemics that they lacked the presence of force they presented in the previous century from which their name *nexʷsƛ̓áy̓əm* (Strong People) derived. With no accurate counts on just what the S'Klallam population was in pre-contact days, we must now rely on speculation by early settlers as to just how horrific the devastation was.

Settlers present during the 1862 smallpox epidemic in Clallam and Jefferson Counties estimated that 1,200 to 1,500 S'Klallam died from the disease. Mathew Fleming, a settler who moved to Clallam County in 1856 and married an Indian woman, swore that he "counted at one time 60 dead on what is known as Cerrish Spit on Sequim Bay, and there were hundreds of bodies found in the woods after the disease had died out." Emily Matheson, a S'Klallam woman born around 1840, also swore that large numbers of the tribe died in 1862.[10]

Health and Healing

Missionary Myron Eells estimated the population loss, comparing 1887 numbers to those twenty-five years earlier:

> Most settlers among the Twanas and Clallams, with whom I have conversed, estimate that twenty-five years ago there were from two and a half to five times as many Indians as there are now. Though this may be exaggerated, yet there certainly has been a great decrease.[11]

The catastrophic loss of life due to new diseases, coupled with the consequent trauma to survivors, undoubtedly impacted traditional healing practices that often proved inadequate against these new diseases.

During the years following the Treaty of Point No Point in 1855, the S'Klallams living at *nexʷqíyt* may not have received any health care assistance from the government, and judging from the relatively stagnant population numbers in the village, infant mortality was probably high compared to the non-Indian regional population.

By 1860, a doctor worked at the mill at Port Gamble, and in 1863, the "New York House" was built to serve as the doctor's home, office, and hospital.[12] In later years, Rose Purser, as well as tribal women like Geneva Ives, Virginia Ives, and Millie DeCoteau, worked at the Port Gamble hospital performing tasks that ranged from reception to feeding patients and emptying bed pans.[13] But even with the close proximity of medical care for the millworkers and their families, it seems that the S'Klallams, well into the 1900s, would instead rely on their traditional remedies. For example, while some S'Klallam babies were born at the Port Gamble hospital, most babies were born at home with the help of community women. Catherine (Anderson) Moran remembered one difficult home birth:

> And Ella—she was married to Ralph George, I think—she was having her baby. . . . Oh, I felt so bad for her . . . 'cause she was having a hard time. And that baby was born butt first. So they tried to think of somebody that had small hands so they could help her. And Old Lady Jones [Jenny Jones] was the only one lady

they could find with the smallest hands. So she pushed that baby back in her . . . and turned it around. I know she had to take and turn her around. Gee, that must have been painful, huh?[14]

Catherine Moran went on to say that cattail was used to ease pain or induce childbirth.

Tuberculosis, commonly known as TB, became a very serious health problem for the S'Klallams, just as it had in other Indian communities. Many died—among them, Geraldine Webster and Lulu (George) Johnson—and every family was touched. The cold, damp atmosphere in the old houses on Point Julia was very conducive to the spread of TB, and it wasn't until 1929 that a TB hospital was opened for Indians at Cushman, on the Puyallup Reservation. Many S'Klallams were sent there, where a school operated through the eighth grade. The only treatment for tuberculosis was rest, and people often spent several years there, away from their families. As a child, Jennarose Charles was unhappy for a long time, missing her sister Eunie while she was hospitalized.[15] And Bill Jones was kept far longer than his TB persisted.[16]

In the early 1900s, Indian hospitals were built in Tulalip and Puyallup, and the boarding school children were given health care at those facilities. Rose Purser recalled:

> One floor (at Cushman Hospital) was devoted to tuberculosis, but tribal members went there for other medical needs too. Rudolph Purser and Bud Purser had their tonsils taken out as young children at Cushman. Their parents took them to the hospital, but then had to leave and come home. Bud admitted crying while there, probably from the discomfort following the procedure and missing his family and home.[17]

Irene (Jackson) Purser went to Cushman to have her tonsils out, contracted pneumonia while there, and was kept there for two years.

Given the travel time in those days to get to the modern facilities and the bad experiences many people had there, routine care for Port

Rose Purser and Dorothy George, two of the excellent CHRs who provided services over the years. The poster, about principles, says: "Follow up on your communications; communicate for tomorrow; make sure your actions support your words; seek to understand." Photo courtesy of Rose E. Purser.

Gamble S'Klallam people still entailed the more traditional remedies. Jake Jones' attitude may have been typical in the early 1900s:

> He never did go to the doctor or nothing. . . . He didn't believe in doctors. When he was 90 some years old, he got pneumonia and we knew if we didn't get him to the doctor right away, he was gonna die and so we finally talked him into . . . "No, I don't want to go to no doctor, I don't believe in doctors. . . ." They give him something for his pneumonia and boy, within a week, he was cleared up. But that's the only time I remember him going to the doctor. . . . He always had Indian remedies to use all the time for his colds and anytime he got sick or anything, he always had Indian medicine.[18]

As S'Klallams began to draw upon Christianity and the Indian Shaker

Church for spiritual strength, spiritual healing practices were often used in conjunction with modern medicines to fight illness and injury. Members of the Pentecostal Church also belived deeply in the healing power of prayer.

Floyd Jones described the Shakers' approach:

> One time, Minnie Webster—she was one of the older ladies down here, married to Jimmy Webster—was on crutches. And she went up there to the Shaker church and sometime during the service, they set her out in the middle of the floor on the chair and they all started shaking her and shaking over her. Pretty soon she got up and she started shaking, jumping and everything like that. Crutches went and she was healed.[19]

Christina Jane Charles' daughter, Monica, a Shaker, also worked on healing the sick:

> Monica's one of them that I like to watch when she's working because she works really hard. . . . She'd be praying and she'd see the soul of that person that was sitting on a chair. The soul'd be way off somewhere and I guess, she'd go in spirit and travel a long ways to get that soul and bring it back. And she'd put it back on that person. And that person feels better and she done take a lot of things off a lot of people.[20]

At some time in the 1930s and 1940s, the Port Gamble S'Klallam began to use the Indian hospitals for health care. As Ron Charles recalls, "I was born at the Tulalip Indian hospital in 1943. My mom said she had to spend almost three weeks at the Tulalip hospital before she got to bring me home."

Through the thirties, forties, and fifties, the government made sporadic, limited and short-lived attempts to provide some healthcare for the Little Boston community. However, day-to-day physician services were not available for routine illnesses. For example, the reservation schoolteacher, Lucille Weisenberger, recalls that in the early 1940s a school doctor came from Tulalip and he gave the children cod liver oil.[21] Rose Purser remembers in the 1940s, there was a two-room government clinic located next to the school where a doctor was available at times. This facility was used for only a short time, and then was abandoned.

Ron Charles remembers his first dental visit:

> Back in the fifties, I recall a bus taking the reservation kids to a dentist in Bremerton, where we were rushed through by a dentist who seemed in a big hurry, and wasn't very sympathetic to many of us experiencing our first visit to a dentist's chair. My six-year-old eyes grew as big as saucers, terrified at seeing a dentist's drill for the first time, but when I cried he told me to stop acting like a baby. I have hated dentist visits ever since.[22]

Rude Purser recalls being taken with his brother to Tulalip for dental care: "We used to call the dentist the 'horse doctor.' They didn't drill out all the cavity, and the fillings would fall out. You ended up getting your teeth all pulled out."

By the 1950s, there were fewer S'Klallam people available who knew how to administer the traditional medicines, and the reservation folks began to rely more on the local doctors. A limiting factor, however, especially in bad economic times, was the inability to pay the medical bills. Reluctantly, some of the doctors might agree to accept partial payments, but many times the Indian people grew tired of the skeptical looks they got when asking for credit, or the lengthy times spent in waiting rooms while everyone else was seen before them, and many simply stayed away from doctors.[23] The consequences were that some Indians lived shorter lives, because some ailments would go untreated and become life threatening.

The Indian Health Service, in 1955, took the responsibility for Indian health care from the BIA, and between the late sixties and early seventies began to obtain enough funding to provide some meaningful services to the rural reservations of Western Washington.

A sign of growth and expansion of comprehensive health services to tribal members was the opening of the long-awaited Wellness Center in 2004

Emergency services, until the 1980s, were limited. During the 1970s, the local pastor, Esko Rentola, many times acted as a first responder, loading a sick or injured person into his personal vehicle, rushing to the hospital with his horn honking all the way. Today, that all seems unbelievable, but nothing else was available at that time.

In those years, there is no question that some people died simply because they did not get to a doctor in time, since the nearest was located some fifteen or twenty miles away.

Funding became available at the reservation level for community health representatives (CHRs). Carol DeCoteau, hired in 1971, was the tribe's first CHR. Ray Ives, Dorothy George, and Thelma Fulton were hired as CHRs over the next few years, followed by Rose and Irene Purser. CHRs focused on preventive services like health education, immunizations, transportation to medical services, rabies shots for pets, environmental health, and establishing a "Well Child Clinic."

The Tribe's Foray into Primary Care

In 1979, the Port Gamble S'Klallam Tribe took a major step toward changing the way health care was delivered on the reservation, when nurse practitioner Dixie Deeter was hired through a contract with the National Health Service Corps.

Prior to Dixie's hiring, health care was administered by an expensive referral system where patients saw local doctors. Consequently, the dollars didn't stretch very far, and funds would run out long before the fiscal year ended. The situation cried out for more care at the reservation level, where dollars could be used more efficiently, but old habits were hard to break, and many refused to use the tribe's clinic.

Dixie slowly won the trust of the Port Gamble S'Klallam people, and soon more and more opted to seek her care in the clinic. She paved the way for the tribe to later open up a larger and better-equipped clinic, which tribal members were required to utilize. Thus, the tribe became a leader in its approach to tribal members' health care, administering what was a very comprehensive and cost-effective health program that was much more sustainable than anything the Indian Health Service ever administered.

Today, in an era when health care is on everyone's mind and many Americans are uninsured, the Port Gamble S'Klallam Tribe really does have universal health care. Tribal members are far healthier than ever before, thanks to the forward thinking of those in the past twenty years who chose to take chances and attempt to improve on the old system.

This chapter has provided a summary and chronology of events, developments, and changes in healthcare practices from those described in the mid-to-late nineteenth century that were grounded in older pre-contact traditions leading up to the present state of health care on the Port Gamble S'Klallam reservation today. From before contact with Euro-Americans, and throughout the period of contact and into the early twentieth century, S'Klallam people relied upon a wide range of healing practices. These practices ranged from the use of locally known medicinal plants to drawing upon and seeking the aid of helping spirits in order to fight biological and spiritual illness.

We have further demonstrated how even in the wake of dramatic and rapid social change that healing practices grounded in traditional knowledge continued to be practiced into the twentieth century and beyond. Following the expansion of government provided health care, which was demonstrated in this chapter to be sporadic, insufficient, and plagued with bureaucratic inefficiencies, community members continued to rely upon the collective help and support of other tribal members for physical and spiritual healing. This aspect of community health continues into the present and is central to contemporary Port Gamble S'Klallam tribal identity.

Over the past years of change, cultural values have provided the basis of strong programs and services, especially as services have become increasingly technologically sophisticated in the recent past. Today, a Health Advisory Board comprised of tribal members provides direction for the health care program, and offers leadership and advice through difficult decision-making processes. Long-established traditional methods of healing have been passed down through the generations, and are often used in addition to the prescriptions from the medical providers. Because of this, the memories of elders are treasured and care is taken to document their experiences and memories. Old family photographs are archived, and artifacts are preserved.

Today, there is a resurgence of traditional dancing and singing. These cultural practices continue to serve as mechanisms for expressing local identity, and as tools for spiritual healing on both an individual and community level in a manner respecting the past as the Tribe moves into the future. In doing so the Port Gamble S'Klallam continue to demonstrate in an ever changing world why they are the *nexʷƛáyəm*— "Strong People."

CHAPTER 12

S'Klallam Baseball

Ron Charles

*"Barn Tom was the best pure hitter I have seen
in Little Boston. What a beautiful swing! He even
looked good striking out, which wasn't all that often."*

—Eugene Purser, 2010

Education played a big role in the introduction of baseball to the S'Klallam community at Port Gamble in the late 1800s. Initially, this was due to the children attending boarding school who were being introduced to the game. In addition, the S'Klallams working at the mill were drawn to the game through their co-workers. Always on the lookout for good baseball players among their workers, the mill strongly encouraged the S'Klallam employees to play for their team. Baseball, termed "America's Pastime," was fast becoming the most popular sport in America, and Indian Country was no exception.

It was not long before the S'Klallams were embracing baseball so enthusiastically that it seemed as if they were the inventors of the game. What was it about baseball that made it the S'Klallam game of choice, and why has it remained so popular still today?

The answer probably has something to do with the fact that Native Americans had a passion for competitive games long before the white man came to America, and baseball may have seemed to them quite similar to games with which they were already familiar. According to Jeffrey Powers-Beck, the author of *The American Indian Integration of Baseball*, "Baseball is a noble game of tradition, of allegiance and camaraderie. It is played at an unhurried pace, with no clock. The character of baseball is consistent with traditional American Indian traits and attitudes toward sport."[1]

Skip (Sonny) George at bat with his older brother Douglas as catcher (Claude "Skip" George, 2009). Photo courtesy of Anderson Moran family.

The role and value of baseball in the S'Klallam community cannot be overstated. Beyond Powers' elegant commentary, playing the game of baseball was a way for players, both individually and as a team, to assert their tribal identity. This chapter will attempt to convey some of what it felt like to be a Port Gamble S'Klallam ballplayer.

S'Klallam youth naturally gravitated toward outdoor activities, as early in life they began to learn their tribe's hunting, fishing, and gathering practices, and in doing so, they ran, jumped, swam, and sometimes invented their own competitive games, which served them well when they were old enough to help harvest the subsistence foods that fed their families. Years of participating in these physical activities tended to produce fast, strong, and agile athletes with very good hand-eye coordination. All of these skills were quite important to the game of baseball.

In 1892, two tribal boys writing letters to friends, as a part of a classroom assignment at the Port Gamble Indian Day School, mention their tribe's baseball team. One student, Thomas Dixter, wrote, "I hope Eddie George will move here to work at the mill, so he can play for our baseball team."[2] His classmate, James Fulton, also wrote, "We have a dandy nine here. We call our nine Boston. They are the champion nine on Sound."[3] The boys seem to be boasting about the Boston men's

Probably a Port Gamble mill team. Bottom row, second from left: Harry Fulton, Sr.

team, and if what they said was true, the S'Klallams must have fielded a team several years prior to 1892.

Eddie George, born in 1863, did indeed move to Port Gamble shortly thereafter, and he would be instrumental in the development of baseball in the S'Klallam community. Eddie played for the Boston team, and would pass on his love of the game to his three sons, Bennie, Willie and Louie. Eddie's grandson, Ted George, talks about how his grandfather tutored his son, Louie, who went on to become one of the greatest pitchers of his time: "Eddie George cut a block from a large old growth fir tree and painted a rectangular block on it representing the strike zone. Louie threw his practice balls at that target and said it also helped his fielding as the ball bounced back to him."[4]

Ted George was born in 1928, a very good player in his own right, and he confirms the emphasis Indian Boarding Schools placed upon baseball, telling about his dad, Bennie, born in 1892: "Bennie George

About 1900, Boston team, most unidentified. Top left: Harry Fulton, Sr. From right: Tommy Charles. Photo courtesy of Ron Charles.

was the captain and center fielder of his Cushman Indian School varsity team. Baseball was so popular at his school that he said they had about six teams."[5]

Sammy Charles was born in 1869, attended Indian Boarding School, and he, along with his brother Thomas, were great players for some of the early Boston teams. Martin Charles, born in 1914, said, "My dad, Thomas Charles, played on the 'Walkaway' team. They called them that because they were so good, they would walk away from all the other teams."[6]

Ted George also notes that great team from the early 1900s. "A very early and highly acclaimed team from the reservation was so successful that they were called the 'Walkways.' Some members mentioned were Joe Tom, Sammy Charles, Cy Webster, Willie, Bennie and Louie George, Harry Fulton Sr., and Peter Jackson."[7] Elder Irene Jackson Purser said, "I met a man long ago from Port Townsend, and he told me that my dad, Peter Jackson, was a member of that great 'Walkaway' team."[8]

Thomas Charles, about 1900, probably dressed in a mill team uniform. Farther of Martin Charles, brother of Sammy Charles. Photo courtesy of Ron Charles.

Ted George also shares this memory about the Northwest of the early 1900s, before there were many roads and cars, when the main mode of transportation around Puget Sound was the "Mosquito Fleet" of small boats:

> Baseball was very popular, the only game in towns and reservations. Competition was very strong, especially among the mill teams. They hired the best players they could find, giving them good and easy jobs so they would play for their teams. Baseball has a long history of being played among Indian tribes. Port Gamble was no exception.[9]

Ron Charles says: "My dad, Martin Charles, who played in the 1930s, told me that, because he was a really good pitcher, the mills would compete for his services, and he would agree to switch teams if he was offered a better job."[10]

Ron Hirschi was raised in a family with a long history in the town of Port Gamble, and he relates the following story that reinforces Ted George's comments regarding the importance baseball played in mill towns years ago:

Many years ago, a Hawaiian man, Brownie Kahalie, arrived in Port Gamble as a deckhand on one of the ships that came in to pick up a load of lumber, and while here it was learned that he was a really talented ballplayer. During his ship's stay dockside in Port Gamble, someone concocted a scheme to cause Brownie to miss the departure of his ship, and afterwards, a job at the mill

These 1910 team members look like they knew how to play some ball! Top left to right: Phillip Howell, unknown, Louie George, unknown, unknown, Harry Fulton Sr. Bottom left to right: Richard Henry, Cy Webster, Bill Garrison and Joe Tom. Photo courtesy of Port Gamble S'Klallam Archives.

was offered to him. Brownie stayed on, took the job at the mill, and was a star player for the company team for many years.[11]

Sammy Charles, born in 1869, played for the Boston team during the late 1800s and early 1900s, and he was legendary for his tough hands, rough and calloused from many years of fishing, canoe building, and millwork. Old-timers say that, with his bare hands, Sammy could toast bread over an open fire, and when catching a game he would sometimes get worked up and toss his catcher's mitt aside and catch barehanded. Many years later, a common saying around the reservation about anyone showing they had tough dukes was that they possessed "Sammy Hands."

On Sammy, Ron Charles recalls:

> We moved in next door to Sammy and Susie Charles in the late 1940s, and by then Sammy was probably close to 80 years old. I loved his baseball stories, and, by radio, he closely followed

the only pro team in the area, the Seattle Rainiers. Hard of hearing, on Rainiers' game days Sammy would have his radio blaring loudly, so the entire neighborhood could hear the game. He sat there listening intently, while he carefully wrote each player's names in his own personal scorebook, and kept score of the game. I don't know if I have ever seen such an avid baseball fan as Sammy.[12]

Harry Fulton Sr., born in 1878, grew up in the old S'Klallam village, and he was a star player for both Boston and the Port Gamble mill baseball team for many years. He was a tall, talented lefty who possessed a blazing fastball, and was recruited to play for several teams during his playing days. Harry had six sons, and each of them was a ballplayer too.

Richard Henry, S'Klallam player, early 1900s. The "W" on his uniform denotes that he was a member of the "Walkaway" team. Photo courtesy of Ron Charles.

Eddie George's sons, Willie, Bennie, and Louie were born in the 1890s, and all followed in their dad's footsteps and became ballplayers. Louie was one of the most talented pitchers of his era, as Ted George recalls:

Louie George was a tall, perfectly coordinated pitcher who was so domineering that he was hired throughout the Northwest to pitch for teams who were to play their rivals, and wanted badly to win. He was riding his Indian motorcycle up on Hansville highway and he wrecked, and took off part of his finger. He always said that is why he was able to throw a pitch like the "clam ball."

Chuck George was the manager of the Boston team about 1950.
Back row: Reg Fulton Sr., Con Sullivan, Ted George, Ken Fulton,
Chuck George, Rude Purser, Len Charles, Calvin Purser, Bud Purser.
From row: Gus Makris, Ivan George, Russ Fulton, Ben Anderson,
Vic Tom, Sr. Photo courtesy of Port Gamble S'Klallam Archives.

Louie played for a Suquamish team that toured Japan around the early 1920s, and won most of the games there. The Japanese players seemed to not know of a curveball. Louie threw a pitch that the Japanese batter thought was going to hit him in the back of the head, so he slightly ducked. It curved, hitting him in the head. He died. Louie played ball into the 1950s and was inducted into the Kitsap old timer's Hall of Fame in the 1990s. He was legendary for his fastball and the originator of a "clam ball" that he threw that rose as the ball neared the place. It was almost impossible to hit. All who saw him said he was definitely a major league prospect had he chosen to pursue it.[13]

Joe Tom, born in 1879, was also one of the great players on early Boston teams, and he passed on his talent to his son, Vic, who was a great athlete that was well known for his tape-measure home runs. Many thought Vic had major-league talent, but in the prime of his career he was drafted into the Army during World War II. Con Sullivan, born in 1933, was himself a good player, and a teammate of Vic's. Recalling his friend, Con said, "Vic Tom was about the best Klallam baseball player I ever saw, but people may not know that he was a great all-around athlete, and a great football player too. He could punt that football a long ways."[14]

Ted George mentions another Boston team from the 1930s whose roster included Herb Charles (catcher), Harry (Jum) Fulton, Martin Charles and Russ Fulton (pitchers), Lyle George (infield), Cecil George (outfield) Bennie George Jr. (third base), Frank Sullivan (second base), and Vic Tom (shortstop). Ted says, "Vic Tom may have been the most talented of those members. He was short, wide, and agile."[15]

Ivan George, born in 1923, said, this of his playing days for Boston: "We went over to Port Gamble and played Pop Olson's team, they were from the mill. We beat the heck out of them, and Vic Tom hit one way out in the bay. He sure could hit that ball a long ways."[16]

Aaron Purser, born in 1923, and his brother Rude, born in 1927, were both great ballplayers. Aaron was a great centerfielder. As Harry (Jum) Fulton said, "Aaron Purser was a young guy when I was pitching for

Reg Fulton, Sr. and Rude Purser, Sr. Photo courtesy of Port Gamble S'Klallam Archives.

Boston. I learned to just lay the ball in there, letting the batter hit it, and Aaron played centerfield. He could catch about anything hit his way."[17] Rude Purser was a pitcher who also threw the famous "clam ball." Ted George remembers, "Back in the forties and fifties, Rude Purser was as good as it gets, and he beat some really good teams. He was always cool, and didn't let anything bother him. One time, Kingston came down and played us, and they had beaten us earlier, but this time, Rude was ready. We beat them, and I bet Rude even remembers the score."[18]

As many old baseball players know, catcher's gear has sometimes been called the "Tools of Ignorance," because it was such a hard, demanding position to play. When playing Indian baseball, it was not uncommon to see the catcher bowled over by an opposing team's base runner when he was attempting to force the catcher to drop the ball. Bennie (Luck) Anderson and Reg Fulton were catchers for the Boston team in the forties and fifties, and both loved the physical intensity and challenge of catching. Ron Charles remembers watching both players:

> I saw Luck Anderson get absolutely creamed by a runner at the plate, but he tagged the runner out, rolled over a few times, and quickly fired the ball to his teammates. I was so impressed, because, if he was hurt, he didn't show it. My uncle, Reg Fulton, was quite a character, and while behind the plate, he loved to give the opposing batters "the business," trying to irritate them. While catching, he kept up a constant chatter directed at the opposing hitters, hoping to distract them, and he delighted in holding up the ball to taunt them when they swung and missed. One time he was playing against the Skokomish Tribal team, and his uncle, Andy Peterson came up to bat. Andy swung and missed at a pitch, and Reg began he familiar routine, when Andy angrily slapped the ball out of Reg's hand. Andy was most likely letting his young nephew know that he had gone too far, and should show more respect for his elder.[19]

Back in the 1940s and '50s, the players, spouses, and fans looked forward to game day, especially when they played other reservation teams, because the whole day became a social event. Rose Purser recalls those days well: "The wives from the home team would prepare a picnic lunch, and after the guys would finish playing, both sides would get together and eat. I just loved those times when we would get together to catch up on news from relatives and friends."[20] Jake Jones, who played in the 1950s, says, "We used to play up at Skok, and they used to treat us really good. They would feed us a meal after the game, and we would do the same here. I don't think anyone does that anymore."[21]

Ron Charles, born in 1943, recalls:

> As a small boy, I couldn't wait until I was old enough to play
> with the big guys. I recall watching Vic Tom hit a tremendous
> homerun one time, clear over the trees at Lofall Park. I recall great
> rivalries with Suquamish, watching Con Sullivan, Rude Purser,
> Reg and Fred Fulton, Russ Fulton, and others battle Bob and Ted
> George, who were pretty good players. Don George was a great
> hitter too. The hardest thrower I ever faced was Skeet Fixico, and
> one of the smoothest players around was Jimmy McCloud. Both
> played for Nisqually. There were some scary times too. Lavern
> Tom was a very good player, and I saw him get hit in the head
> by a fastball. We wore no helmets in those days, and some of us
> thought that pitch might have killed him.[22]

Bernard (Barn) Tom was born in 1943, and old-timers mentioned him
as one of the best players of his era. Barn says, "Each generation in
Boston seems to have a couple of really good players."[23] Harry Fulton,
who played first base for many years, and was a teammate of Barn's,
says, "We were playing in Tulalip, and Don Hatch was going to run Barn
over (Barn was catching), but Barn got real low, and Don went sailing
right over him. Don got a broken jaw out of that one."[24] As Ted George
remembers, "I saw Barn play when he just got out of high school, and
I thought I could get him a scholarship to Olympic College, but I guess
he wasn't ready. Maybe I should have tried harder."[25]

Harry Fulton III was born in 1945, and played and managed the Boston
team for years. Recalling his playing days, he says, "Nisqually was
probably the most talented team we played back then, but we did beat
them at times. Our star pitcher, Eugene Purser, was a lefty, and he did
well against them. Daryl Sullivan was our other great all-around player
back then. The best team Boston ever had was the one that played in
the late 1990s, and I remember them playing a game against Edmonds
Community College, and won both games."[26]

S'Klallam Baseball

Rudy Purser Jr. followed in his dad's footsteps as a very good player, and he recalls how the games could get a bit rowdy: "Skeet Fixico from Nisqually threw a slow change up to Duke Aikman, who just let the ball hit him. Skeet got mad, so the next pitch he threw a fastball right at Duke, who sprawled out in the dirt, and there was almost a big fight over that one.[27]

At times, in the 1950s and '60s, there were attempts to operate all-Indian baseball leagues, but the coordination of schedules was very poor, and the whole idea had to be abandoned. After that, most of the competition for the Boston teams would be during tournaments held at the various reservations, usually as a part of tribal celebrations.

In 1953, some of the reservation kids were excited to learn that Little League was starting to be organized in North Kitsap. That first year, Vic and Lavern Tom were the only two reservation kids to play, but over the years, many others eagerly joined. Little League would play an important part in keeping baseball fever alive in the reservation community, as Babe Ruth baseball did a few years later. Many very talented Boston kids would play for both programs over the years.

Ed Moon was a charismatic, dedicated man who managed the Kingston Little League team for about 33 years in the organization's formative years. During his tenure, he developed some strong relationships with reservation kids and their families. When Little League began, teams were selected simply by geographic area, so the S'Klallam kids automatically played for Ed's Kingston team. This arrangement served Ed well, and he enjoyed much success, in part because of the talented ballplayers from the reservation. However, the league eventually changed the rules, and the teams were selected through a draft system, whereby Ed no longer could count on getting all the Little Boston players. Ed's grandson, Scott Moon, now says, "Even after the league went to a draft, my grandpa still got most of the good reservation players, I guess because he got to know the folks in Boston so well."[28]

Mr. Moon, in his own way, created a welcoming atmosphere for reservation kids through the game of baseball, and in doing so, he helped bridge a communication gap that had long existed between the reservation community and their North Kitsap neighbors.

From the 1970s through the 1990s, the Boston men's team always fielded some very competitive groups. However, many who have followed reservation teams over the years now concede that the best Boston team that played in modern times was the one that came along during the late 1900s. It seemed that there were just an inordinate number of talented Indian players from Boston during those years, and Harry Fulton says, "I think that team might have won the Oakville tournament about 10 years in a row."[29]

For many years, what became known as the "slave game" produced some of the best entertainment for the Boston teams at the end of the season, where one final game would be played between the married men and the single men. The game would give the winners bragging rights for the year, and the losers also had to endure the indignity of serving the winners during the party that followed.

Deadly serious, Con Sullivan would refuse to play if Cubby Bear Sparks umpired the "slave" game. Because he was single, Cubby Bear was always biased against the married men and couldn't be trusted. Cubby Bear and Bob Clements were two guys who seemed to really enjoy the quite thankless job of umpiring, and seemed to have the disposition to handle all the abuse that came with it; abuse that often came from the home fans too.

Indian umpires played an important role, and rarely would the visiting team fully trust the home team to supply officiating that was competent and fair. Ted George says,

> A guy named Joe George, no relation, managed Suquamish way back, and he was well known as the most famous "homer." He was both managing and umpiring a game one time, and he called his player, John Sigo, safe at first, when he was out by a mile. John walked off, and Joe tried to get him to come back, telling him he was safe. John refused, apparently ashamed of

the "homering."[30]

One neighboring reservation team had an umpire who, in the early innings of a game, seemed to be a quite competent, but as the game progressed, his calls became increasingly erratic and inconsistent. It seems that between innings the man would slip behind the backstop, and drink from a bottle of alcohol he had stashed, and the longer the game went on, the worse the man's calls got. Many times he would get unceremoniously fired before the game's end.

The S'Klallam community was well known for its rabid baseball fans, and on game days they turned out to loudly cheer on their guys. They were experts at "getting under the skin" of opposing players. These fans were greatly pleased when their antics could elicit responses from opposing players, causing them to "lose their cool."

Even through the toughest of economic times, players could always find ways to collect enough balls, bats, and equipment, and on a bright summer day nothing could be more therapeutic than a baseball game. Baseball was also a good way to take one's mind off the problems of the day, especially from some of the indignities S'Klallams suffered at the hands of a dominant society not yet prepared to treat Native Americans as equals.

This chapter set out to provide some examples of the prominent role that baseball played in this community from the late nineteenth century until today. Old-time Boston teams, at a time when there were many local pick-up teams, were well known for producing talented baseball players, which resulted in many of them being courted to play for other teams. Because the Boston teams produced such an array of talented players over the years, their winning ways produced a fierce pride within the community for their teams.

Baseball, however, was more than just a sport for the S'Klallam community, and when their players performed well on the field, they were not simply showing how talented they were, they were showing pride in using the game of baseball to express S'Klallam cultural values

In 2009, past Boston players were honored. Photo courtesy of Port Gamble S'Klallam Archives.

and identity.

The old-timers like Eddie George, Harry Fulton Sr., Joe Tom, Sammy and Tommy Charles, and Peter Jackson not only brought the joy of baseball to Little Boston; they exemplified S'Klallam ideals and taught generations of our people what it was to be the "Strong People." They were the ones who taught us the love of the game that many of us will carry the rest of our lives, and for that we are grateful.

CHAPTER 13

Self-Governance and Tribal Government: Into the 21st Century

Greg Anderson and Laurie Mattson

"Harry Robert Fulton Jr. will always be remembered as an honest Chief Judge who loved and worked for the good of his Klallam Indian people."

—Klallam News, 1979

A visit today to the Port Gamble S'Klallam Reservation features a full-fledged tribal government with the capacity to support and improve most aspects of tribal life—a tribe recognized across the country for its leadership and innovative programs. From an annual budget of $229 in 1959, the Port Gamble S'Klallam Tribe grew in fifty years to a multi-million dollar governmental administration. How was this possible? As the Port Gamble S'Klallam people have done throughout their history, they seized the opportunities presented by changes around them—in this case, changes in national Indian policy—and applied their ages-old ingenuity and hard work to build their government and tribal programs. The federal self-governance policy of the 1990s launched an explosion of growth for the tribe; but that growth was also built upon earlier, more modest steps that created a sustainable foundation. The establishment of the first tribal administration center and the tribal court system exemplify these earlier efforts.

Self-Governance and Tribal Government:
Into the 21st Century

Tribal Center under construction, 1976. Photo courtesy of Port Gamble S'Klallam Archives.

A New Tribal Center—A 1976 Dream Come True

The sound of hammers and saws were heard throughout the spring and summer of 1976. A crew of twenty-five tribal members worked under general contractor Tim Ryan Construction to build an 18,000 square foot Tribal Center. The total cost of the facility was $365,000, which was mostly funded by a $300,000 grant from the Title X Program of the Indian Technical Assistance Center. The building, a dream come true, was the result of many meetings by Tribal Council, planners, and community members. The new Tribal Center included a large gymnasium, a kitchen for tribal events, space for offices, and two conference rooms. A new parking lot was built adjacent to the building.

By the first week of October, 1976, staff moved into the new building. On December 11, 1976, a dedication was held in the gymnasium that many dignitaries attended. Floyd Jones presented the welcome, invocation, and dedication prayer. Ed

Sampson and Martha John sang a S'Klallam song. Ted George and Tribal Chair Ron Charles gave speeches. After the dedication ceremony, there was a dinner for the large crowd, estimated to be between 400 to 500 people. The menu included smoked salmon, venison, baked salmon, mashed potatoes, vegetables, green salad, fried bread, clam chowder, and cakes. Then, joyously, a basketball game was held in the new gym.

Chairman Charles' speech expressed his vision of self-determination for the Tribe, and marked the beginning of progressive planning and program implementation:

> Only a few years ago, Indian Tribes, including us, came dangerously close to disappearing into oblivion due to the termination and relocation policies.
>
> Of course we know how the Indian was always expected to blend into the great melting pot of America, and one day all Americans were to be one great brown race of people.
>
> Well, a funny thing happened to the melting pot theory; the Indian failed to cooperate. He didn't desire to be like all the rest of the people, and no amount of prodding from sometimes well-intentioned people could change him.
>
> No one ever understood, or tried to understand, that Indians couldn't be judged or measured according to a foreign value system. It was like trying to fit a square peg in a round hole.
>
> Over the last few hundred years, the Indian has had an ever-changing relationship with the United States and its citizens. We have been called, at times, the Noble Red Man, and at other times, the lazy redskin.
>
> A new era emerged following the termination years, and especially in the last few years, the smaller tribes of Western Washington have made substantial progress. Now, we are being offered something else by the government, and it's called "self-determination." What

does that term mean?

Self-determination will mean as much or as little as we as Indians want it to mean.

It means developing jobs and an economy around our Treaty-guaranteed rights; it means programs instituted by Indians for Indians to obtain better health care, housing, and educational opportunities. Self-determination means Indians doing their own thing, whatever that may be.

The road to self-determination will not be easy, but few really worthwhile things come easily. My hope is that we, as Indians, can work together to implement self-determination, and put aside any differences we might have.

We, the Indian tribes, are only scratching the surface of our potential in many areas, and only by cooperating with one another can we assure ourselves of a smooth road to self-determination."[1]

On a practical level, the self-determination that Charles envisioned required that the tribe act as a sovereign government, with the governmental infrastructure to do so. For example, it meant being able to regulate and enforce the tribe's newly won treaty fishing rights. It meant having a way to protect S'Klallam children from being taken away from their community by state social workers and placed in non-Indian homes. It meant deciding what behavior was unacceptable on the reservation and having the power to enforce these standards. The tribe needed its own judicial system.

Establishment of the Tribal Court
Two years before the Tribal Center dedication, a tribal planning committee consisting of Jim Ives, Ted George, Ron Charles, Diane Sullivan, Jake Jones, Gene Jones and Virginia Ives developed a comprehensive plan that, in part, documented the need for a fully functioning judicial system. At the time, the tribe employed a security

One of the totem poles for the new Tribal Center was carved by Gerald "Jake" Jones. He was assisted by two students, Rudy Wellman and Frank Alexander. Photograph by Kent Soule, Hoot Owl Photography, courtesy of Port Gamble S'Klallam Archives.

officer who would become a law enforcement officer when funds became available for equipment and a car. The plan noted:

"The Tribe also has a fish and game law enforcement officer who protects their hunting and fishing rights. The Port Gamble Tribe has no judicial system or detention facilities. They plan to expand into these areas when funds become available. The Tribe has submitted their law and order code for BIA approval."[2]

The Tribal Council approved a resolution in 1974 requesting that the Bureau of Indian Affairs not only fund a tribal police officer but also equipment, a vehicle, and a judge. On November 16, 1974, in two separate resolutions the Tribal Council appointed Harry Fulton Jr. as tribal judge and another tribal member as clerk of the Tribal Court. The Port Gamble S'Klallam Community Court was established. A slightly later resolution approved a Law and Order Code and commanded its enforcement to the Tribal Court and Police Department.

When appointed, Judge Fulton was retired from the Pope & Talbot Mill, where he had worked for over thirty years. He had also been one of the early founders of the Little Boston Pentecostal Tabernacle Church, where he served in several capacities. For a time, he was both a Tribal Council member and chairman of the tribe's personnel committee. His nickname was "Jum." In so many ways, his leadership and high moral standards made him the perfect choice for the first tribal judge. When Judge Harry Fulton passed away in 1979, Reverend Esko Rentola

Self-Governance and Tribal Government: Into the 21st Century

When appointed, Judge Fulton had retired from the Pope & Talbot Mill where he worked for over thirty years. His leadership and high moral standards made him the perfect choice for the first tribal judge. Photo courtesy of Port Gamble S'Klallam Archives.

eulogized him in the *S'Klallam News:*

> Chief Judge Harry Robert Fulton, Jr., a Klallam Indian of the Port Gamble Indian Reservation, and a member of the National Indian Judges Association was born on the shores of Port Gamble Bay at Little Boston, April 14, 1915. He attended grade school at the old "Little Boston Spit" where the early Klallam village once stood. He later attended the Tulalip Indian Boarding School on the Tulalip Indian Reservation near Marysville, Washington. Legal training in Tribal Law and Order was received at training sessions at the University of Nevada Judicial College in Reno; Phoenix, Arizona; Albuquerque, New Mexico; Salt Lake City, Utah; Port Angeles and Seattle, Washington.
>
> ... Besides being a judge of honesty, integrity, love and fairness to his Klallam Indian people, he often talked from his heart like a loving Father to young people who were summoned to Court.

Those who lacked money were allowed to work out their fines.

. . . Harry Robert Fulton Jr. will always be remembered as an honest Chief Judge that loved and worked for the good of his Klallam Indian people.[3]

While judge, Harry Fulton was involved in meetings to establish a circuit court, now known as the Northwest Intertribal Court System (NICS). After his passing, the tribe began contracting the chief judge and prosecutor services through NICS. Rose Purser became the tribe's first judicial officer in 1977 and later became an associate and appellate judge for the tribe. Purser and NICS were recently honored for thirty years of judicial services to the tribe. Another long time Court employee, Candi (Ives) Seachord, was hired as court administrator in 1987, and served in that capacity for over twenty years. These three tribal members will always be remembered for establishing credibility and integrity in the tribe's judicial system.

The Port Gamble S'Klallam seal with orca whale was designed by former Tribal Chairman, Gerald "Jake" Jones. Courtesy of Port Gamble S'Klallam Archives.

While the tribal court system was initially developed under the thoughtful oversight of Judge Fulton, Rose Purser and Candi (Ives) Seachord, the Law and Order Code (the set of laws that the tribal court would interpret and apply) was gradually built by tribal committees working with Tallis King George, the tribe's attorney for twenty-six years. King George and members of the tribe crafted laws that were unique to the Port Gamble S'Klallam cultural values and way of life. For example, in the Family Code, the S'Klallam definition of "family" and the description of parental duties were thoroughly debated so that the code reflected the S'Klallam way rather than the state's. In recent years, when the tribe

Self-Governance and Tribal Government: Into the 21st Century

was one of the first in the state to take over child support enforcement, the committee polled the community to determine tribal values in key areas and then spent two years adapting the complex child support enforcement system to work for S'Klallam families.

The tribal court, Law and Order Code, and a series of honest, effective tribal councils, gave the Port Gamble S'Klallam tribal government a solid base from which to embark on its next phase of independence from federal and state control.

Greg Anderson presenting the Tribe's position at a 2005 national Self-Governance meeting. Photo courtesy of Port Gamble S'Klallam Archives.

Self-Governance at the Port Gamble S'Klallam Tribe

It was a piercing, cold winter day on the wind-swept National Mall in Washington, D.C. Massive museums, stocked primarily with the memories of a white America, flanked the smooth expanse from the Capitol to the Washington Monument. It was the middle of January in 1993, and the bleak white scene was marked by two shivering, lightly-clad figures leaning into the cold, biting wind as they crossed to the shelter of the sprawl of gray government buildings a block north of Constitution Avenue.

The figures were Ron Charles and Greg Anderson, who served, respectively, as Self-Governance coordinators for the Indian Health Service (IHS) and Bureau of Indian Affairs (BIA) programs for the Port Gamble S'Klallam Tribe. Ron Charles was a tribal councilman and former tribal chairman, while Greg Anderson had served on the staff of Tribal Administration since 1989. Charles and Anderson were in Washington to finalize a self-governance compact with Indian Health Services. The process that brought the two men to this point had been as formidable as the January weather.

Self-Governance and Tribal Government: Into the 21st Century

It had been nearly four years since the tribe had begun federal negotiations, first with the Bureau of Indian Affairs and later with the Indian Health Service, as part of a unique experiment to "prove" that tribal governments could manage their own affairs. Thus, tribal organizations that had existed for hundreds, or even thousands of years, had to "prove" their competence to govern their members to various federal bureaucrats before they would be permitted to permanently self-govern the programs funded by federal agencies.

For 140 years, since the Treaty of Point No Point was signed in 1855, the Bureau of Indian Affairs, Indian Health Service, and their forerunners had been charged with fulfilling their responsibilities under the terms of that treaty. Over the years, many tribes and tribal leaders had voiced their dismay with the quality and quantity of services provided by the federal government. In recognition of these concerns, Congress passed Public Law 93-638, the Indian Self-Determination and Education Assistance Act, in 1975. This act permitted tribal governments to enter into contracts to operate the programs entrusted to the federal government under the terms of treaties and agreements throughout the nation.

After Public Law 93-638 was passed, Port Gamble S'Klallam leaders took advantage to contract a number of programs formerly run by the Bureau of Indian Affairs. Among these were law enforcement, education, Indian Child Welfare, tribal court, forestry, and tribal government. At the same time, the tribe, through its membership in the Point No Point Treaty Council, a consortium of signatories to that treaty, contracted fisheries programs from the BIA. But something was missing. The tribe was operating programs, but the Bureau of Indian Affairs was still calling the shots. This situation was unacceptable, and tribal leaders throughout the nation began to call for a stronger commitment by the federal government for a self-determination policy that truly recognized the proper relationship between tribal governments and the United States. It was the result of the drive and determination of these early leaders that forced the federal government to agree to their demands.

Self-Governance and Tribal Government: Into the 21st Century

The result of this tribally-driven movement was the enactment by Congress, in 1988, of Public Law 100-472, the Self-Governance Demonstration Project. This historic project would allow a few tribes to determine, for themselves, the manner in which funds would be used to provide services to tribal members in concert with the needs, both physical and cultural, of their communities. This was the turning point whereby tribes shifted from sheltering under the protection of the United States, to a true "Government-to-Government" relationship, with the two parties treating each other as equals in the negotiation and administration of federal programs.

It was the middle of 1990 before the first seven tribes inked hard-fought agreements with Bureau of Indian Affairs organizations at agency, area, and headquarters levels. These documents would be referred to as a comprehensive "Compact" and "Annual Funding Agreement" defining the rights and responsibilities for both the BIA and individual tribes.
The Port Gamble S'Klallam was one of eight new tribes in 1990 that began planning to join the first seven tribes by hammering out new agreements that would increase both the scope and funding that had only been touched upon by earlier "PL 638" contracts. The road to equitable and meaningful agreements was not an easy one.

Rick DeCoteau, the first Self-Governance coordinator for the tribe, spent a year in preliminary planning before the tribe was admitted to the demonstration project. The responsibilities, advantages, and disadvantages of each of the 300 line items in the national Bureau of Indian Affairs budget were discussed with the community (through public hearings) and with the tribal council. Council members, including Ron Charles, Jake Jones, Marie Sullivan (Hebert), Floyd Jones, Bud Purser, Betty DeCoteau, Harry Fulton, and Carol DeCoteau, as well as staff members including Dallas DeGuire, Rick DeCoteau, and Greg Anderson, were involved in training sessions on self-governance, budgeting, program definition and analysis, compact language, and tribal finance. Consultants were hired to review organizational structure, accounting systems, the level of services provided to tribal members, and their real need for services.

Page 242

Self-Governance and Tribal Government:
Into the 21st Century

The tribal council established and staffed a tribal office of Self-Governance, and, to protect tribal interests, hired a CPA and attorney to review all documents forthcoming from negotiations.

In March of 1991, the tribe entered into formal negotiations with BIA officials. In between each trip, meetings were held to define tribal shares for each of the 300 BIA line items by:

a. Establishing the federal government's responsibility for *each* line item, and the dollar levels needed to fund that responsibility.

b. Establishing a tribal share for *each* line item. (Many shares were as small as ten to fifteen dollars, but still offered repetitive annual funding to the tribe).

c. Reviewing shares for *each* line item with the tribal council and the community in order to determine if the dollar amount of shares justified taking on the responsibility for that item. (Can the Tribe really take care of road maintenance for a share of $125 per year? Is a $4,280 share enough to administer General Assistance each year? What if Congress reduces funding for General Assistance funding itself? How does the Tribe take care of people if it has taken over that responsibility and the funding is reduced?). Each of these questions required answers, and decisions were made only after long and patient consideration.

After repeated rewrites, a final proposed draft agreement was prepared, presented, renegotiated, and, when agreement was finally reached with BIA officials, submitted for final approval. Finally, on September 30, 1991, the historic Compact with the United States was signed. On January 1, 1992, the Port Gamble S'Klallam Tribe became one of the first fifteen Tribes in America to begin to implement the BIA Self-Governance Demonstration Project.

Self-Governance and Tribal Government:
Into the 21st Century

But all was not over. The tribe still had to redesign the programs for which it elected to assume responsibility in order to fit tribal priorities. The Tribal Council deliberated carefully before designating the following four programs to be the first to receive an increased level of funding in order to properly serve the members of the Port Gamble S'Klallam Tribe: 1) Education; 2) Health; 3) Law Enforcement; and 4) Natural Resources.

The emphasis on health and the success of the self-governance of BIA programs stirred the tribe to plunge headfirst to include Indian Health Service programs into the tribe's self-governance structure. As was the case with the BIA, the tribe entered into extensive considerations and examinations of the issues surrounding the self-governance of IHS programs. Health and Human Services Director Laurie Mattson, with the help of Ron Charles, who had now assumed the responsibilities of IHS Self-Governance coordinator, assembled a team from tribal staff that included Greg Anderson and tribal member Danette Ives, who would later take over as director of health services. The staff also included expert specialists in health issues. The group worked to forge a new plan to provide the best possible health services to all tribal members. But the efforts in Washington, D.C. on that cold winter night in 1993, along with numerous meetings around the country, would soon bear fruit for all tribal members, council, and staff.

In 1994, the Port Gamble S'Klallam Tribe became one of the first in the nation to enter into a Self-Governance Compact with the Indian Health Service. Self-governance gave the tribe the autonomy and flexibility to prioritize local needs. Under the Self-Governance Compact, the tribe assumed the responsibility to provide health care for tribal members. It was a decision that was entered into with the belief that the tribe could better determine and provide health care than the federal government.

With the advent of self-governance, the tribe assumed responsibility for administration of Contract Health Services (CHS). Prior to 1994, tribal members could use the tribe's Health Clinic or receive approval from IHS for health care services from private medical providers. The tribe's management of CHS required that eligible persons use the tribal Health

Clinic as their initial resource and referral center. If specialty or other health care was needed, referrals were made to nearby providers. It was truly a "universal health care" approach, something that the U.S. is still trying to implement for the population at large as of this writing. With the Tribal Health Advisory Committee to provide guidance, the approach has been very successful, and services have grown over the years. In future years, national awards would honor this successful effort. By 2009, 329 Tribes (58%) of the 564 federally recognized tribes had signed IHS Compacts and Agreements with the United States.

The Port Gamble S'Klallam Tribe had taken control of its own destiny, and it now had the basic tools to provide the services needed for, and earned by, its members. Total funding for BIA and IHS programs, which were over 90% of all funds available to Tribal government in 1991, soared from $1 million at that time to a total of $5.1 million in the 2010 budget. But the tribe had taken even greater strides after the early BIA and IHS compacts. By 2010, the total tribal budget had reached $20.7 million, while BIA and IHS programs only totaled 25% of funds available to the tribal government.

The impact that self-governance made on the Port Gamble S'Klallam Tribe was soon felt in other programs. Efforts by staff members such as Marilyn Olson and Tallis King George to help the tribe negotiate the first Tribal Aid to Needy Families (TANF) program in the State of Washington, and to assume the Child Support Enforcement program (one of only nineteen run by tribes in the United States), were indicative of the change in the mind-set brought on by the fundamental concept of self-determination. Both staff members drew upon the skill and expertise of tribal members familiar with the needs and concerns of families both on and off the reservation. The goal of adequate services to the children, families, and elders of the tribe made great strides as these programs and other initiatives began to really make a difference at Port Gamble.

Later, such innovative programs as third-party billings, foster care, and the Washington State Consolidation Project set standards for tribes throughout the United States.

Self-Governance and Tribal Government: Into the 21st Century

The promise of self-governance proved to be much more than a promise. Each and every tribal member of the Port Gamble S'Klallam Tribe has benefited from the foresight and direction set forth by their tribal council and their fellow tribal members. And in the course of this success, the tribe has truly taken its place as a national leader.

On December 12, 2009, Tribal Council Chairman Jeromy Sullivan noted the success of self-governance in a letter to President Barack Obama as follows:

> I am proud of the great strides the Port Gamble S'Klallam Tribe has made over the twenty years since we began to take over the sovereign responsibilities inherent in self-determination. Our community members are stronger, healthier, and economically more self-sufficient. In 150 years under the BIA, we could only count two college graduates in our Tribe of 1,000 men, women and children. Today, 20 years after our initial foray into the arena of self-governance, we can count more than 30 bachelor degrees, two master's degrees, and one law degree. We have truly "pulled ourselves up by the bootstraps" and have repeatedly shown that by Tribes running federal programs more efficiently and responsibly, great things can accrue to Tribal members and their families.

CHAPTER 14

The Beauty and Fabric of Tribal Life

Gina Stevens

*"We are S'Klallam, not because of where we grow
up, how we look or what we have. We are S'Klallam
because it is in the one place no one can change,
steal or replace: it is in our blood, our hearts, and
our minds. That is what makes us S'Klallam and that
never dies. That is why we are the Strong People.
That is why we survive."*

—Young Port Gamble S'Klallam Father, 2009

From the time our ancestors agreed, in 1853, to move across the Bay to make way for the sawmill, and begin building the community which would eventually become the Port Gamble S'Klallam Tribe of today, those hardworking Indian people struggled at times to merely survive during some very tough times. But through the years, the way they lived their lives established customs, norms, and traditions, many of which we still honor today. Some would describe this as our own unique "sense of community," and it speaks to the relationships among those who live within that community.

Our ancestors shared, celebrated, honored, and grieved together, in what was then an isolated, close-knit community that time had forgotten. Since there was not even a road into the old village until the

1930s, and there was no such thing as public assistance in the early days, the helping hands of relatives and neighbors, in times of need, became a way of life. Sharing what was on your table, even in the hard times, was common. Rose Purser recalls life on the reservation during the 1940s: "Share whatever you have with someone that's needy, and anybody who was hungry and didn't have someplace to go, they'd stop in at mealtime."[1] That was the S'Klallam way.

Over the years, individual members have stood out because of their accomplishments and selflessness. There's no doubt their actions impacted the community as a whole, and in some respect they represent the beauty and fabric of S'Klallam life as we know it today. Like others, S'Klallam people act in their individual capacities, but unlike others, they never stop being a part of the community.

Tribal Council member Francine (Jones) Swift reflected on those S'Klallam who made contributions to the tribe:

Our story poles reflect life works that are important to our people. But we cannot forget the grandmas, moms, aunties either. Joe and Josie Anderson donated the land for the Shaker Church, and the cemetery that still remains. Auntie Louisa (Jones) Pulsifer, who was married off to a Skokomish and preserved basketry, weaving, gathering, and dying saved more culture than we can know. Martha John ranks up there as a S'Klallam princess, she contributed so much to our language and culture. Cy Webster, who worked hard to pay the loan off for his house, which was admirable. Star baseball players, Louie George and Victor Tom. Ted George was our first tribal member to graduate from college, and Janis Makris did too, a few years later. Gina Stevens is our first tribal member attorney. We remember the honesty, grace, and integrity with which Candi (Ives) Seachord performed her court and enrollment duties; no one else is like her. We should honor all our tribal chairs too. Uncle Floyd Jones resisted when outsiders wanted to develop the Spit. Ron Charles negotiated for us during the early years of the Boldt decision, and was a fisherman. Jake Jones escorted in the carving of our first canoe. These are people and events that changed our nation. They brought back the longhouse to our community. We are indeed a wealthy people.[2]

The Beauty and Fabric of Tribal Life

The intricacy of the relationships between the people of the community is the very thing that distinguishes Port Gamble S'Klallam people from all others. When someone is first introduced to the reservation, it's not uncommon to hear "everyone waves when I drive on the reservation, why does everyone wave at me?" When you're a S'Klallam, a wave is an effortless, yet genuine, gesture of acknowledgment.

Those who are fortunate and remain involved in the community know a wave is only the beginning; a mere introduction of what it means to truly belong to a community. Being established within the community is to know that "Aunty Dorothy" and "Uncle Ivar" are family, regardless of one's biological relationship, or lack thereof.

Similarly, those who live on the reservation know everyone has a role, and that often a person's role isn't discussed; it's just known. Fred "Brown" Fulton oversees the clambakes we are accustomed to putting on at every event, funeral, and ceremony. To those unfamiliar with the community, a clambake may appear to be a traditional and unusual method for cooking seafood. To the community

S'Klallam tribal members Bethany Swift, Tawny DeCoteau, Shayla DeCoteau, and Francine (Jones) Swift don traditional regalia of cedar, paddles, and button blankets, sharing song and dance and keeping traditions alive. Photo courtesy of Port Gamble S'Klallam Tribe.

members who live, work, and play here, it is a ritual. Brown and others dig the clams, pick the oysters, and catch the crab a day or two in advance of the ceremony. They then gather and deliver rocks and firewood, all the while joking and visiting, as men often do. When the clams are cooked, the elders and guests are served at the dinner table, but most community members choose to stand around the pit, elbow-to-elbow eating the steamed morsels directly from the bed. It is the clambakes that truly set our tribe apart, elicit so much tribal pride, and cause so many visitors to go away happy. Port Gamble is one of the few tribes keeping this tradition alive. We proudly host clambakes for our visitors, including the huge feast we prepare each summer when the canoes visit. It is gratifying to see how the large crowds so enjoy themselves at this event, and some say that it is the highlight of the canoe voyage for them.

Cyrene "Bun" Tooze's Clam Chowder[3]

1 lb. shelled clams (could be little necks, butter clams, or geoduck)
1 onion, chopped
4 potatoes, chopped
2 celery sticks, chopped
3 slices of bacon, chopped
1 carrot, ground
2 cups of milk

Add all ingredients to pot except milk. After all is thickened, add milk. Let simmer. Make sure you simmer long enough to cook bacon and clams. Salt and pepper to taste.

*". . . participating in any activity of the tribe enriches a person's soul
and contributes to the riches of the community as a whole."
Photo courtesy of Port Gamble S'Klallam Tribe.*

The canoe voyage started as the "Paddle To Seattle" in 1989. After a
voyage to Bella Bella a few years later, the journey evolved into an
annual event with participation from many different tribes. A ritual
of Indian communities hosting along the route has evolved as well,
allowing folks to rest, visit, and participate in the various ceremonies,
just as our ancestors did. Canoe skipper Laura Price says:

> That thirteen-day canoe journey to Bella Bella changed my life.
> It opened the doorway for me being S'Klallam. The experience
> helped build the foundation, passion and commitment in me to
> preserve, perpetuate, and celebrate our rich cultural heritage
> for our present and future generations.
>
> I admire and deeply respect our ancestors who by their
> resiliency and strength we owe all this amazing rich culture to.
> Canoe journeys happen every year now. They bring strength
> to our people by giving us a way to connect to our culture. We

The Beauty and Fabric of Tribal Life

"Being on the water is good medicine. It strengthens the body, mind, heart and spirit. It is here on the water and in the longhouses that our ancestors continue to reach out and teach us how to be nexʷƛ̕áy̓əm, the strong people . . . ." This photo from the 1993 Bella Bella Canoe Journey is courtesy of Port Gamble S'Klallam Tribe.

gain confidence, pride, respect, and identity. We know where we belong and are given an opportunity to learn and grow.[4]

As a part of the ceremony, the canoes are greeted in the traditional S'Klallam language when landing in our territory. Three tribal members, Marie Hebert, Karron McGrady, and Laura Price received certificates in the S'Klallam language and have been actively teaching others. As a result, tribal council members and tribal royalty can now greet the canoes in the S'Klallam language instead of English, helping to carry on and revive culture and tradition.

A traditional language component is also incorporated into the Early Childhood Education Program, and language classes are offered, free of charge, to all levels of school-age children. These same children learn the songs and dances of the tribe, and these traditions are incorporated into community events. Every year, the community gathers at the Early Head Start graduation ceremony, where children celebrate their first rite of passage and prepare for the world of academics off-reservation. Parents, aunts, uncles, grandparents and siblings can depend on watching the young ones perform "The Paddle Song," which is often led by Dennis and Kay Jones.

Another custom passed down through the generations, and very much in practice today, teaches us to show respect for those who pass on, and most activities on the reservation come to a halt during a funeral. Cyrene "Bun" Tooze and Lenore Edwards cook turkey and potatoes for the large gatherings, Aunty "Tiny" June Jones makes the fluffiest fry bread, Uncle Floyd Jones offers the sweetest prayers, Joe Price and Paul Hebert lead gatherings with traditional drumming and singing, and the contemporary singing trio—Wayne DeCoteau, Carol DeCoteau and Joyce (Fulton) Bowchop—share songs of comfort. Harry Fulton III also sings solos, as did his father, Harry "Jum" Fulton Jr. A proud group of volunteers always digs the grave for the family, and would be offended if they were not allowed to do so. All of these individuals have established or carried on customs that the entire community continues to benefit from today.

Clambakes, the canoe journey, and other customs are revered because they all encompass a resurgence of culture and re-established historical tradition. But traditions can take on many forms, including contemporary and secular traditions like Halloween. Such traditions are equally embraced by and representative of the beauty of today's community. If you've ever brought your children trick-or-treating here, you know there are certain stops one must make. Grandma Rose Purser takes a Polaroid of the costumed children and shares the photos the next year. Ron and Sharon Charles hand out king-sized candy bars, and Herman and Ellen Price set up their awning and barbecue, sharing hot dogs and chips with all who stop by. It's a holiday the community actively seizes, and the traditions reflect the each community member's welcoming manner.

*When the Early Childhood Education Program began, the Tribe had
a grant for a Foster Grandparent Program. Josephine Sparks, Lina
Charles, Irene Purser and Kate Moran were some of the grandmas
who worked in the program over the years. They are pictured with
children and staff, Loral Wellman and Penny Purser.
Photo courtesy of Ron Charles.*

Other traditions occur with the Tribal government contributing
the human and financial resources necessary to coordinate annual
events the community treasures. Every year, the Tribe sponsors an
elder's honoring for those precious elders turning 55 years of age. The
community comes together to celebrate another rite of passage into elder
status, and we do so with gifts, songs, dance, photos, prayer and humor.

The tribe's elders are often grandparents, and almost every child on the
reservation lives within walking distance of Grandma's house. Children
can stop in if they are hungry or thirsty, if they need a band-aid or
maybe just a hug. Grandparents are a constant they can depend on, and
are always there to meet the needs of their grandchildren. Quite often
the child will bring a friend along as an unspoken testimony to how
great his or her grandparent is.

Rez Humor

Our sense of humor could be the subject of a book on its own. Ted George tells a story that many years ago Uncle Ivar (Ivan George) was driving across the state with his buddies and they got thirsty. They stopped at a tavern and Uncle Ivar asked to buy a six-pack. The bartender said, "I can't sell alcohol to Indians." Uncle Ivar said, "I'm not Indian; I'm Hawaiian." The bartender said, "Well, you'll have to prove it to me." Uncle Ivar said, "Well, if I had my ukulele with me I could sing you a Hawaiian song." Ted says they left without the six-pack, but had a good laugh over it.

U.S. Representative Jay Inslee (back row, far right) joins community members during a celebration in honor of the Little Boston Library receiving an award as "The Best Small Public Library in the U.S." in 1999. Photo courtesy of Port Gamble S'Klallam Tribe.

Whether it's our Early Head Start children or our elders, there's always a story to tell, a memory to recall, or a laugh to share.

With its many new facilities, the community looks very different today. The tribe first became self-governing in the early 1990s, and has since built key facilities like the House of Knowledge complex, which includes a ceremonial longhouse, a new home for the Little Boston Library, an Elders Center, and a Career and Education Center. In 2010, the tribe dedicated a new youth center, which had previously won awards for its health care and social service programs. The tribe was the first, and presently the only tribe in the State of Washington to license its own foster homes, and was a forerunner in developing its own TANF and food stamp programs, determining assistance eligibility on site. Many other tribes across the nation have looked to the Port Gamble S'Klallam Tribe for guidance and assistance in developing their own programs.

Facilities and awards are tangible and easy to observe as marks of success, but they are not representative of the beauty you can only experience by carefully paying attention to the relationships between the people of the community.

The Future

In 2004, the Tribe purchased 391 acres of former DNR land and added it to other small parcels near or adjacent to the reservation. Some of the timber was logged to pay for the land, and within a few months new trees were planted. Land purchases are made not only to add to the tribe's land base, but also to protect the tribe's existing resources from potentially being damaged through development by other buyers. The land is being held in an undeveloped state for future tribal needs. It is a step that we know will be appreciated by our great-great grandchildren, and even farther into the future.

As evidenced by the clambakes, when our tribal members think about home, one of the first things that comes to mind is the beach. Our surrounding marine environment is especially important, because for generations the food it produced has sustained S'Klallam folks. Our elders spoke of those resources being the only thing between them and starvation at times. For example, Angeline was the mother of the large Fulton family, and her children remember that when times were tough, with little food on the table, she would go to the beach and bring home a tub of crab to fill up her kids. Ivan George, speaking on those tough economic times, said, "During the mill strike we moved down to the other side of Hansville. We were doing a lot of fishing and we lived off the beach. Clams, fish, salmon. We sold salmon."[5]

Today, the tribe works diligently to protect Port Gamble Bay. The bay is home not only to a variety of marine and plant life, but to us. It is one of the last bays in Puget Sound that is still open for shellfish harvesting. Since 1853, when the Port Gamble sawmill began operations, the bay

S'Klallam community members gather around clams cooked on a traditional clam bed. Photo courtesy of Port Gamble S'Klallam Tribe.

became the unwilling recipient of a number of hazardous substances. The mill also treated creosote pilings onsite. The sawmill closed in 1997, but industrial operations have continued. This has resulted in long-term releases of additional hazardous substances.

Port Gamble Bay is more than just home to the S'Klallam Tribe. It is historically and culturally significant, but it also serves as a strong economic component for our people. We make our livelihood from the waters of the bay. There are currently no plans for a long-term clean up at the the bay, but the tribe is very committed to this action, and has worked with responsible parties to create a sustainable cleanup act.

We recognize that the only way to guarantee our survival as a tribe is to strongly consider the environment when making decisions about any development. There are always ways to combine development with a healthy environment. Our vision for the tribe, Port Gamble Bay, and the area surrounding us in Kitsap County, is to create an example of how development and environmentalism can work in concert.

While we are looking to build our businesses with an eye on self-sufficiency, we hold each other, our traditional culture, and our natural resources most dear. We have demonstrated determination to remain together as a close-knit family while striving to be a good neighbor. Whether one participates in modern rituals like trick-or-treating, revived traditions like the canoe journey, or the ongoing fight for our natural resources, we know that participating in any tribal activity enriches a person's soul and contributes to the riches of the community as a whole. It is through this very participation and involvement with one another that the Port Gamble S'Klallam remain a unique people with a beautiful reservation to call home.

Afterword

Ron Charles

The group of folks who wrote this book did so because it has long been known that a definitive, true, and accurate history of the Port Gamble S'Klallam people had never been produced and, meanwhile, we were losing elders who possessed valuable cultural knowledge that must be preserved. Waiting any longer would only worsen this problem. We have researched reams of material that has been collected over the years, and we have attempted to write a book that will be of interest and serve to educate tribal members, teachers, and others who want to learn about local tribal history.

We hope that what is written clearly shows how the strength, determination, and wisdom that our S'Klallam ancestors exhibited in the years following the Treaty of Point No Point allowed the generations following them to make positive changes in the community. These changes ultimately enabled the Port Gamble S'Klallams to secure a land base of their own and develop the thriving tribal government we have today.

We hope the book will help the current generation of S'Klallams to understand how important it was that their ancestors never became faint of heart, never gave up on their protests about the unfairness of treaty promises not kept by the U.S. government, and never left the lands where their dead were buried. If they had not demonstrated such determination, there is no question that the Port Gamble S'Klallam Tribe would not exist, as an entity, today.

Looking back at S'Klallam history, readers will recognize that our ancestors have left their indelible marks, in many ways, on our community. How we laugh at our own unique "Rez Humor", how we celebrate, and how we grieve, are all examples of how our ancestors lived, and how they still influence life on the reservation today. Thus, in that way, it could be said that the spirit of our ancestors lives on in

Page 263

the community today.

The spirit of those ancestors is evident in our community today, when we hear almost universal outrage tribal wide in response to proposals for massive development to the uplands surrounding Port Gamble Bay. This development would drastically change the way of life for the S'Klallams because it would poison the local marine environment that remains just as important to our people today as it was to our past generations. Our ancestors would certainly be proud of how the tribal members of today have stepped forward to stop that ill-advised development. We can all be proud of how we have carried on the values and traditions of The Strong People.

The Strong People Committee
Members and Authors

Ron Charles is a Port Gamble S'Klallam tribal elder from the Charles and Fulton families. He served as tribal chairman for twenty-three years, having just stepped down recently, and as a tribal council member for thirty-three years. Charles was a commercial fisherman and active in treaty fishing rights issues and habitat preservation. He wrote Chapters 1 and 12, as well as the Introduction, co-authored Chapters 3 and 11, edited Chapters 10 and 14, and reviewed the entire book for content.

Denise Comstock is the executive director of the Port Gamble S'Klallam Foundation. She coordinated the funding and publication of the history book project.

Joan Garrow is the development officer of the Port Gamble S'Klallam Foundation. She wrote grants to fund the history book project and helped edit the book. Garrow coordinated the final layout, including photographs.

Ted George is a Port Gamble S'Klallam tribal elder from the George and Purser families. He was the first of his tribe to receive a Bachelor's degree and the first to work as a schoolteacher. George was active in education issues on the national level, including his former position as a presidential appointee to the National Council on Indian Education. George wrote Chapter 9 and the Foreword.

Ron Hirschi is an ecologist and author whose books for young readers include the popular *Seya's Song*. He was formerly the Port Gamble S'Klallam Tribe's fisheries biologist and cultural resources specialist, and he currently serves as a board member on the Port Gamble S'Klallam Foundation. His family has lived in S'Klallam country for eight generations. Hirschi wrote Chapter 4.

Emily Mansfield is a former attorney who has worked on contract for the Port Gamble S'Klallam Tribe for eighteen years, including setting up the tribe's archives. She co-authored Chapters 3 and 9, wrote Chapters 5–8, compiled the Historical Timeline, Reference List and Index, and helped edit the book.

Laurie Mattson is Port Gamble S'Klallam Executive Operations Director. She has worked for the tribe for over thirty-four years. Mattson co-authored Chapters 11 and 13. She coordinated the selection, captioning, and placement of the book's photographs.

Sharon Purser is a Port Gamble S'Klallam community member, having married into the Purser family. She is currently the tribe's Legal Department assistant and was formerly director of the Natural Resources Department. Purser wrote Chapter 10, assisted in the collection of photographs for the book, and organized the Baseball Honoring Pie Social, which provided much of the material for Chapter 12.

Billie Jo Reynolds is a Port Gamble S'Klallam tribal member from the Ives family. As the tribe's former archives assistant, she compiled documents and photographs for chapter authors.

Gina Stevens is a Port Gamble S'Klallam tribal member from the Jones family. She is the Tribal Attorney, having been the first Port Gamble S'Klallam to earn a Juris Doctorate degree. Stevens helped create the tribal archives while working for the Legal Department before becoming an attorney. Stevens wrote Chapters 2 and 14.

Additional Author and Designer

Greg Anderson is the Port Gamble S'Klallam Self-Governance Coordinator. He has worked for the tribe for twenty-one years. Anderson co-authored Chapter 13.

Jeffrey Veregge is a Port Gamble S'Klallam tribal member from the Sullivan family. He is an artist and designer. Veregge designed the cover and artwork for the book, and helped prepare it for publication.

INTRODUCTIONS

[1] The publications *Pride Is Our Heritage* and *Our Lives* may be purchased from the Port Gamble S'Klallam Tribe. Transcripts of the elder interviews from the 2005 Oral History Project are held in the tribal archives.

[2] The way the old S'Klallams pronounced words is difficult to put on paper, because one cannot accurately portray the sounds they made when they spoke. Sammy Charles, in trying his best to tell a *Seattle Post-Intelligencer* reporter in 1947 how to pronounce the tribe's name, said it was "*Nooksclime.*"

Endnotes

CHAPTER 1 – THE S'KLALLAM MIGRATION
TO PORT GAMBLE BAY

[1] Lower Elwha Tribe. *Elwha Klallam Calendar*. Port Gamble S'Klallam Tribe Archives. 1999.

[2] The Jamestown S'Klallam, in their history by Joseph Stauss, *The Jamestown S'Klallam Story*, xxv, noted the discrepancy between the shorter lists of winter villages compiled by Erna Gunther, Edward Curtis, and George Gibbs and the longer list of settlements identified by S'Klallam people: "Some of the differences in the lists can be explained by a largely anthropological-created distinction between winter, or 'permanent,' villages and summer, or 'temporary,' fishing sites or stations. In sharp contrast to these arbitrary categories, we know that S'Klallam people lived at the mouth of virtually every good fishing stream and gathered on all the best beaches throughout their homeland. What did it matter if the shelter erected was not permanent? It could and would be rebuilt at the next visit. When S'Klallam stayed seasonally at fishing sites, they certainly considered them, regardless of the type of roof over their heads, permanent and crucial to sustaining their way of life. Both winter and summer communities, or villages, were equally important and integral to S'Klallam life."

[3] Chemakum is also spelled Chimakum, or Chimacum.

[4] Barbara Lane, Identity, Treaty Status and Fisheries of the Port Gamble Indian Community (1977): 2.

[5] Henry Allen, a Skokomish/S'Klallam man, told anthropologist William Elmendorf that Port Gamble Bay was a Twana camping site. His brother Frank said the area was anciently Suquamish and then S'Klallam. W.W.Elmendorf, *Structure of Twana Culture*. Research Studies, Monographic Supplement no. 2 vol. 28, no. 3. (September, 1960): 55.

[6] Astrida Onat. *National Register of Historic Places Report*. 1991:

section 7:8; section 8:1. Recent preliminary examination suggests that use may have been significantly longer than 1,000 years (Personal communication with archaeologist Josh Wisniewski, 2011).

[7] *S'Klallam Tribe v. US.* Indian Claims Commission, Dkt 123, Findings of Fact and Opinion. 5 ICC 680 at 684 and 699.

[8] *The Loggers* (1976), 63.

[9] *Ibid.,* 57.

[10] Waterman, *Puget Sound Geography.* "Geographical Names in the Clallam and Chimakum Area." [1920].

[11] "Little Boston, Picturesque Indian Village, Vanishing." *Seattle Times,* May 23, 1937. Graphic Section: 5

[12] Charles E. Roblin, "Report to Commissioner of Indian Affairs." January 31, 1919.

[13] Frank Lynch. "Plenty Smart Those Paleface Bostons, But Why Steal Body." *Seattle Post-Intelligencer*, August 26, 1947.

[14] Keller to Foster: March 7, 1854. Papers of Josiah Keller, Yale University.

[15] University Commissioners to Pope & Talbot, dba Puget Mill Co. Deed. September 16, 1863; Charles Gates. "Daniel Bagley and the University of Washington Land Grant, 1861–1868." *Pacific Northwest Quarterly*, Vol. 52, No. 2 (April 1961): 56.

[16] *The Loggers.* 1976, 58

[17] John Peabody Harrington. Reel 16, frame 1062.

[18] Erna Gunther, *Klallam Ethnography* 1, no. 5. (Seattle: University of Washington, Publications in Anthropology, 1927): 180.

Endnotes

[19] J.P. Harrington. Reel 16, frames 1009, 1103, 1114; Erna Gunther Notebook, 1924: 21.

[20] S'Klallam Census, Port Gamble, 1898; Edwin Eells, S'Klallam Census, Seabeck, 1877.

[21] Edwin Eells, S'Klallam Census, Port Gamble, 1877. Joseph Anderson's birth date is noted as 1850 on the headstone on his grave. 1862 is the birth date given in the "Original Clallam Roll" of 1926.

[22] J.P.Harrington. Reel 16, frames 0303, 0375, 0400, 0429, 1008.

[23] J.P. Harrington. Reel 16, frame 0632.

[24] Settlers and government agents gave Indian people English names that they, the whites, could pronounce and remember.

[25] J.P. Harrington. Reel 16, frame 0429. The Prince of Wales eventually moved to Jamestown. The Prince family are his descendants.

[26] Claude and Betty George Interview, August 21, 2006: 28; Edwin Eells, S'Klallam Census, Dungeness, 1877; Irene Purser, Ed Purser and Clara Jones Oral History, ca. 1974.

[27] Lambert. The House of the Seven Brothers, Trees, Roots and Branches of the House of Ste-tee-thkum. (Port Orchard: Publishers Printing, [1960] 1972): 19.

[28] Martinez, Ruth. Interview with Tallis Woodward, n.d.

[29] Erna Gunther Notebook, Burke Museum, n.d.; Correspondence, 1913.

[30] Solomon most likely came to Port Gamble Bay in the early 1880s as a man in his twenties. Tracing the whereabouts of Indian people through the early censuses is difficult and unreliable. English names given to Indians by whites were often changed over time or the same name was given to several people; ages given on the censuses were

usually a wild guess and the spelling of Indian names depended on the Anglo census takers' ability to discern unfamiliar sounds. Tracking Solomon before he came to Port Gamble requires piecing together clues that may or may not actually refer to him: in the 1877 Indian census, "Solomon" and "George" are listed together in Dungeness and on the 1878 Annuity Roll, Solomon is listed with George, father of Port Gamble's Eddie George. In 1880, an Indian named "Solomon" was working at the sawmill in Port Discovery. These may all be the same Solomon who, by 1885, had migrated east to Port Gamble, where he lived with his wife, Katie, and, later, with his second wife, Susie (1877 S'Klallam Census; Edwin Eells, March 1, 1878, List of Clallam Indians belonging to Skokomish; 1880 Federal Census, Washington Territory, Jefferson County, Pt. Discovery).

[31] Edwin Eells. Report, March 15, 1878.

[32] Erna Gunther Notebook, Burke Museum, n.d.

[33] Edwin Eells. Report, March 15, 1878; J.P. Harrington. Reel 16, frame 1098.

[34] J.P. Harrington. Reel 16, frames1041, 0367, 1024; Sam Sparks. Oral History, 1998.

[35] J.P. Harrington. Reel 16, frames 0553, 0571, 1028; Erna Gunther Notebook, Burke Museum, n.d.

[36] Aaron Purser, Rudolf Mark Purser, Orville Bud Purser in *Pride is our Heritage*, 11, 18, 19.

[37] Winfield Scott Ebey. Journal: Feb. 8, 1856; Gunther Fieldnotes, Book 1924: 47.

[38] Rev. Myron Eells. *The Indians of Puget Sound.* (Walla Walla: Whitman College, [1894] 1986): 181

Endnotes

[39] Rev. Myron Eells. "Puget Sound Indians: Locomotion and Transportation," *American Antiquarian* 10, no. 1 (January 1888): 27.

[40] Eells, Edwin, *Autobiography*, 1871 – 1882, 3.

[41] George Dickey, ed. Journal of Occurrences at Fort Nisqually. [1833-1859] 1989.

[42] Barbara Lane. Background of Treaty Making in Western Washington, 1977.

[43] Irene (Fulton) Purser in *Pride Is Our Heritage*, 3.

[44] Keller to Foster: September 29, 1854. Papers of Josiah Keller. Americana Collection: 280. Beinecke Rare Book Library, Yale University.

[45] Commander Swartout to Secretary of Navy, November 23, 1856 and December 8, 1856.

[46] See, in general, descriptions by Reverend Myron Eells, Edwin Eells and William Elmendorf, *Twana Narratives*.

[47] Harry Fulton Jr. Interview, ca. 1976.

CHAPTER 2 – TREATY OF POINT NO POINT:
RIGHTS THAT LIVE TODAY

[1] 21.03.02 PGST Law and Order Code, Family Code.

[2] Port Gamble S'Klallam. Confidential interview #6 conducted by Melody Bidtah with a tribal member family to develop an Indian Child Welfare Practice Manual. March 4, 2008: 4.

[3] Kickingbird, et al. *Indian Treaties.* Albuquerque: Institute for the Development of Indian Law, 1980; As early as the 1500s, treaties were used in the New World by the Spanish, and later the French, Dutch, and the British, in order to seek peace with the then-powerful Indian Nations, and to obtain land. In the 1700s, the strength of the Indian confederations would convince the British that treaties were the preferred approach in dealing with the Natives, especially when they were already at war with the French.

Tribal sovereignty preceded the development of the U.S. Constitution. The framers of the U.S. Constitution specifically recognized the sovereignty of Indian tribes. Congress is identified as the governmental branch authorized to "regulate commerce with foreign Nations, and among the several states, and with the Indian tribes."

[4] Records of the Proceedings of the Commission to hold Treaties with the Indian Tribes in Washington Territory and the Blackfoot Territory. n.d.

[5] Jerry Gorsline, ed. *Shadows of Our Ancestors, Readings in the History of Klallam-White Relations* Dalmo'ma Anthology 8. (Pt. Townsend: Empty Bowl, 1992): 57.

[6] Treaties with the Indian Tribes in Washington Territory.

[7] Gorsline. *Shadows of Our Ancestors.* (1992): 40.

[8] Treaties with the Indian Tribes in Washington Territory; Treaty of Point No Point, 1855.

Endnotes

[9] Treaties with the Indian Tribes in Washington Territory; http://www.oregonencyclopedia.org

[10] Treaties with the Indian Tribes in Washington Territory. *Chits-ah-mah-han* was changed by non-Indians to *Chetzemoka*.

[11] Treaty of Point No Point, 1855.

[12] Ibid.

[13] Lambert, *The House of the Seven Brothers*, [1960] 1972. The spelling is not an exact match, where *Tulmetum* is spelled with two "t's," not three, but it is close enough to assume the treaty signer is the same man Lambert referred to as the father of Lord Jim Balch, Chief.

[14] Ibid. Lambert, chapter 2.

[15] *United States v. Washington*, 384 F.Supp. 312 (W.D. Wash. 1974).

[16] Lewis Kamb, "The Boldt Decision very much alive 30 years later." *Seattle PI*, February 12, 2004.

[17] Barbara Lane, Karen James, and Emily Mansfield, "Hunting and Gathering Practices of the S'Klallam and Skokomish Indians and the Treaty of Point No Point," June 1997: 1.

[18] Ibid., Part I-10.

[19] Port Gamble S'Klallam Law and Order Code, Title 18, (adopted 1986).

[20] Barbara Lane, et al, "Hunting and Gathering Practices of the S'Klallam and Skokomish Indians and the Treaty of Point No Point," 1997: 1.

[21] Port Gamble, Jamestown and Lower Elwha Tribes, "Tribes provide insight on Treaty hunting rights." *North Kitsap Herald*, February 26, 2010.

CHAPTER 3 – THE S'KLALLAM NATURAL WORLD

[1] *Che-lam-teh-tat*, Skokomish Indian at Treaty of Point No Point, 1855.

[2] Irene Fulton Purser, in *Pride Is Our Heritage*, 3; Martin Charles, in *Pride Is Our Heritage,*10*;* Henry J. Phillips Interview, 1936. Washington Pioneer Project, Washington State Library.

[3] Irene Fulton Purser, in *Pride Is Our Heritage*, 3.

[4] Gene Jones Interview, November 21, 2005: 22.

[5] Ted George Interview, August 11, 2006.

[6] For S'Klallam territory and resources in general see Barbara Lane, "Identity, Treaty Status and Fisheries of the Port Gamble Indian Community," Report prepared for *U.S. v. Washington*, 1977; Erna Gunther, *Klallam Ethnography*; T.T. Waterman, "Geographical Names in the Clallam and Chimakum Area," *Puget Sound Geography*, unpublished manuscript, ca. 1920; Karen James, "S'Klallam Shellfish Report," 1993; Barbara Lane, Karen James and Emily Mansfield, "Hunting and Gathering Practices of the Skokomish and S'Klallam and the Treaty of Point No Point," 1997; Jacilee Wray, *The Salmon Bank: An Ethnohistoric Compilation,* 2003.

[7] Chart from Gunther, *Klallam Ethnography*: 198, 199.

[8] Erna Gunther Notebooks, Book III, 1923 and Book 1924. ; E.G. Swindell Jr., Report, 1942.

[9] Sparks, Webster, Buttner in J.P.Harrington, Roll 16: 0308, 0285, 0313, 0307, 0301, 0288, 0300.

[10] T.T. Waterman. "Names of places on Hood Canal in the vicinity of Seabeck," *Puget Sound Geography*, vol. 1 (1920): Site 112. As one of the important traditional S'Klallam and Skokomish fisheries, it is fitting that in recent years the tribe played a major role in the preservation of

Endnotes

this lagoon (Ron Hirshi, 2009).

[11] For example, in 1873 when the Indian Agency instructed agents to require Indians to stay on their reservations, Edwin Eells responded that the Skokomish and S'Klallam had to be away most of the time to fish (Smith to Milroy, Circular of October 21, 1873; Eells to Smith, December 2, 1873).

[12] Sec. 5694, Remington's Revised Statutes of Washington, Annotated, vol. 7: 35, 36; McChesney to Commissioner of Indian Affairs, October 28, 1915; Ron Charles Interview, November, 2008. Indians were permitted to fish without a state license on-reservation, on a reservation river within five miles outside the reservation boundaries, or for a half mile offshore in salt waters bordering a reservation. The law's exception for reservation rivers did not help the Port Gamble S'Klallam because at that time they had neither a river nor a reservation.

[13] Martin Charles in *Pride Is Our Heritage*, 10. Kate Moran Interview, March 17, 1992.

[14] Dorothy Day George Interview, February 27, 2006: 5, 6, 12, 14, 16.

[15] For example, Emily Chubby Webster joined other S'Klallam families from Jamestown trolling and selling to the Port Angeles cannery when the mill at Jamestown closed. George Sparks even boarded a ship from Neah Bay to venture to the Bering Sea to hunt fur seals. In 1914, Martin Charles' mother was working at the Port Washington clam cannery when he was born.

[16] Rose Purser Interview, February 7, 2006: 4; February 10, 2006: 7.

[17] "We can no longer hunt and fish in accordance with our treaty rights . . . we are compelled to buy a hunters' and fishermen's license to do these. The U.S. District Attorney's office has declined to defend us in a case where a game warden arrested two of our tribesmen for having an old dead duck in the back yard after the close of the season." (S'Klallam Tribe, Resolution from Tribal Council Meeting, May 11 and 12, 1914).

Fourteen Port Gamble S'Klallam men signed the resolution.

[18] Con Sullivan Interview, February 7, 2006: 3, 6.

[19] Ted George Interview, October 26, 2006: 19; August 11, 2006.

[20] Dorothy Day George Interview, February 26, 2006: 5, 6, 12, 14, 16.

[21] Rose Purser Interview, February 7, 2006: 15.

[22] Christine Charles and Monica Charles Interview, November 21, 2005: 10, 11.

[23] Irene Jackson Purser Interview, April 14, 2006: 10.

[24] Christine Charles and Monica Charles Interview, November 21, 2005: 7, 11.

[25] Claude and Betty George Interview, August 14, 2006: 12.

[26] Rose Purser Interview, February 7, 2006: 2, 4; Ron Charles Interview, October 22, 2008.

[27] Jake Jones and Floyd Jones Interview, September 14, 2005; Ron Charles Interview, October 22, 2008.

[28] Ron Charles Interview, November, 2008; George Sparks in J.P. Harrington, Roll 16, 1108; Christine Charles in *Pride Is Our Heritage*, 12.

[29] Ron Charles, March 2009.

[30] Ron Hirshi, 2009.

[31] Ivan George Interview, August 31, 2005: 6, 7, 11, 15, 16.

[32] Christine Charles and Monica Charles Interview, November 21, 2005: 7, 11.

Endnotes

[33] Pulsifer has sometimes been spelled Pulcifer.

[34] Dorothy Day George Interview, February 27, 2006: 5, 6, 12, 14, 16.

[35] Gene Jones Interview, November 21, 2005: 22.

[36] Ted George Interview, August 11, 2006.

[37] Martha John Interview, ca. 1974.

[38] Gertrude Adams Interview, August 18, 2006: 7.

[39] Claude George Interview, August 14, 2006: 12, 25. Ivan George is often called "Uncle Ivar".

[40] Martin Charles <u>in</u> *Pride Is Our Heritage*, 10.

[41] Alice George Fulton <u>in</u> *Pride Is Our Heritage*, 9.

[42] William Jones Interview, November 29, 2005: 2, 3; November 21, 2005.

[43] Archaeological data from Point Julia was predominantly shellfish (Personal communication, archaeologist Josh Wisniewski).

[44] Ivan George Interview, August 31, 2005: 11, 21.

[45] Victor Tom and Bernard Tom Interview, September 27, 2005: 6.

[46] Irene Purser Interview, ca. 1976; Ted George Interview, August 11, 2006.

[47] Ron Charles Interview, November, 2008; Lloyd Fulton <u>in</u> *Pride Is Our Heritage,* 10; James Fulton <u>in</u> *Pride Is Our Heritage,* 23.

[48] Irene Jackson Purser Interview, February 7, 2006: 6.

[49] Martha George Interview, ca. 1974: 7.

[50] Ivan George Interview, August 31, 2005: 6, 7, 11, 15, 16.

[51] Martin Charles in *Pride Is Our Heritage*, 10.

[52] Rose Purser Interview, February 7, 2006: 2, 4.

[53] Lloyd Fulton in Pride Is Our Heritage, 10.

[54] Claude and Betty George Interview, August 14, 2006: 25.

[55] Ivan George Interview, August 31, 2005: 7, 11, 15, 16.

[56] Lloyd Fulton in Pride Is Our Heritage, 10.

[57] Ron Charles Interview, November 2008.

[58] American Friends Service Committee, *Uncommon Controversy,* 1975 edition; *Puyallup Tribe v. Department of Game of Washington, et al,* 391 U.S. 392 (1968); *U.S. v. Washington*, 354 F. Supp. 312 (W.D. Wash. 1974); *U.S. v. Washington*, 873 F. Supp. 1422 (W.D. Wash. 1994).

[59] Ted George, November 2010.

[60] William Jones Interview, November 29, 2005: 8, 9.

[61] Claude and Betty George Interview, August 14, 2006: 44, 45.

[62] Claude George Interview, August 14, 2006: 43, 44.

[63] *U.S. v. Washington,* 873 F. Supp. 1422 (W.D. Wash. 1994). Judge Rafeedie's decision was upheld in 1998 by the 9th Circuit Court of Appeals.

[64] Karen James, "S'Klallam Shellfish Report," 24.

[65] Lahti Rahn, "Klallam Band's pools will be home to salmon," *Bremerton Sun*, June 27, 1975; Ron Charles Interview, November, 2008.

Endnotes

[66] Ron Hirshi, 2009.

[67] William Jones Interview, November 29, 2005: 3; November 21, 2005: 29, 34.

[68] Erna Gunther notebooks, Acc. # 614-1, Box 2, Fld 14. Book 1924: 23, 24; Lane, et al, "Hunting and Gathering Practices," 1997; Harrington, Roll 16, 0505.

[69] Washington State Game Warden, Annual Report, Washington Public Documents, 1898-1900, 116; *Ward v. Race Horse*, 163 U.S. 504 (1896); *Mason Co. v. Archie Adams and Harry Lewis,* No. 1115, Mason Co. Superior Ct, Appearance Docket, Microfilm C 18, May 21, 1909; Robert Lewis <u>in</u> *Duwamish et al. v. U.S.* 1927, 608.

[70] Lane, et al, 1997, "Hunting and Gathering Practices" 2: 25; Session Laws 1905:351, 352; Session Laws 1929, 600; Washington State Game Commissioners, Annual Report, Washington Public Documents, 1933–1934, vol. 3, 9; Harrington, Roll 16, 0391; 16 U.S.C. 251; Lester Jackson <u>in</u> Indian Claims Commission, Dkt. No. 143, June 17, 1952, vol. 1, 23–33; Con Sullivan Interview, February 7, 2006: 7; Dorothy Day George Interview, February 27, 2005: 7.

[71] Ivan George Interview, August 31, 2005: 11, 21.

[72] Harrington, Roll 16, 520, 439; Thomas Bishop to Commissioner of Indian Affairs Sells, December 24, 1915.

[73] William Jones Interview, November 29, 2005: 3; November 21, 2005, 34.

[74] Jake Jones Interview, September 14, 2005: 21.

[75] Irene Jackson Purser Interview, February 7, 2006: 7.

[76] Ted George Interview, August 11, 2006.

[77] Clara Jones, Martha George, Reada Taylor, Bennie George Jr. Interview, 1972.

[78] Ted George, November, 2008.

[79] William Jones Interview, November 21, 2005: 22; Jake Jones Interview, September 14, 2005: 14, 15; Gene Jones Interview, November 21, 2005: 22, 25; November 22, 2005: 31; Con Sullivan Interview, February 7, 2006: 5, 6, 8.

[80] Irene Jackson Purser Interview, February 7, 2006: 5, 6, 8.

[81] Dorothy Day George Interview, February 27, 2006: 5, 6.

[82] Virginia Jones Ives in *Pride Is Our Heritage*, 7.

[83] Martha John Interview, ca. 1973.

[84] Irene Jackson Purser Interview, February 7, 2006: 5; April 14, 2006: 10.

[85] Jake Jones, September 14, 2005: 17.

[86] Ivan George Interview, August 31, 2005: 6, 7; Louise John Sparks in Harrington, Roll 16, 506–509.

[87] Christine Charles Interview, November 23, 2005: 6.

[88] Louise Buttner in Harrington, Reel 16, 1043.

[89] William Jones and Gene Jones Interview, November 21, 2005: 27.

[90] Irene Jackson Purser Interview, February 7, 2006: 7.

[91] Christine & Monica Charles Interview, November 23, 2005: 23; Dorothy Day George Interview, September 27, 2005: 5; Ivan George Interview, August 31, 2005: 10,11; Gene Jones Interview, November 22, 2005: 5.

Endnotes

[92] Ron Charles Interview, November 2008.

CHAPTER 4 – THE MILL

[1] Ron Charles, 2008.

[2] J.P. Harrington, 1910, Roll 16: 0361.

[3] Pope and Talbot, Inc. "The Port Gamble Centennial, 1853-1953." Pope and Talbot Archives, 2-13 (1953): 40–44.

[4] David Smith, Essays in New England History: Northeast Corner. (Routledge Press, 2002).

[5] James Elliot Defebaugh, "History of the Lumber Industry of America." *The American Lumberman,* 1907.

[6] Gene Jones, Interview, 1995.

[7] Martha John Interview, 1975.

[8] Martin Charles Interview, June 8, 1997 and January 10, 2005.

[9] Daisy Cotter Hirschi Interview, 1976.

[10] Russell Fulton Jr. Interview, 2008.

[11] LaVerne Hirschi Interview, 2008.

[12] John S. Garner, The Company Town: Architecture and Society in the Early Industrial Age. Oxford University Press, 1992.

[13] Harry Fulton Sr. Interview, ca. 1974.

[14] Collin Thrush. *Native Seattle, Histories from the Crossing-Over Place.* Seattle: University of Washington Press, 2007.

Endnotes

[15] Edmond Meany. "Twana and Clallam Indians Aborigines of Hood Canal." *Seattle P.I.* Magazine Section (October 22, 1905): 6.

[16] Louisa Pulsifer Interview, 1974.

[17] Russell Fulton Jr. Interview, 2008.

[18] Harry Fulton III Interview, 2009.

[19] Gina Beckwith et al, "Port Gamble S'Klallam." In Olympic Peninsula Intertribal Cultural Advisory Committee. *Native Peoples of the Olympic Peninsula,* 2002. Edited by Jacilee Wray.

[20] Ibid.

[21] Ted George Interview, October 26, 2006: 9.

[22] Josiah P. Keller, Papers, Yale University.

[23] Ibid.

[24] Ibid.

[25] Egan, Timothy, *The Good Rain*.

[26] U.S. Federal Census. 1880. Washington Territory, Jefferson County.

[27] Gene Jones Interview, November 22, 2005.

[28] Floyd Jones Interview, 2008.

[29] Ibid.

[30] Port Gamble Museum Ledger #83.

[31] Daisy Cotter Hirschi Interview, 1976.

[32] Pacific Telephone and Telegraph Company. May 1948 with Purser number added by Daisy Hirschi circa 1948. Tribal Archives.

[33] Rose Purser Interview, 2008.

[34] Floyd and Jake Jones Interview, 2008.

[35] Washington Emergency Relief Administration, Kitsap Co. to Indian Agency, October 5, 1934.

[36] Rude Purser Interview, 2008.

[37] "Port Gamble Employees of McCormick Lumber Co.", 1934.

[38] Rude Purser Interview, 2008.

[39] Rose Purser Interview, 2008; Rose Purser Interview, February 10, 2006: 2, 3.

[40] Ibid.

[41] Laurel Wellman Interview, 2008.

[42] Ron Charles Interview, November 18, 2008.

[43] Harry Fulton Interview, February 2009

[44] Kelly Baze, December 2009.

Endnotes

CHAPTER 5 – PORT GAMBLE S'KLALLAM LAND

[1] Frank Lynch. *Seattle P.I,* August 26, 1947.

[2] Martha John, Notebook, 1953.

[3] Terry to Commissioner of Indian Affairs, August 20, 1897.

[4] S'Klallam Census, 1877.

[5] Kate Anderson Moran Interview, March 17, 1992.

[6] General Land Office. Trust Patent to U.S. for Joseph Anderson, 1891.

[7] Indian Homestead Act of 1875; Indian Homestead Act of 1884.

[8] Edwin Eells,"To All Persons Whom It May Concern," 1889.

[9] Johnson to Commissioner of Indian Affairs, October 18, 1909; General Land Office, Patent in fee in lieu of trust to Joseph Anderson, April 11, 1910.

[10] Cyrus Webster's father, James Webster Sr., was Chemakum from the Port Townsend area. Cyrus Webster was born in 1890. Henry Lambert (b. 1869) was from the Port Angeles area. See Chapter 1 for more information about these families.

[11] Joseph Anderson, Deed to N.M. Pulsifer, June 17, 1913; Joseph Anderson, Deed to Cyrus Webster, May 26, 1915; Joseph Anderson, Deed to Henry Lambert, August 24, 1916.

[12] James Henry, Certificate 8010, February 23, 1886.

[13] Harrington, Roll 16, 0301.

[14] Kitsap County Historical Society, *Kitsap County History,* Book 2 (1977): 81, 82. Another possible reason for choosing the location was that it was less than a half mile north of a site that had been used frequently as a camp and burial place in earlier times. Another Indian family had built a cabin at the other site, but moved away before 1888.

[15] James and Emma Henry and their son William—Ruth Martinez' father—lived at Point Julia during some of the time they were homesteading the land on Hood Canal. In 1888, the Henrys were listed on the Port Gamble S'Klallam census with a brother, Clallam Willie. (S'Klallam Census, 1888). On the 1877 S'Klallam census from Port Gamble, James Henry, aka Joshua, was listed by himself. After living on Point Julia, the Henrys sold part of their cottage on the Spit to house the Port Gamble Day School teacher.

[16] Charley Jones and wife, Deed to James Henry, January 6, 1903.

[17] Ron Charles Interview, April 2007.

[18] Ruth Martinez Interview with Tallis King George, n.d.

[19] James Mead, Deed to Charley Jones, December 8, 1886; James Mead, Deed to Solomon, December 8, 1886; James Mead, Deed to Cook House Charley, December 8, 1886. 1870 Federal Census, Washington Territory, Kitsap County, Port Gamble.

[20] Solomon, Deed to Eddie George, May 26, 1911.

[21] Old Solomon and his second wife, Susie, took care of the children of Solomon's late daughter Alice—Irene, Arnold and Russell—along with Dora and Emily (Webster), Susie's children from her previous marriage to Howard Chubby of Jamestown. (Irene Fulton Purser in *Pride is Our Heritage*, 3). Solomon worked hard to support his large family, keeping the same job at the mill for at least fifty-three years. (Swain to Johnson, June 13, 1913. This letter, written in 1913, suggests that Solomon started working at the mill in 1860. This may conflict with the census information tracing Solomon from Dungeness to Port Discovery in 1880. Or it may

be that Solomon did the same job in several different mills for 53 years). Harry Fulton applied for an allotment at Skokomish, the home of his wife Angie, but was turned down because the tract was not available. (Eells to Commissioner of Indian Affairs, 1909).

[22] Mildred Fulton DeCoteau in *Pride Is Our Heritage*, 17.

[23] Annie George et al, Deed, January 27, 1902.

[24] Martin Charles, in *Pride is Our Heritage,*10; Tommy Charles, Deed, October 30, 1930.

[25] Sammy Charles, Deed to U.S., August 8, 1916; Collier to Secretary of Interior, November 2, 1940. Jennarose Charles Fulton in *Pride Is Our Heritage,* 9; Jane Charles in *Pride is Our Heritage*, 12; Christine Jane Charles Interview, November 21, 2005: 1; Gene Jones Interview, November 22, 2005: 18, 19. Sammy and Susie Dick Charles had the house nearest and facing the mill side of the bay. In this prime location, they provided "ferry" service back and forth across the bay for Ruth Henry's family when they came from the Chico area to Port Gamble to visit (Ruth Martinez Interview with Tallis King George, n.d.). Later, Sammy and Susie used the proceeds from the sale of his big boat to buy other land inland, off the Kingston-Port Gamble highway, some distance from Point Julia. There, in the early 1930s, they built a home and lived until Sammy retired from the mill.

[26] Annual Report to the Commissioner of Indian Affairs, 1872.

[27] Claude and Betty George Interview, August 21, 2006: 28.

[28] When Annie George died in 1926, a dispute arose between her son, Sammy Charles, and her husband, Eddie George, as to who should inherit her various properties. Annie had informally indicated her desires about inheritance of her Coontown land and some lots she owned in Port Townsend but she had not made a formal will. Her arrangements did not include Eddie. Eddie apparently understood

that in the absence of a proper will, the law favored the husband. He contacted a lawyer and had the property title transferred to his name (Martha John Notebook, 1927). When Eddie's house burned down in 1933, the younger Georges re-built a second home over the ashes of the first (Ivan George Interview, August 31, 2005: 5, 6, 11, 18). The community held a dance to raise money for rebuilding (Martha John Oral History, ca. 1975).

[29] Pride is Our Heritage, 8, 14, 15.

[30] Louisa Pulsifer Interview, 1974. Lucy was Cowitchan and Snohomish but lived at Skokomish. Louisa's first marriage was to Doctor Charley, a Twana man.

[31] Little is known about Jim Williams except that he was born in 1861 at Pysht.

[32] Annie George and Eddie George, Deed to William George, June 7, 1905.

[33] Louisa Pulsifer Interview, 1974.

[34] Erik Peterson, Deed to Jacob Jones, September 28, 1903. The site where Jacob and Jenny Jones bought their land was called *tITts* by the S'Klallam, after their nickname for the bearded white man who had lived there (Harrington, Roll 16). Here, Jacob and Jenny built a farm with a gravity-fed water supply, two big fields of vegetables, chickens, ducks, pigs, cattle, and milk cows.

[35] Johan George Schmidt, Deed to Edward Purser, March 12, 1921. The sale was made August 4, 1919.

[36] Irene (Jackson) Purser, <u>in</u> *Pride is our Heritage*, 15.

[37] State of Washington, Deed to George Dan. Howell, October 18, 1897. G.C. Howell is shown as the owner of the adjoining 40 acres on a 1909 Metzker tax assessor's map.

Endnotes

[38] George and Nancy Howell had three sons, Phillip (b. 1889), George (b. 1904), and Robert (b. 1912). They gave Phillip five acres of their land in 1916. In later years, Phillip published a book of Native place names, *Dictionary of Indian Geographic Names*, gathered Indian stories, and was active in the Federation of American Indians in the 1920s. He also acted in several films that were shot in San Juan County (Phillip Hugh Howell, *Dictionary of Indian Geographic Names: The Origin and Meaning of Indian Names,* 1948; Phillip Howell, "Raven Steals Daylight," 1926.)

[39] George D. and Nancy Howell, Deed to Bennie George, July 13, 1918; George Dan Howell, Deed to Louis John, December 12, 1927. Martha John was the daughter of Sammy Charles and his first wife, Nancy, who was Samish. After her mother died when she was four-and-a-half Martha spent half her time with her mother's people on Guemes Island and half her time with her father at Port Gamble (Karen Gorham, "Martha John, Grand Old Lady of S'Klallam," in Kitsap County Historical Society, *History of Kitsap County,* 2: 109, 1977).

[40] Karen Gorham, "Martha John, Grand Old Lady of S'Klallam," 2: 109.

[41] Carl Cubby Sparks, Delores Sparks Sullivan, Maxine Sparks Walbridge, in *Pride is our Heritage*, 17, 20, 23.

[42] Kitsap County Historical Society, *Kitsap County History* 2, 159.

[43] Bill Pulsifer (b. 1879) was Josie (Pulsifer) Anderson's brother. Lizzie (b. 1880) was the sister of Harry Fulton Sr.

[44] Tyee Jack, his two wives, Mary and Nancy, and their children remained on the Port Gamble censuses until 1899; however, they could have been counted among their S'Klallam counterparts even while living on the Canal.

[45] Irene Jackson Purser Interview, April 14, 2006: 4.

Page 292

[46] Swain to Wilson, June 12, 1915.

[47] Cy Webster, Emily Webster and Louise Adams Butler Webster Buttner in Harrington, Reel 16, 0356.

[48] Irene Jackson Purser Interview, April 14, 2006: 10.

[49] Jacilee Wray, "The Salmon Bank: An Ethnohistoric Compilation."

[50] Mary Littleman Probate, 1915.

[51] General Land Office, Deed to U.S. in trust for Mary Littleman, March 7, 1892. By 1892, two of Mary Littleman's children had died. After Mary's death, her two remaining daughters both married men from Little Boston: Susie married Tommy Charles and Mary (the younger) married James Fulton, Jr., leaving two daughters when she died of tuberculosis in 1903. Agatha Fulton (b. 1899) was legally adopted by her grand uncle, Henry Lambert when she was four years old. Lydia Fulton (b. 1897) was raised by her aunt, Susie (Littleman) Charles (J.P. Harrington, Roll 16). Mary's heirs were Susie (Littleman) Charles, Lydia (Fulton) Dick and her husband, Nelson, and Agatha (Fulton) Steilacoom and her husband, John.

[52] Myron Eells, "Skokomish Agency Field and Work." *American Missionary* 34 (1880), 308; Joseph Stauss, *The Jamestown S'Klallm Story,* 2002, 145.

[53] Olympic Peninsula Intertribal Cultural Advisory Committee, *Native Peoples of the Olympic Peninsula: Who We Are,* 23, 25, 35, 36.

[54] Harrington Roll 16, Frames 0445-0448. Gorsline, 1992: 158.

[55] Johnson to Commissioner of Indian Affairs, Dec. 4, 1911.

[56] McChesney, Special Supervisor to Commissioner of Indian Affairs, October 28, 1915.

Endnotes

[57] Johnson to Commissioner of Indian Affairs, March 21, 1913.

[58] Leonidas Swain to Commissioner of Indian Affairs cited in Hauke, 2nd Asst. Commissioner of Indian Affairs to Johnson, January 13, 1913.

[59] Johnson to Commissioner of Indian Affairs, October 24, 1910.

[60] Act of March 4, 1911; Hawke, 2nd Asst. Commissioner of Indian Affairs to Johnson, May 20, 1911, quoted in part in Johnson to Commissioner of Indian Affairs, May 8, 1911.

[61] H.B. 22868, introduced by Rep. Warburton.

[62] In a Petition to remove the S'Klallam from a bill before Congress authorizing Quinault allotment, they wrote "We declare our adherence to our tribe and as such, uphold our treaty of 1855 and protest against the action of the government or its agents in treating us as individuals and furthering our adoption unto other tribes." (S'Klallam Tribe, Petition, June 15, 1912.) The bill, H.R. 22868 never passed. The Indian Office determined that no special legislation was needed to allot to the S'Klallam and others because a previous law, the Act of March 4, 1911, could be interpreted broadly enough to include them. Meanwhile, the Quinault processed 500 applications for enrollment in April, 1912, accepting most of them. They later reconsidered their hasty generosity and nearly all were dropped. (McDowell to Board of Indian Commissioners, November 1, 1920, 9).

[63] Charlie Fitzgerald to Tulalip Agent, June 25, 1912.

[64] Peter Jackson, Minutes of Council of the Clallam Tribe, May 11, 1914. On the other hand, some S'Klallam leaders reasoned, if the government was so willing to give away land at Quinault, why not grant it to the S'Klallam outright, in fee (not in trust), including all the timber, so that the S'Klallam could sell that land and purchase land in their home territory with the proceeds (Fitzgerald and Peterson to Secretary of Interior, January 6, 1913).

[65] Resolution of Clallam tribal council, May 11, 1914. Only the Port Gamble signatories are listed here.

[66] Peter Jackson to President, June 12, 1913.

[67] In the government's view, it had fulfilled the Treaty by establishing the Skokomish Reservation for the S'Klallam; the fact that they declined to move there was their choice (Merritt, Commissioner of Indian Affairs to Poindexter, August 27, 1915.)

[68] See for example Jackson to Commissioner of Indian Affairs, October 4, 1912. Ironically, these efforts ultimately resulted in an appropriation of money to individual S'Klallam people rather than to the tribe as a tribe. The S'Klallam leaders, however, never lost sight of their status.

[69] Port Gamble S'Klallam Census 1904 and 1905. In one of his many letters to the Commissioner of Indian Affairs, Peter Jackson invoked the wisdom of these elders. He implored the Commissioner to send a commission "to deal direct with the old people who knows [sic] what the tribe have received from the Government, and also what they have not received." "Our old people that were present at the signing of the Treaty are getting old," Jackson wrote, "We want their statements taken." (Hauke, Commissioner of Indian Affairs to Johnson, January 13, 1913).

[70] Peter Jackson, Minutes of Council of the Clallam Tribe, May 11, 1914.

[71] For example, Washington's Senator Poindexter badgered the Commissioner of Indian Affairs to find a solution to the S'Klallam's land deficiency other than removal to Quinault. He wrote " . . . in view of the Indians' love for his accustomed home, an effort to remove this remnant of the Clallam tribe to the Quinault Reservation would be most unhappy for them and would result in their early extermination." (Poindexter to Commissioner of Indian Affairs, September 24, 1915.)

[72] Eliot to Chair, Board of Ind. Commissioners, January 1, 1915.

Endnotes

[73] Christine Charles Interview November 21 and 23, 2005: 7.

[74] McChesney, Special Supervisor to Commissioner of Indian Affairs, October 28, 1915.

[75] Thomas Bishop, *An Appeal to the Government to Fulfill Sacred Promises Made 61 Years Ago.* December 24, 1915. The S'Klallam parted ways with Bishop's cause, however, when he focused on collecting over 2,000 applications from landless Indians for allotment at Quinault.

[76] Roblin created a roll of over 4,000 landless Indians based on genealogical proof of each family's Indian heritage. The roll completed by Charles Roblin in 1919 did not directly result in any tangible benefits for the unalloted people but he did collect a treasure trove of genealogical information. Roblin's final report marginalized most of the individuals on the roll as descendants of Indian women who dropped their tribal affiliations to marry white men. Roblin saw them as mixed-blooded people with no real Indian connections, spurred on by Bishop to claim allotment rights. (Roblin to Commissioner of Indian Affairs, January 31, 1919.)

[77] The Indian Office's insistence that it owed nothing to the S'Klallam crumbled in the face of contrary recommendations by the Board of Indian Commissioners, the Roblin Report, the Washington congressional delegation, and former superintendent McChesney himself. In 1921, the Office sent Walter Dickens to a S'Klallam Council at Jamestown to discuss their treaty claims. (Dickens to Commissioner of Indian Affairs, February 15, 1922).

[78] Dickens, Ibid.

[79] The claim Ritchie drafted for the S'Klallam was originally intended to enable the tribe to sue the U.S. in the Court of Claims along with other tribes pursuing this approach. (Ritchie to Commissioner of Indian Affairs, January 9, 1922).

[80] Richie negotiated hard for $600,000 but Congress cut the amount

back even further (Dickens to Commissioner, May 23, 1926; Work to Senator Harreld, January 26, 1924; 43 Stat. 1102). The Act provided for up to $15,000 of the $400,000 to be paid to the attorney.

[81] After the court determined how much money was due to each treaty tribe, it deducted from the settlement all monies the government had spent "for the benefit" of the tribes since the signing of the treaties. In the case of the tribes of western Washington, the grand total after the offset amounted to nothing. (*Duwamish et al. v. U.S.*)

[82] Burke to Dickens, March 24, 1926.

[83] Dickens to Commissioner, May 23, 1926; *North American Indian*, VI, No. 49, April 23, 1926. S'Klallam who did not attend the meeting had until May 10 to submit written applications. If a person had been living apart from the tribe, more information was needed. Few individuals submitted applications that could not be verified as having S'Klallam blood. The difficulty was in the 760 applications from people with undisputed S'Klallam blood who the Committee refused to recognize because they lacked current affiliation with the tribe.

[84] Dickens to Commissioner, May 23, 1926. The Agent complained that the Committee restricted recognition to "a clannish few who have stood together since the event of the Treaty."

[85] Tulalip Agency Superintendent to Sam Charles, n.d.; Beckwith, "Land and its Significance," 7. Of the 1225 hopefuls, 533 S'Klallam were officially enrolled. The shares of under-aged children were retained until they reached the age of majority, with interest on their share dispersed to their parents.

[86] Anderson to Sir, November 24, 1931.

[87] Stanton to Indian Agent, September 18, 1934.

[88] Kitsap County Treasurer's Return on Tax Sale, October 8, 1938 (The Anderson property sold to Kitsap County for $125.28); Kitsap County

Treasurer's Return on Tax Sale, October 8, 1938 (The Pulsifer property taxes due were $8.69); Kitsap County Treasurer's Tax Deed after tax judgment, August 31, 1936 (The George parcel was sold for $21.29); Kitsap County Assessor's Map, 1936. Documentation on the other parcels has not yet been found.

[89] Tommy Charles, Deed, October 30, 1930. The land owned by Henry Lambert and by Jim Henry was out of their hands by 1955 but it is not known whether they sold their parcels or lost them in tax foreclosures.

CHAPTER 6 – THE LITTLE BOSTON COMMUNITY

[1] Ted George Interview, October 26, 2006, 14.

[2] Pride Is Our Heritage, 17.

[3] Christine Charles and Monica Charles, November 21 and 23, 2005: 36, 37.

[4] Kate Moran Interview, March 17, 1992.

[5] Myron Eells, *The Twana, Chemakum and Klallam Indians of Washington Territory.* Smithsonian Institution, Annual Report (1887), 605, 611; Myron Eells, "Indians of Puget Sound: Measuring and valuing," *American Antiquarian* 10, no. 3, (May, 1888), 174; Francis Norbert Blanchet, S.J., *Historical Sketches of the Catholic Church in Oregon.* [1878] 1983, 96–99.

[6] Myron Eells, *The Twana, Chemakum and Klallam Indians of Washington Territory.* Smithsonian Institution, Annual Report (1887), 605, 615.

[7] Often, adaptation and tradition were mixed in unique ways. For example, an Indian agent reported that the S'Klallam spent the cash they earned at the mill for possessions which they kept until a quantity had been collected. Then the whole was given away at a great potlatch feast. (Myron Eells, *Twana, Chemakum and Klallam,* 605, 615; Henry Webster, 1862 Annual Report of the Commissioner of Indian Affairs.) By the late 1880s, potlatches were becoming less frequent, but the tradition of sharing the fruits of one's labors is still strong today.

[8] Papers of Josiah P. Keller, Western Americana Collection, Yale University; U.S. Coast Survey Map, 1856. The archeological survey of Point Julia for the National Historic Register could fix no definite date for the construction of the houses. Onat's guess was late 1850s or 1860s (Astrida Onat, Application for National Register of Historic Places, Point Julia, Washington, Sec. 7:4, Sec. 8:6). However, Keller's 1862 sketch of

Endnotes

Port Gamble Bay showed only a house and two hog sheds on the Point Julia side of the Spit. Keller's papers were not available to the Onat study. Pope and Talbot's historian stated no date either (Coman, *Time, Tide and Timber*). In 1871 Indian agent Edwin Eells described S'Klallam houses in the "old plank house style." (Edwin Eells, Autobiography, 1914, Bk. 3) This suggests that the Little Boston houses may have been built after 1871.

[9] In the 1800s, Native people distinguished between the English newcomers—the "King George men"—and the Americans—the "Bostons." Myron Eells, *Twana, Chemakum and Klallam*, 605, 623.

[10] Harry Fulton Jr. Interview, ca. 1974

[11] Louise Pulsifer Interview, 1974

[12] Harry Fulton Jr. Interview, ca. 1974: 4, 5.

[13] Rose Purser Interview, February 10, 2006: 4, 7; February 7, 2006: 6.

[14] Vic Tom Jr. and Bernard Tom Interview, September 27, 2005: 2.

[15] William W. Elmendorf, Twana Narratives: Native Accounts of a Coast Salish Culture, 64, 88.

[16] 125 Indians also came from Sooke, across the Strait, 25 from Port Discovery and 25 from Port Townsend. (Myron Eells, *Twana, Chemakum and Klallam*, 605, 662, 665.)

[17] Myron Eells, "Puget Sound Indians: Locomotion and Transportation," 1888, 26.

[18] Ibid.

[19] Myron Eells, Twana, Chemakum and Klallam, 607.

[20] Myron Eells, "Skokomish Agency Field and Work," (1880), 308.

[21] Kate Moran Interview, March 17, 1992.

[22] Harry Fulton Jr. Interview, ca. 1974: 2; Ivan George Interview, September 13, 2005: 12.

[23] Harry Fulton Jr. Interview, ca. 1974: 2; Kate Moran Interview, March 17, 1992.

[24] Martha John Interview, 5.

[25] Gene Jones Interview, November 22, 2005: 18, 19.

[26] Christine and Monica Charles Interviews, November 21, 2005: 5; November 23, 2005: 14.

[27] Gene Jones Interview, November 22, 2005: 8.

[28] Harrington, Roll 16, Frame 1064, 1020.

[29] Harry Fulton Jr. Interview, ca. 1974: 6.

[30] Con Sullivan Interview, February 7, 2006: 11; March 29, 2006: 8.

[31] Darlene Peters in Gene Jones Interview, November 22, 2005: 20.

[32] Kate Moran Interview, March 17, 1992.

[33] Myron Eells, Twana, Chemakum and Klallam, 605, 615.

[34] Ted George Interview, October 26, 2006: 25. Martha's mother was Julia John, part of the Sigo family. Richard Purser was Martha's stepfather.

[35] Irene Purser Interview, April 14, 2006: 26, 27.

Endnotes

[36] Ted George Interview, October 26, 2006: 31.

[37] Christine Charles and Monica Charles Interview, November 21, 2005: 3; November 23, 2005: 14.

[38] Jake Jones and Floyd Jones Interview, September 14, 2005: 7; September 22, 2005: 1, 2.

[39] Rose Purser Interview, February 7, 2006: 5; February 10, 2006: 3.

[40] Claude George and Betty George Interview, August 14, 2006: 37.

[41] Jake Jones and Floyd Jones Interview, September 14, 2005: 21, 7; September 22, 2005: 4, 5; Ted George Interview, October 26, 2006: 32.

[42] Kate (Anderson) Moran Interview, March 17, 1992; Christine Charles and Monica Charles, November 23, 2005: 9).

[43] Rose Purser Interview, February 7, 2006: 4, 9, 10; Jake Jones and Floyd Jones, Interview, September 14, 2005: 7, 21; September 22, 2005: 4, 5; Con Sullivan Interview, February 7, 2006: 8.

[44] Ivan George Interview, August 31, 2005: 11, 15, 20; September 13, 2005: 5.

[45] Dorothy George, Interview, February 27, 2005: 8.

[46] Jake Jones and Floyd Jones, Interview, September 14, 2005: 21, 7; September 22, 2005: 4, 5.

[47] Harry Fulton Jr. Interview, ca. 1974.

[48] Con Sullivan Interview, March 29, 2006: 18.

[49] Martha John Interview, ca. 1974: 3.

[50] Harmon to Hammond, January 31, 1918.

[51] Martha John Interview, ca. 1974: 4.

[52] Claude George Interview, August 14, 2006: 28, 29; Harmon to Wilson, February 1, 1927; Cushman Superintendent to Harmon, February 9, 1917; Swain to Wilson, July 7, 1917; Kate Anderson Moran, March 17, 1992.

[53] Kate Anderson Moran Interview, March 17, 1992.

[54] Jake Jones and Floyd Jones Interview, September 14, 2005: 1, 2; September 22, 2005: 3, 7.

[55] Ivan George Interview, August 31, 2005: 17; Harry Fulton Jr. Interview, ca. 1974, 6.

[56] Martha John interview, ca. 1974: 3.

[57] Ivan George Interview, August 31, 2005: 5, 6, 11, 14, 18.

[58] Rose Purser Interview, February 7, 2006.

[59] Jake Jones and Floyd Jones Interview, September 14, 2005: 12; Harman to Hammond, January 31, 1918; Con Sullivan Interview, March 29, 2006: 7.

[60] Claude George Interview, August 14, 2006: 28, 29; Kate Anderson Moran Interview, March 17, 1992; Karen Gorham, "Grand Old Lady of S'Klallam," *Bremerton Sun,* April 23, 1977; Christine Charles Interview, November 21, 2005: 20; Dorothy Day George Interview, September 26, 2006: 15; Irene Jackson Purser Interview, April 14, 2006: 20; Shirley Loeffler in *Pride is Our Heritage*, 23.

[61] Irene Jackson Purser Interview, April 14, 2006: 30.

[62] Ted George Interview, October 26, 2006: 2, 9.

Endnotes

[63] Ed Friedrich, "This Corner Will Stand for the Georges," *Bremerton Sun*, June 29, 1999; Wm. Ramsey, "Saving the Corner Store, in Name Only," *Bremerton Sun,* July 1, 1998.

[64] Myron Eells, *Twana, Chemakum and Klallam,* 605, 659, 660.

[65] Harry Fulton Jr. Interview, ca. 1974, 6; Ivan George, September 13, 2005, 24; Irene Jackson Purser Interview, April 14, 2006, 12, 5.

[66] Victor and Bernard Tom Interview, September 27, 2005: 16.

[67] Rose Wellman Purser Interview, February 7, 2006: 2, 4; February 10, 2006: 2, 3.

[68] Irene Jackson Purser Interview, April 14, 2006: 5, 12.

[69] Rose Purser Interview, February 7, 2006: 2, 4, 11, 16, 19; Jake Jones and Floyd Jones Interview, September 22, 2005: 23.

[70] Ted George Interview, October 26, 2006: 14.

[71] Ron Charles Interview, March 2007.

[72] Ed Puser, "Port Gamble Locals" and "Clallam Indians Strike: Fight Ten Hour Day." *Real American*, April 7, 1922.

[73] Claude George Interview, August 14, 2006: 31, 32, 36.

[74] Kitsap County Historical Society, *Kitsap County: A History.* Central Kitsap Section: 16, 29. One or more Sackmans married S'Klallam, but we do not have enough information about these families to comment on them.

[75] Rose Wellman Purser Interview, February 7, 2006: 7.

[76] Irene Jackson Purser Interview, April 14, 2006: 10.

[77] Swain Report, May 7, 1915; Swain to McChesney, June 1, 1914; McChesney to Swain, June 3, 1914; Rose Purser Interview, February 10, 2006: 7, 17.

[78] Ted George Interview, October 26, 2006: 14.

[79] Ted George Interview, October 26, 2006: 28.

[80] Ron Charles, *The S'Klallam View*, January 2009.

[81] Sharon Purser Interview, April 2009.

[82] Ted George Interview, November 5, 2008.

Endnotes

CHAPTER 7 – THE NEW RESERVATION

[1] Ivan George Interview, September 13, 2005: 12, 25.

[2] John Collier Congressional Testimony on the Indian Reorganization Act, Collier Papers Microfilm, A 6833, Roll 29II, 498 [1076]. Under the General Allotment Act of 1887, reservations were divided into allotments, which were granted to individual Indians. Land in excess of the parcels allotted were then sold to non-Indians. Further loss of reservation lands occurred when Indian allotments were taken out of trust so that their owners could sell, inevitably, to non-Indians.

[3] The 1920 Tulalip Agency Report lamented that the agent had no control over the Little Boston S'Klallam because they were not living on government land (Tulalip Agency, Report, October 5, 1920: 40).

[4] 48 Stat. L. 984. From a contemporary perspective, the IRA had its shortcomings; for example, boilerplate tribal constitutions left too much control in the hands of the Department of Interior. At the time, however, the Act represented a major, positive breakthrough in Indian policy.

[5] The Tribe was third only to the Mississippi Choctaw and the Swinomish Tribes. (Zimmerman, Asst. Commissioner of Indian Affairs to Gray, Director Land Utilization Division, August 10, 1935).

[6] U.S. Dept. of Interior, Indian Office Land Division, Memo, August 28, 1935; Ade to Commissioner of Indian Affairs, September 10, 1936. The IRA authorized $2,000,000, but Congress halved the appropriation. Still, the Tulalip Agency made such a strong case for Port Gamble S'Klallam that the Tribe remained a top priority. (Zimmerman, Commissioner of Indian Affairs to Upchurch, August 16, 1935).

[7] Zimmerman, Ibid.

[8] Tulalip Agency, Appraisal Report, September 25, 1946; T.W. Wheat, "Statement Concerning the Project," December 12, 1935.

[9] Natural Resources Board Questionnaire – Clallam (Public Domain)" n.d.

[10] McCormick Lumber Company, "Offer to sell lands to the U.S.," September 30, 1935.

[11] Port Gamble S'Klallam Reservation Proclamation, June 16, 1938.

[12] Daiker, Commissioner of Indian Affairs to Secretary of Interior, June 15, 1939. The Indian Office later decided that their failure to hold a vote on the IRA was not a bar to organizing under the Act. The Act would apply unless a Tribe voted *against* it, which the S'Klallam had not done.

[13] Kenneth Meiklejohn, Solicitor Memo, September 27, 1938.

[14] Peter Jackson to LaVatta, March 23, 1939.

[15] George LaVatta to Commissioner of Indian Affairs, March 17, 1938.

[16] Joseph Stauss, *The Jamestown S'Klallam Story,* 153; Olympic Peninsula Intertribal Cultural Advisory Committee, *Native Peoples of the Olympic Peninsula,* 26.

[17] Kenneth Meiklejohn, Solicitor Memo, September 27, 1938; Kenneth Meiklejohn, Memo n.d. (ca. post–1938); Kenneth Meiklejohn, Memo June 17, 1937. An early draft of a Constitution and By Laws for the Clallam Tribe was dated 1934 (S'Klallam Tribe, Clallam Constitution, August 16, 1934). La Vatta met with the recently constituted Business Committee and then the whole community, two-thirds of whom were present at the meeting. He presented a draft constitution that was unanimously approved, demonstrating the Tribe's desire to organize formally. This draft was waylaid and revised for several years. (George LaVatta to Commissioner of Indian Affairs, August 24, 1935.)

Endnotes

[18] U.S. Dept. of Interior, Indian Office, Land Division, Minutes of Meeting, 1935.

[19] Upchurch to Commissioner of Indian Affairs, December 6, 1938; Tulalip Agency, Report on 1938 Program.

[20] Upchurch to Commissioner of Indian Affairs, March 20, 1936.

[21] Ivan George Interview, August 31, 2005, 25.

[22] Upchurch to Commissioner of Indian Affairs, August 23, 1938; Port Gamble Indian Council, March 1, 1939.

[23] Herrick, Asst. Commissioner of Indian Affairs to Upchurch, February 14, 1939; Tulalip Agency Report, ca. December, 1940.

[24] Upchurch to Jackson, March 27, 1939; Vigeant to Upchurch, December 14, 1938.

[25] Port Gamble Indian Council, March 1, 1939.

[26] Kitsap County Board of Commissioners, December 6, 1937; Rue, Kitsap County Commissioner to Senator Bone, April 13, 1938; Bone to Commissioner of Indian Affairs, July 29, 1938; Karl Leonard to Senator Walgren, April 3, 1942; Upchurch to Commissioner of Indian Affairs, April 12, 1938; Tulalip Agency, Report, ca. December, 1940; Kitsap County Board of Commissioners, Minutes, March 6, 1939; Lucille Weiesenburg Interview, June 25, 2007.

[27] Lucille Weisenburger Interview, June 25, 2007: 8, 9.

[28] Tulalip Agency Report, ca. December, 1940.

[29] The Trust Fund received $20,000 under the 1938 Rehabilitation Trust Agreement, and $13,000 under the 1939 Rehabilitation Trust Agreement (Zimmerman, Commissioner of Indian Affairs to Upchurch, November 15, 1940). The twenty homes were not enough for all the

S'Klallam who needed one. For example, Joseph Patsy applied for an assignment of land so that he could move his family from Hadlock to the new reservation. Apparently the houses were all assigned to others (Patsy to Collier, March 31, 1936).

[30] Upchurch to Commissioner of Indian Affairs, October 15, 1940.

[31] Vigeant to Upchurch, May 18, 1939; Port Gamble S'Klallam Tribe, Resolution, December 3, 1938.

[32] Tulalip Agency Report: ca. December, 1940; Harry Fulton Jr. Interview, ca. 1976: 3.

[33] Christine Charles Interview: November 21, 2005: 9.

[34] Thelma Fulton Oya in *Pride Is Our Heritage*, 14.

[35] Harry Fulton Interview, ca. 1976: 3; Mildred Fulton DeCoteau in *Pride Is Our Heritage*, 17.

[36] Port Gamble Indian Tribe, Community Lot List, n.d.

[37] Russell Fulton Jr. in *Pride Is Our Heritage*, 14.

[38] Betty Wellman George in *Pride Is Our Heritage*, 5. The Wellmans had previously lived in Port Ludlow and Centralia, following employment opportunities in the sawmills (Rose Wellman Purser Interview, February 7, 2006: 1, 2).

[39] Zimmerman, Asst. Commissioner of Indian Affairs to Senator Bone, June 15, 1938; Karl Leonard to Senator Walgren, April 3, 1942.

[40] Rose Wellman Purser, October 2008.

[41] Vigeant to Upchurch, October 17, 1940; Upchurch to Commissioner of Indian Affairs, October 31, 1940; Port Gamble Tribe, Resolution, November 14, 1940; Upchurch to Vigeant, February 21, 1941. In 1941,

the Project was not approved by the CCC, but between the Tribe and the Agency, it was built anyway (Murphy to Upchurch, May 16, 1941; Tulalip Agency, Report, March 26, 1947).

[42] Rose Wellman Purser Interview, February 7, 2006: 17; Tulalip Agency, Planning Committee Report, 1944-1945.

[43] Rose Wellman Purser Interview, February 7 2006: 17.

[44] Ibid.

[45] Karl Leonard to Senator Walgren, April 3, 1942; Zimmerman, Commissioner of Indian Affairs to Senator Walgren, April 15, 1942; Tulalip Agency, Planning Report, 1947.

[46] Dorothy (Day) George in *Pride Is Our Heritage*, 16.

[47] Rose Wellman Purser Interview, February 7, 2006: 17.

[48] Aaron Purser in Pride Is Our Heritage, 11.

[49] Wm. Ramsey, "Saving the Corner Store, in Name Only," *Bremerton Sun*, July 1, 1998.

[50] Ted George in Pride Is Our Heritage, 13.

CHAPTER 8 – EARLY TRIBAL GOVERNMENT

[1] According to anthropologist Wayne Suttles, before the arrival of whites, the S'Klallam had no "head chiefs" with authority outside their own villages (Wayne Suttles. "Central Coast Salish." *Handbook of North American Indians* 7, 464). Erna Gunther, however, wrote that when whites arrived, Lord Jim, of Dungeness, was recognized as chief of all the S'Klallam (Erna Gunther, *Klallam* Ethnography, 261). For the treaty negotiations and later, for other purposes, government officials designated "chiefs" with whom they could deal.

[2] Irene Jackson Purser Interview, April 14, 2006: 11. The Enrollment Committee set up in 1926 to determine eligibility for claims payment (described in Chapter 5) is another good example of how heads of families conferred together to make decisions.

[3] Edwin Eells. Census of the S'Klallam Tribe, December, 1877; Port Gamble S'Klallam Tribe, Base Roll, 2; Frank Lynch. "Plenty Smart, Those Paleface Bostons, But Why Steal Body?" *Seattle P.I.* August 26, 1947.

[4] Harry Fulton Jr. Interview, ca. 1976: 5.

[5] Edwin Eells. "To All Persons Whom It May Concern." 1889.

[6] Dorothy George Interview, February 26, 2006: 18; Ivan George Interview, September 13, 2005: 28; Harry Fulton Jr. Interview, ca. 1976: 5; Irene Jackson Purser Interview, April 14, 2006: 11; Ted George in *Pride Is Our Heritage*, 13.

[7] Ed Purser was officially a Suquamish tribal member, but he was such an integral part of the Port Gamble S'Klallam community that he often assumed leadership roles—including service on the Business Committee—during these early years of formal organization.

[8] La Vatta to Commissioner of Indian Affairs, March 16, 1937; Jackson to La Vatta, November 22, 1938.

Endnotes

[9] Ibid.

[10] La Vatta to Jackson, September 9, 1938. The Bill of Rights was added by amendment in 1991; guardians for minors and incompetents was added by amendment in 1980.

[11] When the question arose in 1937 as to whether the Port Gamble S'Klallam were a tribe (or band) and therefore eligible to organize under the Indian Reorganization Act, the Indian Office's attorney answered a resounding "Yes!" Even without a reservation, the federal government recognized that S'Klallam people had stayed together as a *tribe*, clustered in three distinct groups. Kenneth Meiklejohn, Solicitor Memo, September 27, 1938; Kenneth Meiklejohn, Memo n.d. (post-1938); Kenneth Meiklejohn, Memo June 17, 1937; Jennings, Indian Organization Field Administrator to La Vatta, May 26, 1938.

[12] Kenneth Meiklejohn, Memo, June 17, 1937; Memo to Indian Organization, September 27, 1938.

[13] Amended Constitution and Bylaws of the Pt. Gamble Band of S'Klallam Indians.

[14] Harry Fulton Jr. Interview ca. 1976: 5.

[15] Ron Charles Interview, May 2008.

[16] Libby, Superintendent to Purser, August 8, 1963.

[17] Port Gamble S'Klallam Tribe, Community Council minutes, April 17, 1950.

[18] Ron Charles Interview, May 2008.

[19] Floyd Jones and Jake Jones Interview, November 7, 2005: 12, 13.

[20] Con Sullivan Interview, March 29, 2006: 15.

[21] Superintendent to Foster, Area Director, April 19, 1956 in Tallis King George, "The Twenty-Seven Year Saga of the Port Gamble S'Klallam Membership Roll." It was not until 1982 that an amendment added the Business Committee to the constitution.

[22] George to Superintendent Ringey in Tallis King George, "The Twenty-Seven Year Saga of the Port Gamble S'Klallam Membership Roll," July 6, 1958.

[23] Larsen to Purser in Tallis King George, "The Twenty-Seven Year Saga of the Port Gamble S'Klallam Membership Roll," November 19, 1953; Memo to Superintendent in Tallis King George, "The Twenty-Seven Year Saga of the Port Gamble S'Klallam Membership Roll," August 30, 1960.

[24] Tallis King George, "The Twenty-Seven Year Saga of the Port Gamble S'Klallam Membership Roll"; Port Gamble S'Klallam Tribe, Constitution and By Laws, Article II; Superintendent to George in Tallis King George, "The Twenty-Seven Year Saga of the Port Gamble S'Klallam Membership Roll," November 15, 1955; Resolution of the Community Council, February 24, 1947; Everett Agency to Aaron Purser in Tallis King George, "The Twenty-Seven Year Saga of the Port Gamble S'Klallam Membership Roll," July 5, 1962.

[25] Memo to Superintendent in Tallis King George, "The Twenty-Seven Year Saga," August 30, 1960; Everett Agency to Portland Area Tribal Operations, May 13, 1966.

[26] Tallis King George, "The Twenty-Seven Year Saga"; Resolution of the Port Gamble Community Council, June 4, 1970; Port Gamble S'Klallam Tribe, Adoption Ordinance, June 25, 1970; Notice of Deadline for Membership Applications, November 1, 1972; Port Gamble S'Klallam Tribe, Resolution of the Community Council, June 9, 1974; Port Gamble S'Klallam Tribe, Resolution of the Business Committee, June 25, 1974.

[27] Memo re. Port Gamble Meeting, November 16, 1965.

Endnotes

[28] Con Sullivan Interview, March 29, 2006: 15.

[29] Bitney to L. Jackson, January 1, 1953; Ted George to Western Washington Agency, March 17, 1958.

[30] Floyd Jones and Jake Jones Interview, November 7, 2005: 13, 14.

[31] Magnusson to Foster, Area Director, September 19, 1958; Memo re. Port Gamble Meeting, November 16, 1965.

[32] Dorothy George to Ringey, July 6, 1958.

[33] Floyd Jones and Jake Jones Interview, November 7, 2005: 12, 13.

[34] Rose Purser Interview, February 7, 2006: 17.

[35] Superintendent to DeCoteau, June 25, 1970; Superintendent to Purser, June 23, 1964.

[36] Floyd Jones and Jake Jones Interview, November 7, 2005: 12, 13.

[37] Ron Charles Interview, 2008.

[38] Chart compiled from Port Gamble S'Klallam legal department and Ron Charles.

CHAPTER 9 – INDIAN CLAIMS COMMISSION

[1] John Collier, Congressional Testimony on the Indian Reorganization Act, Collier Papers Microfilm, A 6833, Roll 29II, 498 [1076].

[2] Public Law 726, August 13, 1946.

[3] Findings of Fact and Opinion, December 2, 1957, *S'Klallam Tribe v. US,* Indian Claims Commission Dkt. 134, 5 I.C.C. 680.

[4] Fred Noland to Klallam Tribe, September 10, 1975; E.L. Crawford to Herbert Taylor, August 6, 1968.

[5] Findings of Fact and Opinion, October 1, 1970, *S'Klallam Tribe v. US,* Indian Claims Commission Dkt. 134, 23 I.C.C. 512. The amount of compensation stated in the treaty was for the entire area ceded under the Treaty of Point No Point Treaty, which included Skokomish lands as well as S'Klallam lands. The Commission looked at population estimates for Skokomish and S'Klallam at treaty times and decided that the S'Klallam share of the treaty compensation was sixty-five percent of the $60,000.

[6] Additional Findings of Fact and Opinion, November 5, 1976, *S'Klallam Tribe v. US,* Indian Claims Commission Dkt. 134, 39 ICC 134. In an extremely twisted tangle of logic, the Commission treated the purchase of the Elwha Reservation differently from the Port Gamble Reservation. The purchase price of the Elwha Reservation was not offset because the land was within the "Klallam Tract," the part of the ceded area compensated for by the ICC. The Commission said the US was simply returning to the ElwhaTribe lands it had acquired under the Treaty and deprived them of for 78 years. Since the Port Gamble area had been used jointly by several tribes, the Commission had previously excluded it from the "Klallam Tract." The reservation purchase, therefore, was ruled to be an expenditure, not a "return of lands taken."

Endnotes

CHAPTER 10 – EDUCATION

[1] Treaty of Point No Point, 1855, Article XI; Edwin Eells, Address at Cushman Indian Trades School, June, 16, 1910.

[2] Francis Paul Prucha, *The Great Father, The United States Government and the American Indians* (Lincoln: University of Nebraska Press, [1984] 1991 edition). 158-164.

[3] Johnson, Supt. Cushman School to Swain, Little Boston teacher, September 2, 1913.

[4] Ted George Interview, August 11, 2006.

[5] Harry Fulton Jr. Interview, ca. 1976.

[6] Ruth (Henry) Martinez in *Pride is our Heritage*, 6.

[7] Annual reports to the Commissioner of Indian Affairs, 1892–1905.

[8] Swain to Johnson, August 3, 1913 and August 28, 1913.

[9] Harman to Hammond, January 19, 1918.

[10] Sammy Charles, Deed to U.S., August 8, 1916. In 1958, the U.S. declared the property to be "surplus" and it was sold to the highest bidder.

[11] Zimmerman, Asst. Commissioner of Indian Affairs to Senator Bone, June 15,1938; Karl Leonard to Senator Walgren, April 3, 1942.

[12] Dorothy George in *Pride is our Heritage*, 16.

[13] Ivan George in Pride is our Heritage, 7.

[14] Upchurch to Commissioner of Indian Affairs, April 30, 1938.

[15] Francis Paul Prucha, *The Great Father,* 278, 286, 287.

[16] Little Boston School Board to Governor Martin, September 23, 1940.

[17] Ted George Interview, 2009.

[18] Mildred DeCoteau in *Pride is our Heritage,* 17.

[19] Floyd Jones in Pride is our Heritage, 7.

[20] Ron Charles Interview, 2010.

[21] Jake Jones in Pride is our Heritage 16.

[22] Ron Charles Interview, 2010.

[23] Lloyd Fulton in Pride is our Heritage.

[24] During the 1950s, 109 tribes were "terminated" from Federal services, a policy that had disastrous results for the tribes involved. The Port Gamble S'Klallam Tribe seemed to be targeted for the same fate, but fortunately Port Gamble S'Klallam leaders resisted the Bureau officials' attempts to include the tribe in that debacle.

CHAPTER 11 – HEALTH AND HEALING

[1] Jake Jones Interview, September 22, 2005, describing his grandfather, Jacob Jones (b. 1869).

[2] Louisa Pulsifer Interview, 1974.

[3] Chimphila umbellata.

[4] Floyd Jones in *Pride Is Our Heritage*, 7.

[5] Dorothy Day George Interview, September 27, 2006.

[6] Erna Gunther. Ethnobotany of Western Washington, The Knowledge and Use of Indigenous Plans by Native Americans. Seattle: University of Washington Press, [1945] 1973.

[7] *Klallam History from Manuscript & Memory*, Port Gamble S'Klallam Tribe Title IV Curriculum Project, ca. 1975: 88.

[8] T. T. Waterman. Puget Sound Geography [1920], 69.

[9] Vancouver 1998: 1.241 in Boyd 1999: 30

[10] Mathew Fleming Affidavit and Emily Matheson Affidavit in William Richie to Commissioner of Indian Affairs, January 9, 1922.

[11] Myron Eels, *The American Antiquarian* 9, no. 5. September 1887.

[12] www.portgamble.com/pdf/port_gamble_walking_tour.pdf, pg. 4.

[13] Rose Purser Interview, June 26, 2008.

[14] Catherine Moran Interview, March 17, 1992.

[15] Lucille Weisenberger Interview, June 25, 2007.

[16] William Jones Interview, November 29, 2005.

[17] Rose Purser Interview, June 25, 2008.

[18] Gerald "Jake" Jones Interview, September 22, 2005.

[19] Floyd Jones Interview, September 22, 2005.

[20] Christina "Jane" Charles Interview, November 21, 2005.

[21] Lucille Weisenberger Interview, June 25, 2007.

[22] Ron Charles, June 25, 2008.

[23] Rose Purser Interview, June 25, 2008.

CHAPTER 12 – S'KLALLAM BASEBALL

[1] Jeffrey Powers-Beck. *The American Indian Integration of Baseball.* (Lincoln: University of Nebraska Press, 2004): Foreword.

[2] Papers of Martha John. Quote by Thomas Dixter, son of Jenny (later Jenny Jones).

[3] Papers of Martha John. Quote by James Fulton.

[4] Ted George Interview, 2010. Unless otherwise noted, all quotes and memories related in this chapter were obtained at a Little Boston Baseball honoring event held at the Port Gamble S'Klallam longhouse in 2009.

[5] Ted George Interview, 2010

[6] Martin Charles Interview, 1994.

[7] Ted George Interview, 2010.

[8] Irene Jackson Purser Interview, 2010.

[9] Ted George Interview, 2010.

[10] Ron Charles Recollection, 2010.

[11] Ron Hirshi Recollection, 2010.

[12] Ron Charles Recollection, 2010.

[13] Ted George Interview, 2010.

[14] Conrad Sullivan Interview, 2010.

[15] Ted George, 2010.

[16] Ivan George, 2010.

[17] Ron Charles Recollection of Jum Fulton conversation.

[18] Ted George, 2010.

[19] Ron Charles Interview, 2010.

[20] Rose Purser Interview, 2010.

[21] Jake Jones Interview, 2010.

[22] Ron Charles Recollections, 2010.

[23] Bernard Tom, 2010.

[24] Harry Fulton III, 2010.

[25] Ted George Interview, 2010.

[26] Harry Fulton Interview, 2010.

[27] Rudy Purser Jr. Interview, 2010.

[28] Scott Moon Interview, 2010.

[29] Harry Fulton III Interview, 2010

[30] Ted George Interview, 2010.

CHAPTER 13 – SELF-GOVERNANCE
AND TRIBAL GOVERNMENT

[1] Ron Charles, excerpt from speech to dedicate the new Tribal Center, December 11, 1976.

[2] Klallam Indian Tribe, Comprehensive Plan, 1974: 17.

[3] Klallam News, 1979.

Endnotes

CHAPTER 14 – THE BEAUTY AND FABRIC OF TRIBAL LIFE

[1] Rose Purser Interview, February 7, 2006: 7.

[2] Letter from Francine (Jones) Swift, 2008.

[3] From the Port Gamble S'Klallam Tribe's website, www.pgst.nsn.us

[4] Laura Price. *Healing of the Canoe Project.* University of Washington. DVD.

[5] Ivan George Interview, September 13, 2005: 2.

References

Adams, Gertrude. Interview. Port Gamble S'Klallam Oral History Project. August 18, 2006.

Adams, Mary Ann (nee Mary Ann Williams) and George Adams. Deed to Annie George. Washington State Archives, King County Branch. Kitsap County Deeds, Vol. 57 Deeds: 15. April 30, 1904 (Recorded April 10, 1908).

American Friends Service Committee. *Uncommon Controversy.* Seattle: UW Press, 1975.

Anderson, Joseph. Deed to N.M. Pulsifer. June 17, 1913. Kitsap County Recorders Office. Vol. 96 Deeds: 333.

———. Deed to Cyrus Webster. May 26, 1915. Kitsap County Recorders Office. Vol. 96 Deeds: 235.

———. Deed to Henry Lambert. August 24, 1916. Kitsap County Recorders Office. Vol. 104 Deeds: 586.

———. Letter to Sir. I.I.M. Files: Anderson. Bureau of Indian Affairs, Everett Office. 1931.

Annual Report of the Commissioner of Indian Affairs. Washington: Government P rinting Office. 1872, 1892-1905.

Baze, Kelly. Interview by Ron Hirschi. December, 2009.

Beaulieu, F.D., Clerk, Taholah Agency. Letter to N.O. Nicholson, Superintendent Taholah Agency. May 27, 1936. National Archives, Seattle. RG 75. Taholah Agency. Decimal File 115.

Beckwith, Rogina. "Land and its Significance to the Spirit of the Port Gamble S'Klallam People." Research Paper for Evergreen State College. Port Gamble S'Klallam Tribe Archives. 1998.

Berlew, E.K., Acting Secretary of the Interior. Port Gamble Band of Clallam Indians Reservation Proclamation. Bureau of Indian Affairs, Everett Office. June 16, 1938.

Indians Reservation Proclamation. Bureau of Indian Affairs, Everett Office. June 16, 1938.

Bishop, Thomas. *An Appeal to the Government to Fulfill Sacred Promises Made 61 Years Ago.* December 24, 1915. Northwest Federation of American Indians. National Archives, D.C. RG 75. Central Classified Files. Cushman Agency. File: 95702-1913-313.

Bitney. Letter to Lester Jackson. Bureau of Indian Affairs, Everett Agency. January 1, 1953.

Blanchet, Francis Norbert, S.J. *Historical Sketches of the Catholic Church in Oregon.* Fairfield, WA: Ye Galleon Press, [1878] 1983.

Bone, Senator. Letter to Commissioner of Indian Affairs. Original source citation lost. Copy in Port Gamble S'Klallam Archives. July 29, 1938.

Bureau of Land Management. Township survey map, T27N, R2E, W.M. Surveyed by John Trutch. 1859. http://www.blm.gov/or/landrecords/survey/ySrvy1.php.

Burke, C.H., Commissioner of Indian Affairs. Letter to Walter Dickens, Tulalip Superintendent. March 24, 1926. National Archives, D.C. RG 75. Central Classified Files. General Services, 51087-1919-013, Part 1.

Charles, Christine and Monica Charles. Interviews. Port Gamble S'Klallam Oral History Project. November 21 and 23, 2005.

Charles, Ron. Speech to dedicate tribal center. Port Gamble S'Klallam Archives, December 11, 1976.

———. "Fulton Family Reunion," *Port Gamble S'Klallam News.* September 2004.

———. Interviews. Port Gamble S'Klallam Oral History Project. October 22 and November 2008.

———. *The S'Klallam View.* January 2009.

———. Interview. Port Gamble S'Klallam Oral History Project. March, 2009.

Charles, Sammy and Susie. Deed to U.S. August 8, 1917. National Archives, Seattle. RG 75. Puyallup Agency. Correspondence with the CIA, 1907-1920. Forestry-Land Heirship. Box 7. Fdr: Land Sales [Port Gamble Day School], 1916 – 1920. [Pt. G. File: CIA Corresp.: Port Gamble School.]

Charles, Tommy. Deed to Niels Beck. October 30, 1930. Washington State Archives, King County Branch, Kitsap County Deeds, Vol. 176 Deeds: 141.

"Clallam Tribe in Big Meeting to O.K. Claims," *The North American Indian.* vol. 6, no. 49 (April 23, 1926.): 1. National Archives, Seattle. RG 75. Tulalip, 476, Records Relating to Clallam Enrollment. Box 1. Fldr: App for Enrollment.

Collier, John, Commissioner of Indian Affairs. 1934. Congressional Testimony on the Indian Reorganization Act. In Collier Papers Microfilm. A 6833, Roll 29II, 498 [1076].

———. Letter to Secretary of Interior. November 7, 1940. National Archives, Seattle. RG 75. Tulalip Agency. Records of Tribal Councils, Box 480. File: Pt. Gamble 1935-1952, 1 of 2.

Coman, Edwin T. Jr. *Time, Tide and Timber: A Century of Pope and Talbot.* Stanford: Stanford University Press, 1946.

Crawford, E.L. Letter to Herbert Taylor. Port Gamble S'Klallam Tribe Archives, August 6, 1968.

Cushman Superintendent. Letter to Harmon. February 9, 1917. National Archives, Seattle. RG 75. Puyallup. Correspondence with Day School Teachers, 1913-1918. Box 2. Fldr: Pt. Gamble Day School.

Daiker, Fred H., Commissioner of Indian Affairs. Letter to Secretary of Interior. June 15, 1939. National Archives, D.C. RG 75. E 1012, Records of Indian organization Division. Box 35. Tulalip Agency. 068-9764A.

Defebaugh, James Elliot. "History of the Lumber Industry of America," *The American Lumberman.* 1907.

Dickens, W.F., Tulalip Agent. Letter to Commissioner of Indian Affairs. February 15, 1922. National Archives, Seattle. RG 75. BIA Western Washington Agency, Operations Branch General Corresp. 1914-1951. Box 259. Fldr: Indian Claims Commission

———. Letters to Commissioner of Indian Affairs. May 23 and May 31, 1926. National Archives, D.C. RG 75. General Service. 51087-1919-013.

Dickey, George, ed. *The Journal of Occurrences at Fort Nisqually: Commencing May 30, 1833; Ending September 27, 1859.* Tacoma: Ft. Nisqually Historic Site, Metropolitan Park District of Tacoma, Washington. 1989.

Duwamish et al. v. USA. Testimony. U.S. Court of Claims, No. F-275. vol. 1. Seattle: Argus Press. 1927.

Ebey, Winfield Scott. Journal. University of Washington Special Collections and Manuscripts. Accession No. 127. 1856.

Eells, Edwin. Letter to E.P Smith, Commissioner of Indian Affairs. Original source citation lost. Copy in Port Gamble S'Klallam Archives, December 2, 1873.

———. Census of the S'Klallam Tribe. Port Gamble S'Klallam Tribe Archives, December, 1877.

———. Letter to Commissioner of Indian Affairs: List of Clallam Indians belonging to Skokomish. Plaintiff's Exhibit 115. *Skokomish Tribe v. United States.* Indian Claims Commission, Dkt. 296. March 1, 1878.

———. Report. March 15, 1878. Washington State Historical Society. Edwin Eells Collection. Box 3, Folder 8.

———. "To All Persons Whom It May Concern." Source: Anderson Family. Port Gamble S'Klallam Tribe Archives, 1889.

———Letter to Commissioner of Indian Affairs. 1909. National Archives, Seattle. RG 75. Puyallup. Correspondence with CIA, 1907–1920. Box 6. Fldr: Land Allotments, 461–3262.

———. Address at Cushman Indian Trades School, June, 16, 1910. Washington State Historical Society. Eells, Box 3, Folder 2.

———*Autobiography.* 1914. Washington State Historical Society. Edwin Eells, Box 1.

Eells, Myron. "Skokomish Agency Field and Work," *American Missionary* 34. (October, 1880): 308.

———. *The Twana, Chemakum and Klallam Indians of Washington Territory.* Smithsonian Institution, Annual Report 1889. Facsimile Reproduction, 1971, The Shorey Book Store, Seattle, WA.

———. *American Antiquarian* 9, no. 5 (September, 1887).

———. "Puget Sound Indians: Locomotion and Transportation," *American Antiquarian* 10, no.1 (January 1888): 26.

———. "Indians of Puget Sound: Measuring and Valuing," *American Antiquarian* 10, no. 3 (May, 1888): 174.

———. *The Indians of Puget Sound: The Notebooks of Myron Eells.* Walla Walla: Whitman College, [1894] 1986.

Egan, Timothy. *The Good Rain.* Vintage Press, 1991.

Eliot, ——. Letter to Board of Indian Commissioners. January 1, 1915. National Archives, D.C. RG 75. E. 121. Central Classified Files. General Services. 101–1915 to 101–1918. Box 29. 14361-15-101. [Pt. G. File: Bd. of Ind. Commr. Reports, 1915 – 1932].

Elmendorf, William W. *The Structure of Twana Culture.* Research

Studies, Monographic Supplement no. 2 vol. 28, no. 3. (September, 1960). Pullman: Washington State University, 1960.

———. *Twana Narratives: Native Accounts of a Coast Salish Culture.* Seattle: U.W. Press, 1993.

Everett Agency. Letter to Portland Area Tribal Operations. Bureau of Indian Affairs, Everett Agency. May 13, 1966.

———. Notice of Deadline for Membership Applications. November 1, 1972.

Ficken, Robert E. *The Forested Land: A History of Lumbering in Western Washington.* Seattle: University of Washington Press, 1987.

Fitzgerald, Charles. Letter to Tulalip Agent Buchanan. June 25, 1912. National Archives, D.C. RG 75. Cushman Agency. Central Classified Files. File: 66386-1912-21.

Fitzgerald, Charles and A.P. Peterson. Letter to Secretary of Interior. January 6, 1913. National Archives, D.C. RG 75. Central Classified Files. Cushman. Decimal 313. Box 5126. File: 5329-1910.

Friedrich, ed. "This Corner Will Stand for the Georges." *Bremerton Sun.* June, 29, 1999.

Fulton, Harry Jr. Interview. Port Gamble S'Klallam Tribe Archives, ca. 1976.

Fulton, Harry III. Interview by Ron Hirschi, February 2009.

Fulton, Russell Jr. Interview by Ron Hirschi, 2008.

Garner, John S. *The Company Town: Architecture and Society in the Early Industrial Age.* Oxford University Press, 1992.

Gates, Charles M. "Daniel Bagley and the University of Washington Land Grant, 1861 - 1868." *Pacific Northwest Quarterly* 52, no. 2 (1961).

General Land Office. Trust Patent to United States in trust for Joseph Anderson. Final Cert. No. 4059. Feb. 10, 1891. BIA Title Plant, Portland, Ore. Documents from Western Washington Public Domain Land Index, Res. Code 130.

———. Trust Patent to United States in trust for Mary Littleman, widow of George Littleman. March 7, 1892. Public Room Document Cards for T35N, R3W, Bureau of Land Management, Portland, OR.

———. Fee Patent in lieu of Trust to Joseph Anderson. Final Cert. No. 4059. April 11, 1910. BIA Title Plant, Portland, Ore. Documents from Western Washington Public Domain Land Index, Res.

Code 130.

George, Annie and Eddie. Deed to William George. Kitsap County Recorder's Office. vol. 57 Deeds: 16, 17. June 7, 1905.

George, Annie, Tommy Charles and Sammy Charles. Deeds to Annie George, Tommy Charles and Sammy Charles. January 27, 1902. Kitsap County Recorder's Office. Deeds and Mortgages, Box 1857-1883 (sic: dates extend beyond 1883): 355-358.

George, Claude and Betty. Interview. Port Gamble S'Klallam Oral History Project, August 14, 2006.

George, Dorothy Day. Interview. Port Gamble S'Klallam Oral History Project, February 27, 2006.

George, Ivan. Interviews. Port Gamble S'Klallam Oral History Project, August 31 and September 13, 2005.

George, Martha. Interview. Port Gamble S'Klallam Tribe Archives, ca. 1974.

George, Ted. Letter to Western Washington Agency. March 17, 1958. Bureau of Indian Affairs, Everett Agency.

———. Interviews. Port Gamble S'Klallam Oral History Project, August 11 and October 26, 2006.

———. Interview. Port Gamble S'Klallam Tribe Archives, November 5, 2008.

———. "S'Klallam Baseball." Port Gamble S'Klallam Tribe Archives.

———. "Klallam Claims Case." Port Gamble S'Klallam Oral History Project, 2009.

Gorsline, Jerry, ed. *Shadows of Our Ancestors: Readings in the History of Klallam-White Relations.* Dalmo'ma Anthology 8. Pt. Townsend: Empty Bowl, 1992.

Gunther, Erna. Field Notebook. Burke Museum. Erna Gunther Collection. n.d.

———. Field Notebook 3, 1923. UW Special Collections & Manuscripts. Gunther Collection. Acc.# 614-001. Box 2, Fldr. 15.

———. Field Notebook, 1924. UW Special Collections & Manuscripts. Gunther Collection. Acc.# 614-001, Box 2, Fldr. 14.

———. *Klallam Ethnography* 1, no. 5 (Seattle: University of Washington, Publications in Anthropology, 1927): 195, 212.

———. Field Notebook. January 21, 1936. UW Special Collections &

Manuscripts. Gunther Collection. Acc.# 614-001, Box 2, Fldr 17.

———. *Ethnobotany of Western Washington, The Knowledge and Use of Indigenous Plans by Native Americans.* Seattle: University of Washington Press, [1945] 1973.

Harmon, Port Gamble Day School Teacher. Letter to Wilson. 1917. National Archives, Seattle. RG 75. Puyallup. Correspondence with Day School Teachers, 1913-1918. Box 2. Fldr: Pt. Gamble Day School.

———. Letter to Hammond. January 19, 1918. National Archives, Seattle. RG 75. Puyallup. Correspondence with Day School Teachers, 1913-1918. Box 2. Fldr: Pt. Gamble Day School.

———. Letter to Hammond. January 31, 1918. National Archives, Seattle. RG 75. Puyallup. Correspondence with Day School Teachers, 1913-1918. Box 2. Fldr: Pt. Gamble Day School.

Harrington, John P. *The Papers of John Peabody Harrington.* 1910. National Anthropological Archives. Smithsonian Institution. Microfilm Roll 16.

Hawke, 2nd Asst. Commissioner of Indian Affairs. Letter to Johnson. May 20, 1911. National Archives, D.C. RG 75. Central Classified Files. Cushman Agency. Decimal 313. Box 5126. File: 5329-1910-313.

Henry, James. Indian Homestead Certificate 8010. February 23, 1886. National Archives, Seattle. RG 49. Washington Tract Books.

Herrick, Assistant Commissioner of Indian Affairs. Trust Agreement for Relief and Rehabilitation Grant to Unorganized Tribe. December 13, 1938. National Archives, Seattle. RG 75. Tulalip Agency. Decimal 242. Pt. Gamble Rehabilitation. 280, Box 30.

———. Letter to Upchurch. February 14, 1939. National Archives, D.C. RG 75. Central Classified Files. Tulalip Agency. File: unknown. Copy in Port Gamble S'Klallam Archives.

Hirschi, Daisy Cotter. Interview. Hirschi Family Collection, 1976.

Hirschi, LaVerne. Interview. Hirschi Family Collection, 2008.

Howell, George Dan. Deed to Bennie George. July 13, 1918. Kitsap County Recorder's Office. vol. 116 Deeds: 247, 248.

———. Deed to Louis John. December 12, 1927. Washington State Archives, King County Branch. Kitsap County Deeds, vol. 638 Deeds: 500.

Howell, Philip Hugh. "Raven Steals Daylight." Port Gamble S'Klallam Tribe Archives, 1926.

———. *Dictionary of Indian Geographic Names: The Origin and Meaning of Indian Names.* American Indian Historical Society, 1948.

Jackson, Lester. Letter to Upchurch, quoting letter from Department of Interior. March 14, 1939. National Archives, D.C. RG 75. Tulalip Agency. Box. 1. Decimal File 003. Fld: 003 Misc. Corres, 1935–40. [Pt. G. File: Misc. Corresp. 1935–40.]).

———. Indian Claims Commission, Dkt. No. 143. *S'Klallam Tribe v. U.S.*, vol. 1 (June 17, 1952).

Jackson, Peter. Letter to Commissioner of Indian Affairs. October 4, 1912. National Archives, D.C. RG 75. Central Classified Files. Cushman. Decimal 313. Box 5126. File: 5329-1910.

———. Letter to Mr. President. June 12, 1913. National Archives, D.C. RG 75. Central Classified Files. Cushman. 66386-1912-211.

———. Minutes of Council of the Clallam Tribe, May 11, 1914. National Archives, D.C. RG 75. Central Classified Files. Cushman Agency. File: 3405-1914-054.

———. Letter to George La Vatta. November 22, 1938. National Archives, Seattle. RG 75. Tulalip Agency. Records of Tribal Council, 1925–1952, Muckleshoot, Port Gamble. Box 480. Folder: Pt. Gamble, 1935-1942 [2 of 2].

James, Karen. "S'Klallam Shellfish Report." Prepared for *U.S. v. Washington.* Copy in Port Gamble S'Klallam Tribe Archives, 1994.

Jennings, Joe, Field Administrator in charge of Indian Organization. Letter to George LaVatta. April 13, 1938. National Archives, Seattle RG 75. Tulalip Agency. Records of Tribal Council, 1925–1952, Muckleshoot, Port Gamble. Box 480. Folder: Pt. Gamble, 1935-1942 [2 of 2].

John, Martha. Notebook diary. Port Gamble S'Klallam Tribe Archives, 1927.

———. Interview. Port Gamble S'Klallam Tribe Archives, ca. 1974.

Johnson, Superintendent. Letter to Commissioner of Indian Affairs. October 18, 1909. National Archives, D.C. RG 49. Bureau of Land Management. General Land Office, Seattle. Homestead Final Certificate Case File No. 4059.

———. Letter to Commissioner of Indian Affairs. October 24, 1910. National Archives Seattle. RG 75. Taholah Agency. Box 1. Letters Sent to CIA, 1908-1914. File: May 17, 1909–Nov. 19, 1909. [Pt. G. File: Taholah Agent – CIA Corresp.].

———. Letter to Commissioner of Indian Affairs. December 4, 1911. National Archives, Seattle. RG 75. Puyallup. Correspondence with CIA, 1907-1920, Box 6. Fldr: Land allotments, 461-3262.

———. Letter to Commissioner of Indian Affairs. March 21, 1913. National Archives, Seattle. RG 75. Taholah Agency. Box 1. Letters Sent to CIA, 1908-1914. File: March 7, 1913–Sept. 15, 1913. [Pt. G. File: Taholah Agent – CIA Corresp.].

———. Letter to L. Swain, Little Boston teacher, September 2, 1913. National Archives, Seattle. RG 75. Puyallup. Correspondence with Day School Teachers, 1913-1918. Box 2. Fldr: Pt. Gamble Day School.

Jones, Charley and Lucy. Deed to Jim Williams. March 8, 1889. Kitsap County Recorder's Office. vol. F, Deeds and Mortgages: 211.

———. Deed to James Henry. January 6, 1903. Washington State Archives, King County Branch, Kitsap County Deeds, vol. 64, Deeds: 111.

Jones, Clara, Martha George, Reada Taylor and Benny George Jr. Interview. Port Gamble S'Klallam Tribe Archives, 1972.

Jones, Gene. Interviews. Port Gamble S'Klallam Oral History Project, November 21 and 22, 2005.

Jones, Jake and Floyd Jones. Interviews. Port Gamble S'Klallam Oral History Project, September 14, 22 and November 5, 2005.

———. Interview by Ron Hirschi, 2008.

Jones, William. Interviews. Port Gamble S'Klallam Oral History Project, November 21 and 29, 2005.

Kamb, Lewis. "The Boldt Decision Very Much Alive 30 Years Later." *Seattle P.I.*, February 12, 2004.

Keller, Josiah. Papers of Josiah Keller. 1853 *et seq*. Americana Collection: 280. Beinecke Rare Book Library, Yale University.

Kickingbird, Kirke et al. *Indian Treaties*. Albuquerque: Institute for the Development of Indian Law, 1980.

King George, Tallis. "The Twenty-Seven Year Saga of the Port Gamble S'Klallam Membership Roll." Port Gamble S'Klallam Tribe

Archives, n.d.

Kitsap County Board of Commissioners. Minutes of Meeting. December 6, 1937. Washington State Archives, Puget Sound Branch. Kitsap Co. Commissioners Journals, vol. 5. Accession No. 93–PS–0055 and 0057.

———. Minutes of Meeting. March 6, 1939. Washington State Archives, Puget Sound Branch. Kitsap Co. Commissioners Journals, vol. 5. Accession No. 93–PS–0055 and 0057.

Kitsap County Historical Society. *Kitsap County: A History.* Kitsap County Historical Society, 1977.

Kitsap Country Treasurer. County Treasurer's Tax Deed after tax judgment. August 31, 1936. Kitsap County Recorder's Office. Vol. 206 Deeds pp. 47, 76.

———. Treasurer's Return on Tax Sale. October 8, 1938. Kitsap County Treasurer's Office. Tax Foreclosure No. 615 and 616.

La Vatta, George, Field Agent. Letter to Commissioner of Indian Affairs. August 24, 1935. National Archives, D.C. RG 75. E 121. Tulalip Agency. 00–1934–066. Box 6.

———. Letter to Commissioner of Indian Affairs. March 16, 1937. National Archives, Seattle. RG 75. Tulalip Agency. Records of Tribal Council, 1925-1952, Muckleshoot, Port Gamble. Box 480. Folder: Pt. Gamble, 1935-1942 [2 of 2].

———. Letter to Commissioner of Indian Affairs. March 17, 1937. National Archives, Seattle. RG 75. Tulalip Agency. Records of Tribal Council, 1925-1952, Muckleshoot, Port Gamble. Box 480. Folder: Pt. Gamble, 1935-1942 [2 of 2].

———. Letter to Commissioner of Indian Affairs. September 9, 1938. National Archives, Seattle. RG 75. Tulalip Agency. Records of Tribal Council, 1925-1952, Muckleshoot, Port Gamble. Box 480. Folder: Pt. Gamble, 1935-1942 [2 of 2].

Lambert, Mary Ann. *The House of the Seven Brothers, Trees, Roots and Branches of the House of Ste-tee-thkum.* Port Orchard: Publishers Printing, [1960] 1972.

Lane, Barbara. "Identity, Treaty Status and Fisheries of the Port Gamble Indian Community." Report prepared for *U.S. v. Washington.* Port Gamble S'Klallam Tribe Archives, 1977.

———. "Background of Treaty Making in Western Washington." Vienna, VA: Institute for the Development of Indian Law, n.d.

Lane, Barbara, Karen James and Emily Mansfield. "Hunting and Gathering Practices of the Skokomish and S'Klallam and the Treaty of Point No Point." Report prepared for Point No Point Treaty Council, 1997.

Leonard, Karl, Assembly of God Church. Letter to Senator Walgren. April 3, 1942. National Archives, D.C. RG 75 E. 1007. Records of the Rehabilitation Division. Project Records, 1935–1944. Box 46. File: 6090-P-2. General Correspondence, Jan. 2, 1941–present.

Libby, Superintendent. Letter to Purser, August 8, 1963. Bureau of Indian Affairs, Everett Agency.

"Little Boston, Picturesque Indian Village, Vanishing." *Seattle Times.* Graphic Section 5, May 23, 1937.

Little Boston School Board. 1940. Letter to Governor Martin, September 23, 1940. National Archives, Seattle. RG 75. Tulalip. Box 480. Fldr: Pt. Gamble, 1935–1942.

Littleman, Mary. Probate #32975-1915. File 350. Bureau of Indian Affairs. Portland, Titles and Records. 1915.

Lower Elwha S'Klallam Tribe. *Elwha Klallam Calendar.* Port Gamble S'Klallam Tribe Archives, 1999.

Lynch, Frank. "Plenty Smart, Those Paleface Bostons, But Why Steal Body? Last of Clallams Cling to Site of Ancestors." *Seattle P.I.* August 26, 1947.

Magnusson, Warren. Letter to Foster, Area Director. Bureau of Indian Affairs, Everett Agency, September 19, 1958.

Martinez, Ruth. Interview with Tallis Woodward King George. Port Gamble S'Klallam Tribe Archives, n.d.

Mason Co. v. Archie Adams and Harry Lewis. No. 1115, Mason Co. Superior Ct. Appearance Docket, Microfilm C 18. May 21, 1909.

Mead, James. 1886. Deeds to Charley Jones, Solomon and Cook House Charley. December 8, 1886. Kitsap County Recorder's Office. Deeds and Mortgages, Box 1857-1883 (sic: dates extend beyond 1883): 534-539.

Meany, Edmond. "Twana and Clallam Indians Aborigines of Hood Canal." *Seattle P.I.* sec 6, October 22, 1905.

Meiklejohn, Kenneth, Attorney, Indian Organization. Solicitor's

Memorandum to Indian Organization. June 17, 1937. National Archives, D.C. RG 75. E 1012, Records of Indian organization Division. Box 35. Tulalip Agency. 068-9764A.

———. Solicitor's Memorandum to Indian Organization. September 27, 1938. National Archives, D.C. RG 75. E 1012, Records of Indian organization Division. Box 35. Tulalip Agency. 068-9764A.

———.Solicitor's Memorandum to Indian Organization, ca. October 1938.

National Archives, D.C. RG 75. E 1012, Records of Indian organization Division. Box 35. Tulalip Agency. 068-9764AMerritt, E.B., Commissioner of Indian Affairs. Letter to Senator Miles Poindexter. August 27, 1915. National Archives, D.C. RG 75. Cushman Agency. Central Classified Files. File: 95702-1913-313.

Moran, Kate. Interview. Port Gamble S'Klallam Tribe Archives, 1992.

McChesney, Special Supervisor. Letter to Swain. June 3, 1914. National Archives, Seattle. RG 75. Puyallup. Correspondence with Day School Teachers, 1913-1918. Box 2. Fldr: Pt. Gamble Day School.

———. Letter to Commissioner of Indian Affairs. October 28, 1915. National Archives, Seattle. RG 75. Puyallup Indian Agency. Correspondence with the Commissioner, 1907-20, Land Population-Purchases. Box #7; Fd: Land-Records, 1915-1919.

McCormick Lumber Company. "Offer to sell lands to the U.S." September 30, 1935. National Archives, Seattle. RG 75. Tulalip. Records of Tribal Councils, 1925-52. Box 480, Fldr; Pt. Gamble (2 of 2).

———. Deed to United States in trust for Port Gamble Band of Clallam Indians. March 12, 1936. Kitsap County Recorder's Office. Deeds, vol. 212: 238-244.

McDowell. Report to Board of Indian Commissioners. November 1, 1920. National Archives, D.C. RG 75. E. 1388. Special Reports of the Bd. of Ind. Commrs. 19-15-1933. Box 1. Vol. 3. [Pt. G. File: Reports of the Bd. of Ind. Commrs, 1915 - 1932.]

Murphy, D.E., Director, Indian Division, CCC. Letter to Upchurch, 1941. National Archives, D.C. RG 75. E.1007. Records of the Rehabilitation Division. Project Records, 1935-1944.Box 46. File: 6090-P-2. General Correspondence, Jan. 2, 1941-present.

"Natural Resources Board Questionnaire-Clallam (Public Domain)" n.d. National Archives, Seattle. RG 75. Tulalip Agency. Box 479. File: Corresp. on IRA Land Acquisition.

Nicholson, N.O., Superintendent, Taholah Agency. Letter to Commissioner of Indian Affairs. February 6, 1931. National Archives, Seattle. RG 75. Taholah Agency. Decimal File 115.

―――. Letter to F.E. Briggs. April 29, 1931. National Archives, Seattle. RG 75. Taholah Agency. Decimal File 115.

―――. Letter to Mr. Michel, Game Protector. March 7, 1934. National Archives, Seattle. RG 75. Taholah Agency. Decimal File 115.

Noland, Fred, Attorney. Letter to Klallam Tribe. September 10, 1975. Port Gamble S'Klallam Tribe Archives.

Olympic Peninsula Intertribal Cultural Advisory Committee. *Native Peoples of the Olympic Peninsula: Who We Are.* Edited by Jacilee Wray. Norman: University of Oklahoma Press, 2002.

Onat, Astrida. Report for Bureau of Indian Affairs. Application for National Register of Historic Places: Point Julia, Washington. Washington State Department of Archaeology and Historic Preservation, 1991.

Pacific Telephone and Telegraph Company. Port Gamble S'Klallam Tribe Archives, May 1948.

Patsy, Joseph. 1936. Letter to Collier, Commissioner of Indian Affairs. Original source citation lost. Port Gamble S'Klallam Archives.

Peters, Darlene. Interview with Gene Jones. Port Gamble S'Klallam Oral History Project, November 22, 2005.

Peterson, Erik. Deed to Jacob Jones. September 28, 1903. Kitsap County Recorder's Office. Vol. 36 Deeds p. 664.

Phillips, Henry J. Interview. Washington Pioneer Project. Washington State Library. Washington Pioneer Project Record, 1936–1937: King Co. Box 3, File P,Q.

Poindexter, Miles, Senator. Letter to Merritt, Commissioner of Indian Affairs. 1915. National Archives, D.C. RG 75. Cushman Agency. Central Classified Files. File: 95702-1913-313.

Pope and Talbot, Inc. "The Port Gamble Centennial, 1853–1953." Pope and Talbot Archives, 2-13 (1953):40–44.

Port Gamble Day School Journal. Port Gamble S'Klallam Tribe Archives, 1892.

"Port Gamble Employees of McCormick Lumber Co." 1934. National Archives, D.C. RG 75. E. 121. Tulalip Agency. 00-1934-066. Box 6.

Port Gamble Museum. Ledger #83. n.d.

Port Gamble S'Klallam Tribe. Port Gamble Indian Council Resolution Approving CCC Program. March 1, 1939. National Archives, Seattle. RG 75, 476, Box 1. File: Working Plan Report.

———. Constitution and By Laws of the Port Gamble Band of S'Klallam Indians. Approved by Fred H. Daiker, Assistant Commissioner of Indian Affairs and Oscar L. Chapman, Assistant Secretary of the Interior. June 15, 1939. Certification of Adoption by Port Gamble Band, August 5, 1939. Port Gamble S'Klallam Tribe Archives.

———. Resolution. November 4, 1940. National Archives, D.C. RG 75 E. 1007. Records of the Rehabilitation Division. Project Records, 1935-1944. Box 46. File: 6090-P-2. General Correspondence, Jan. 2, 1941-present.

———. Port Gamble Indian Community Lot List. n.d. [post-1940]. National Archives, Seattle. RG 75, Tulalip Agency, Box 480.

———. Community Council Minutes. April 17, 1950. National Archives, Seattle. RG 75. Tulalip Agency, Box 481.

———. Resolution of the Port Gamble Community Council. Port Gamble S'Klallam Tribe Archives, June, 4 1970.

———. Adoption Ordinance. Port Gamble S'Klallam Tribe Archives, June 25, 1970.

———. Base Roll of Port Gamble S'Klallam Tribe. Port Gamble S'Klallam Tribe Archives, 1974.

———. Comprehensive Plan. Port Gamble S'Klallam Tribe Archives. n.d.

———. Resolution of the Community Council. Port Gamble S'Klallam Tribe Archives, June 9, 1974.

———Resolution of the Business Committee. Port Gamble S'Klallam Tribe Archives, June 25, 1974.

———. *Klallam History from Manuscript & Memory*. Port Gamble S'Klallam Tribe Title IV Curriculum Project. Port Gamble S'Klallam Tribe Archives, ca. 1975.

———. *Klallam News*. Port Gamble S'Klallam Archives, 1979.

———. Title 18. Port Gamble S'Klallam Law and Order Code, 1986.

———. Amended Constitution and By Laws of the Port Gamble Band of S'Klallam Indians. Port Gamble S'Klallam Tribe Archives, 1993.

———. *Pride Is Our Heritage.* Newspaper publication of the Port Gamble S'Klallam Tribe, 1994.

———. 21.03.02, Family Code, adopted December 11, 2001. Port Gamble S'Klallam Law and Order Code, 2001.

———. Confidential interview #6 conducted by Melody Bidtah for Indian Child Welfare Practice Manual, March 4, 2008, 2008.

Port Gamble S'Klallam, Lower Elwha Klallam, and Jamestown S'Klallam Tribes. "Tribes Provide Insight on Treaty Hunting Rights." *North Kitsap Herald*, February 26, 2010.

Powers-Beck, Jeffrey. *The American Indian Integration of Baseball.* Lincoln: University of Nebraska Press, 2004.

Price, Laura. *Healing of the Canoe.* Port Gamble S'Klallam Tribe and University of Washington. DVD.

Prucha, Francis Paul. *The Great Father: The United States Government and the American Indians.* Lincoln: University of Nebraska Press, [1984] 1991 edition.

Pulsifer, Louisa. Interview. Port Gamble S'Klallam Tribe Archives, 1974

Purser, Ed. "Port Gamble Locals" and "Clallam Indians Strike: Fight Ten Hour Day." *The Real American.* April 7, 1922.

Purser, Irene Fulton. Interview. Port Gamble S'Klallam Tribe Archives, ca. 1976.

Purser, Irene (Fulton), Ed Purser and Clara Jones. Oral History Interview. Port Gamble S'Klallam Tribe Archives, ca. 1974.

Purser, Irene (Jackson). Interviews. Port Gamble S'Klallam Oral History Project.

Purser, Rose. 2006. Interviews, February 7 and February 10, 2006. Port Gamble S'Klallam Oral History Project, February 7 and April 14, 2006.

———. Interview by Ron Hirschi. 2008.

Purser, Rude. Interview by Ron Hirschi. 2008.

Puyallup Tribe v. Department of Game of Washington, et al, 1968. 391 U.S. 392.

Rahn, Lahti. "Klallam Band's Pools Will Be Home to Salmon." *Bremerton Sun.* June 27, 1975.

Ramsey, William. "Saving the Corner Store, in Name Only," *Bremerton*

Sun. July 1, 1998.

Records of the Proceedings of the Commission to hold Treaties with the Indian Tribes in Washington Territory and the Blackfoot Territory. n.d.

Ritchie, William. Letter to Commissioner of Indian Affairs. January 9, 1922. National Archives, Seattle. RG 75 BIA Western Wash. Agency, Tribal Operations Branch General Corres. 1914-1951. Box 259. File: Indian Claims Commissioner's File. [Pt. G. File: Claims, 1916 - 1923].

Roblin, Charles. Report to Commissioner of Indian Affairs. January 31, 1919. National Archives, Seattle. M-1343. Roll 1. [Pt. G. File: Roblin, 1919].

Rue, Chair, Kitsap County Board of Commissioners. Letter to Senator Bone. April 13, 1938. National Archives, Seattle. RG 75, Tulalip Agency. Records of Tribal Councils 1925–52. Box 480. File: Port Gamble 1935–42 (2 of 2). [Pt. G. File: Land. 1935 - 38].

Schmidt, Johan George. Deed to Edward Purser. March 21, 1912. Kitsap County Recorder's Office. 129 Deeds: 269.

Shackleford, Charlotte. "Donation Land Claims." *Building a State: Washington, 1889 - 1939.* Tacoma: Washington State Historical Society, 1940.

S'Klallam Tribe Census. 1898. Port Gamble S'Klallam Tribe Archives.

S'Klallam (Klallam, Clallam) Tribe. Petition. June 15, 1912. National Archives, D.C. RG 75. Central Classified Files. Cushman. Decimal 313. Box 5126. File: 5329–1910.

———. Resolution from Tribal Council Meeting. May 11 and 12, 1914. National Archives, D.C. RG 75. Central Classified Files. Cushman Agency. File: 3405–1914–054.

———. Minutes of meeting of December 15, 1921. National Archives, Seattle. RG 75 BIA Western Wash. Agency, Tribal Operations Branch General Corres. 1914-1951. Box 259. File: Indian Claims Commissioner's File. [Pt. G. File: Claims, 1916 - 1923].

———. Clallam Constitution. August 26, 1934. National Archives, D.C. Indian Organization Division Records, Box 35, Tulalip. 068-9764A.

S'Klallam Tribe v. US. Findings of Fact and Opinion. December 2, 1957.

Indian Claims Commission, Dkt. 134. 5 ICC 680.

———. Findings of Fact and Opinion. October 1, 1970. Indian Claims Commission, Dkt. 134. 23 ICC 512.

———. Additional Findings of Fact and Opinion. November 5, 1976. Indian Claims Commission, Dkt. 134. 39 ICC 134.

Smith, David. *Essays in New England History: Northeast Corner.* Routledge Press, 2002.

Smith, E.P., Commissioner of Indian Affairs. Letter to R.H. Milroy. Circular of October 21, 1873. Original source citation lost. Copy in Port Gamble S'Klallam Archives.

Solomon. Deed to Eddie George. May 26, 1911. Kitsap County Recorder's Office. Vol. 75 Deeds: 174.

Sparks, Sam. Oral History. Port Gamble S'Klallam Tribe Archives, 1998.

Stanton, Lloyd Bowen. Letter to Indian Agent. September 18, 1934. I.I.M. Files: Anderson. BIA, Everett Office.

State of Washington. Deed to Geo. Dan. Howell. October 18, 1897. Washington State Archives. Natural Resources Department Accession. Book 148. Original Tract Book.

———. Deed to George Dan Howell. January 19, 1905. Washington State Archives, King County Branch. Kitsap County Deeds, Vol. 43 Deeds: 244.

Stauss, Joseph H. *The Jamestown S'Klallam Story: Rebuilding a Northwest Coast Indian Tribe.* Sequim: Jamestown S'Klallam Tribe, 2002.

Sullivan, Con. Interviews. Port Gamble S'Klallam Oral History Project, February 7 and March 29, 2006.

Superintendent, Everett Agency. Letter to Purser. June 23, 1964. Bureau of Indian Affairs, Everett Agency.

———. Superintendent, Everett Agency. Letter to DeCoteau. June 25, 1970. Bureau of Indian Affairs, Everett Agency.

Superintendent, Tulalip Agency. Letter to Sammy Charles, 1926. National Archives, Seattle. RG 75. Tulalip Agency, 476. Records related to Clallam Enrollment, Box 1. Fldr: Corresp. re. payment to Clallam (3 of 3).

Suttles, Wayne. "Central Coast Salish." *Handbook of North American Indians.* Vol. 7. Washington, D.C.: Smithsonian Institution.

Swain, Leonidas. Swain to CIA in Hauke, 2nd Asst. CIA to Johnson:

January 13, 1913. National Archives Seattle. RG 75. Puyallup Agency. Correspondence with the CIA, 1907-1920. Forestry-Land Heirship. Box 6. Fdr: Land Allotments 3735-5887. [Pt. G. File: CIA Correspondence: Land, 1913].

———. Letter to Johnson, Superintendent. August 3, 1913 and August 28, 1913. National Archives, Seattle. RG 75. Puyallup. Correspondence with Day School Teachers, 1913-1918. Box 2. Fldr: Pt. Gamble Day School.

———. Letter to McChesney. June 1, 1914. National Archives, Seattle. RG 75. Puyallup. Correspondence with Day School Teachers, 1913-1918. Box 2. Fldr: Pt. Gamble Day School.

———. Report. May 7, 1915. National Archives, Seattle. RG 75. Puyallup. Correspondence with Day School Teachers, 1913-1918. Box 2. Fldr: Pt. Gamble Day School.

———. Letter to Wilson. June 12, 1915. National Archives, Seattle. RG 75. Puyallup. Correspondence with Day School Teachers, 1913-1918. Box 2. Fldr: Pt. Gamble Day School.

———. Letters to Wilson. July 7 and July 9, 1917. National Archives, Seattle. RG 75. Puyallup. Correspondence with Day School Teachers, 1913-1918. Box 2. Fldr: Pt. Gamble Day School.

Swartout, Commander S. Letters to Secretary of Navy. November 23 and December 8, 1856. National Archives, D.C. RG 45. Records of the Navy, M-147, Roll 15.

Swift, Francine (Jones). Letter to History Book Committee. Port Gamble S'Klallam Tribe Archives, 2008.

Swindell, E.G. Jr. Report on Source, Nature, and Extent of the Fishing, Hunting and Miscellaneous Related Rights of Certain Indian Tribes in Washington and Oregon Together with Affidavits Showing Location of a Number of Usual and Accustomed Fishing Grounds and Stations. United States Office of Indian Affairs, Division of Forestry and Grazing. Plaintiff's Exhibit 127. *Skokomish Tribe v. U.S.* Indian Claims Commission, 1942.

Terry, Frank. Letter to Commissioner of Indian Affairs. August 20, 1897. *ARCIA for 1897*:293. Washington: Government Printing Office, 1897.

Thrush, Collin. *Native Seattle, Histories from the Crossing-Over Place*. Seattle: University of Washington Press, 2007.

Tom, Victor and Bernard Tom. Interview. Port Gamble S'Klallam Oral
    History Project, September 27, 2005.

Treaty of Point No Point. Executed by the United States and the
    Skokomish, S'Klallam, and Chemakum Tribes. January 26, 1855.
    Copy in Port Gamble S'Klallam Tribe Archives.

Tulalip Agency. Report to Commissioner of Indian Affairs. October 5,
    1920. National Archives, D.C. RG 75. Tulalip Agency. Central
    Classified Files. File: 90736-1920-916.

———. Report on 1938 Program Grants, 1939. National Archives,
    Seattle. RG 75, Tulalip, Dec. 242. Port Gamble Rehabilitation.
    280, Box 30. [Pt. G. File: Rehabilitation Project. 1938-56].

———. Report on 1939 Program Grants, 1940. National Archives,
    Seattle. RG 75, Tulalip, Dec. 242. Port Gamble Rehabilitation.
    280, Box 30. [Pt. G. File: Rehabilitation Project. 1938-56].

———. Report of Planning Committee of Tulalip Indian Agency,
    Washington, 1944-1945. National Archives, D.C. RG 75. Tulalip
    Agency. Records of Tribal Councils, 1934-52. Box 479. Fldr:
    Report of Planning Committee, 1944-54.

———. Appraisal Report. September 25, 1946. Original source citation
    lost. Copy in Port Gamble S'Klallam Archives.

———. Report. March 26, 1947. Original source citation lost. Copy in
    Port Gamble S'Klallam Archives.

United States Department of Interior, Indian Office. Minutes of Meeting,
    Land Division, Credit Division & Rehabilitation Division. 1935.
    National Archives, Seattle. Portland Area Office Jurisdictional
    Files of Realty Office, 1935-1961, Box 182. File: IRA Misc. 2 of 2.

United States House of Representatives. House Bill 22868. 1910. National
    Archives, D.C. RG 75. Central Classified Files. Cushman Agency.
    Decimal 313. Box 5126. File: 5329-1910.

U.S. v. Washington. U.S. District Court, Western District, Washington.
    Civil No. 9213, Phase I. 384 F. Supp. 312. 1974.

———. 873 F. Supp 1422 (W.D. Wash. 1994).

United States of America. Patent in fee in lieu of trust to Joseph
    Anderson, April 11, 1910. National Archives, D.C. RG 49. Bureau
    of Land Management. General Land Office, Seattle. Homestead
    Final Certificate Case File No. 4059.

United States Federal Census. Washington Territory, Jefferson County, Pt. Discovery, 1880.

University Commissioners. Deed to Pope and Talbot, dba Puget Mill Co. September 16, 1863. Kitsap County Recorder's Office. Vol. 1A, 1871-77, 230.

Upchurch, O.C. Letter to Commissioner of Indian Affairs. March 20, 1936. National Archives, Seattle. RG 75. Taholah Agency. Decimal File 105.2, Rehabilitation.

———. Letter to Commissioner of Indian Affairs. April 12, 1938. National Archives, D.C. RG 75. Entry 1007. Records of the Rehabilitation Division, 1935-1944. File 76096-P-2.

———. Letter to Commissioner of Indian Affairs, April 30, 1938. National Archives, Seattle. RG 75. Tulalip. Records of Tribal Councils, 1925-1952. Box 480. Fldr: Pt. Gamble, 1935-1942 (2 of 2).

———. Letter to Commissioner of Indian Affairs. August 23, 1938. National Archives, Seattle. RG 75. Tulalip Agency. Dec. File 242, Box 30, Fldr. 242, Commissioner Correspondence, 1938-1939.

———. Letter to Commissioner of Indian Affairs. December 6, 1938. National Archives, D.C. RG 75. Entry 1007. Records of the Rehabilitation Division, 1935-1944. File: 76096-P-2.

———. Letter to Lester Jackson. March 27, 1939. National Archives, D.C. RG 75. Tulalip Agency. Box. 1. Decimal File 003. Fld: 003 Misc. Corres, 1935-1940. [Pt. G. File: Misc. Corresp. 1935-40.]

———. Letter to Commissioner of Indian Affairs. October 15, 1940. National Archives, D.C. RG 75. Entry 1007. Records of the Rehabilitation Division. Project Records, 1935-1944. Box 46. File: 6090-P-2.

———. Letter to Commissioner of Indian Affairs. October 31, 1940. National Archives, D.C. RG 75. Entry 1007. Records of the Rehabilitation Division, 1935-1944. File: 76096-P-2.

———. Letter to Vigeant. February 21, 1941. National Archives, D.C. RG 75 E. 1007. Records of the Rehabilitation Division. Project Records, 1935-1944. Box 46. File: 6090-P-2. General Correspondence, Jan. 2, 1941-present.

Vigeant, X. 1938. Letter to Upchurch. December 13, 1938. National Archives, D.C. RG 75. Entry 1007, Records of the Rehabilitation

Division, 1935-1944. File 76096-P-2.

————. Letter to Upchurch. May 18, 1939. National Archives, Seattle. RG 75. Tulalip Agency. Decimal 242. Commissioner Correspondence on Rehabilitation, 1938-39.

————. Letter to Upchurch. October 17, 1940. National Archives, D.C. RG 75 E. 1007. Records of the Rehabilitation Division. Project Records, 1935-1944. Box 46. File: 6090-P-2. General Correspondence, Jan. 2, 1941-present.

Ward v. Race Horse. 1896. U. S. Supreme Court. 163 U.S. 504.

Washington Emergency Relief Administration, Kitsap Co. Letter to Indian Agency, October 5, 1934. Bureau of Indian Affairs, Western Washington Agency, I.I.M. Account Files: Anderson.

Washington State Game Commission. Annual Report Game Commissioners. Washington Public Documents, 1933-1934, vol. 3 (1933):9.

Washington State Game Warden. Annual Report of Game Warden, 1898-1900 (1900): 116.

Waterman, T. T. *Puget Sound Geography*. "Geographical Names in the Clallam and Chimakum Area." Manuscript No. 1864. National Anthropological Archives, Smithsonian Institution. 1920. Microfilm at University of Washington, A3435, and University of California Museum of Anthropology Archives.

Webster, Henry. Report. *Annual Report of the Commissioner of Indian Affairs for 1862*. Washington: Government Printing Office, 1862.

Weisenburger, Lucille. 2007. Interview. June 25, 2007. Port Gamble S'Klallam Oral History Project.

Wellman, Laurel. Interview by Ron Hirschi. 2008.

Wheat, T.W., Land Field Agent. Letter to J.M. Stewart, Director of Lands, Office of Indian Affairs. December 12, 1935. National Archives, Seattle. RG 75. Tulalip Agency. Archives Box #478. Port Gamble Project-Indian Reorganization Act Land Purchase.

Williams, Richard L. *The Loggers*. Time-Life Books, 1976.

Wray, Jacilee. "The Salmon Bank: An Ethnohistoric Compilation." Prepared for San Juan Island National Historical Park, 2003.

Zimmerman, William, Jr., Commissioner of Indian Affairs. Letter to L.C. Gray, Director, Land Utilization Division, Resettlement

Administration. August 10, 1935. National Archives, Seattle. RG 75. Tulalip Agency. Dec. 479. File: Corresp. on IRA Land Acquisition.

———. Letter to O.C. Upchurch, Superintendent. August 15, 1935. National Archives, Seattle. RG 75. Tulalip Agency. Dec. 479. File: Corresp. on IRA Land Acquisition.

———. Letter to O.C. Upchurch, Superintendent. August 16, 1935. National Archives, Seattle. RG 75. Tulalip Agency. Dec. 479. File: Corresp. on IRA Land Acquisition.

———. Letter to Senator Bone. June 15, 1938. National Archives, Seattle. RG 75. Tulalip Agency. Records of Tribal Councils 1925–52. Box 480. File: Pt. Gamble, 1935–42 (2 of 2).

———. Letter to Upchurch. November 15, 1940. National Archives, D.C. RG 75 E. 1007. Records of the Rehabilitation Division. Project Records, 1935–1944. Box 46. File: 6090-P-2. General Correspondence, Jan. 2, 1941–present.

———. Letter to Walgren, U.S. Senate. April 14, 1942. National Archives, D.C. RG 75 E. 1007. Records of the Rehabilitation Division. Project Records, 1935–1944. Box 46. File: 6090-P-2. General Correspondence, Jan. 2, 1941–present.

WEBSITES
www.portgamble.com/pdf/port_gamble_walking_tour.pdf.
www.pgst.nsn.us

STATUTES
Federal
16 U.S.C. 251
25 U.S.C. 465, Indian Reorganization Act of 1934
43 U.S.C. 189, Act of March 3, 1875, Indian Homestead Act of 1875
43 U.S.C. 190, Act of July 4, 1884, Indian Homestead Act of 1884
43 Statutes at Large 1102, Act of March 3, 1925
Act of March 4, 1911
Act of August 13, 1946, Public Law 726. Indian Claims Commission Act
General Allotment Act of 1887 (Dawes Act), 24 Statutes at Large 388

State
Session Laws of the State of Washington. 1905:351, 352; 1929:600.

Index

A

Adams
    George, 10, 96, 108, 126
    Gertrude, 44, 62
    Mary Ann, 19, 153
Aikman, John, 31
Allen
    Frank, 119
    Henry, 119
    Ron, 179
allotment policy, 91, 144
American Indian Movement, 52
Anderson
    Bennie, 26, 224, 226
    Joseph, 9, 84, 92-94, 105, 108, 112, 113, 130, 139, 160
    Josie, 9, 80, 92-94, 98, 122, 126, 132, 249
    One-Armed Peter, 9
Anderson, Greg, 233, 240, 242, 244
aquaculture, 57
Assembly of God Church, 129, 150

B

Bainbridge Island strawberry cannery, 132
baseball, 217-231
basket socials, 137
basketry, 67, 74, 132, 249
    clam basket, 24, 49
Battle of Port Gamble, 18
Baze, Kelly (Sullivan), 71, 88

Bella Bella, 253
berries, 4, 17, 24, 36, 45, 62-67, 84
    commercial harvest, 32, 38, 132
    preserving, 63, 64
    salmonberries, 32
    soapberry, 32
    squossum, 32, 64
Bishop, Thomas, 109
Blue, Brantely, 176
Board of Indian Commissioners, 106
boarding school, 89, 185-187, 189, 209, 217, 219
    Chemawa, 186

C

Chinook Jargon, 23, 121
Chits-a-mah-han, 24. 101
Chubby, Howard, 13
Civilian Conservation Corps, 148
Clallam Bay, 1, 8, 10, 13, 17, 33 101 111
Cliffside, 59
Collier, John, 144
Cook
    Johnny, 11
    Mrs. John, 15
Coontown, 13, 77, 93-97, 99, 102, 111, 113, 123-126, 130, 131, 143, 155, 189
Cotter, Henry, 75
Cowitchan First Nation, 15, 115, 116
Crawford, E.L., 179
Cultus John, 15
Cushman Hospital, 31, 209

D

Daebler, Lorraine, 178
dancing, 18, 35, 137, 216
DeCoteau
    Betty, 242
    Carol, 168, 174, 214, 242, 255
    Mildred (Fulton), 115, 132, 151, 196, 208
    Rick, 242
    Shawn, 57
    Warren, 170
    Wayne, 255
DeGuire, Dallas, 242
Dexter, *Niatum*, 14
Dexter (Dixter)
    Thomas, 218
Discovery Bay, 60, 64, 111, 207
Donation Land Act, 4
Dosewallips River, 53, 61
Doyle, Dicky, 170
Driftwood Keys, 44, 59
duck, 32, 33, 37, 45, 58, 60. 61, 128
Duckabush River, 53
Duke of York, 10, 11, 24, 101
Dungeness, 10, 13, 15, 101, 111, 177, 178
Dungeness River, 33, 53, 58
Dye's Inlet, 94, 138

E

Ebey, Colonel Isaac, 18
Ediz Hook, 101
education, 109 183-199
 Port Gamble S'Klallam graduates, 195-199
 traditional S'Klallam, 183-185
Edwards, Leonore, 155
Eells, Edwin, 16, 17, 92
Eells, Myron, 117, 119, 120, 135, 208
Eglon, 157, 196
Eglon Slough, 67
elections, 162, 163, 171
Elwha River, 33, 53, 58, 59, 101
Elwha River Dams, 58
environmental protection – fishing habitat, 57
Erland's Point, 138
Evans, Governor Dan, 55
Evergreen State College, 199

F

farms, 17, 94, 97, 112, 123-131, 141
fish
 bullhead, 124
 candlefish, 34
 cod, 32, 34, 39, 44, 46, 74
 flounder, 34
 grunt fish, 32, 44
 halibut, 33, 34
 herring, 32, 34
 octopus (devil fish), 39, 44
 salmon, *see Salmon*
 smelt, 32, 34
fishing, 8, 14, 16, 17, 35, 36, 68, 99, 117, 128, 145, 164
 commercial, 53, 54
 gillnetting, 53
 illegal non-indian, 55
 protest fisheries, 52
 rights, see Treaty rights
 state restrictions, 39, 41, 50, 51
 tribal management, 57, 236, 237
 trolling, 43
Fort Nisqually, 17, 37
Foulweather Bluff, 39, 148, 177
Frank's Landing, 51
Fulton

Alice (George), 45
Alice (Solomon), 94, 97
Angie (Peterson), 14, 41, 259
Daisy (Garrison), 36, 154. 203
Fred, 127, 227, 250
Harry III, 78, 87, 88,213, 227, 242, 255
Harry Jr.,36, 47, 76, 119-122, 128, 137, 151, 153, 162, 173, 186, 225, 233, 237-239, 255
Harry Sr., 13, 14, 19, 84, 94, 95, 108, 135, 219, 220, 222, 223, 231
James, 9, 14, 84, 218
Jennarose (Charles), 167
Jim, 83
Ken, 224
Lloyd, 48, 50, 83
Mary (Littleman) (the daughter), 25
Reg, 83, 244-226
Russell Jr., 42, 43, 52, 154, 173, 224
Russell Sr., 43, 75, 85, 87, 135, 153, 173, 191, 225
Susie, 9
Thelma, 38, 132, 214
Tracy, 88
funeral, 250

G

gambling, 120
Garrison
    Anna, 108
    Bill, 40, 108
    George (aka Joseph), 138
    Jane, 138
    John, 138
gathering, 41, 62-68, 91, 117, 148, 164, 197
    alder, 204
    bear grass, 67
    berries, *see Berries*
    blackberries, 46, 63, 67
    camas, 14, 33
    cattail, 76, 209
    crabapple, 204
    devil's club, 204
    dogwood, 203
    foxglove, 204
    Prince's Pine, 202
    rights, 24, 26, 27, 33, 107
    seaweed, 204
    skunk cabbage, 202
    squirrel tail, 203

sweet grass, 67
vetch, 204
General Allotment Act, 176
George, 10, 106
    Annie Charles, 96
    Bennie Jr., 160, 162, 166, 171, 173
    Bennie Sr., 97, 110, 113, 120, 122, 134, 135, 141, 157, 173, 177, 219, 223
    Betty (Wellman), 48, 154
    Bob, 227
    Cecil, 225
    Chuck, 224
    Claude "Skip", 26, 41, 44, 48, 54, 55, 83,96, 125, 126, 137, 153, 218
    Don, 227
    Dorothy (Garrison), 36, 40, 44, 59, 63, 127, 130, 132, 138, 156, 166-168, 173, 190, 203, 210, 214
    Eddie, 10, 11, 13, 94, 96, 105, 106, 108, 121, 137, 186, 218, 219,
    Ella, 208
    Ellen (Sigo), 49, 63, 67, 121, 131, 138
    Emore, 135
    Ivan (Uncle Ivar), 44, 45, 47, 49, 59, 64, 131, 140, 148, 190, 224, 225, 257
    Louie, 108, 220, 222, 223, 249
    Lucy (Emore), 10, 97
    Lyle, 135, 225
    Martha, 46, 61, 97, 122, 134
    Ralph, 153, 208
    Ted, 39, 61, 78, 124, 133, 139, 143, 157, 166, 170, 173, 175, 178, 183, 196, 198,219, 221, 224, 235, 249
    William, 39, 96, 105, 108, 113, 131, 153, 160, 223
George's Corner, 46, 98, 134
Great Depression, 112, 128, 132, 134, 137, 143, 147, 148
Grinnel, Elaine, 178

H

Hadlock, 14, 101, 123
Haida Tribe, 25
Hall, Mabel, 15
Hamma Hamma River, 35, 53
Hansville, 39, 64, 196, 259
Harman, August, 188
Hazel Point, 46, 48
health, 201-216
Hebert
    Marie, 67, 137, 174, 195, 242, 254
    Paul, 255
Henry
    Emma (Sly), 1, 13, 93

James, 1, 13, 93, 96, 99, 107
    Louise (Sigo), 94, 138
    Richard, 222, 223
    William, 93
Hirschi
    Daisy Cotter, 75
    LaVerne, 75
    Ron, 57, 67, 71, 221
Hoh Tribe, 102
Hoko River, 1
Hood Canal, 2, 5, 8, 17, 22, 33, 35, 36, 43, 44, 53, 58, 59, 62, 91, 93, 98, 99, 101, 119, 135,
    177, 186
hop fields – Indian harvesters, 18, 32, 37, 38
housing, 74, 119, 147, 153
Howell
    Dan, 16
    George, 16, 97, 105, 107, 113
    Nancy, 16, 97
    Phillip, 107, 113, 222
Hudson's Bay Company, 17, 37, 80, 117
hunting, 2, 28, 32, 35, 45, 51, 58-62
    deer, 59
    duck, 60
    elk, 33, 51, 59, 61
    state limitations on, 59
    treaty rights, 22, 24-27, 39
Hyasman, Dolly, 42

I

illness, 128, 211
Indian Child Welfare
    practice manual, 22
Indian Child Welfare Act, 133
Indian Child Welfare Program, 241
Indian Claims Commission, 175-182
    "Klallam Tract", 180
    offset phase, 180
    S'Klallam judgment, 180
    valuation phase, 179
Indian Claims Commission Act, 176
Indian Education Act of 1972, 198
Indian Health Service, 213, 240
Indian Homestead Act, 78, 91
    restrictions, 92, 93
Indian homesteads, 92, 99
Indian Island, 10, 96, 101

Foster, 42, 58, 76, 129, 132, 135, 138, 155, 157, 160, 170, 173. 191, 195
Gene, 44, 67, 236
Jacob, 14, 72, 76, 97, 108, 126, 131, 201, 202, 210
Jake, 60, 63, 64, 72, 124, 174, 196, 226, 236, 237, 242, 249
Jenny, 14, 63, 97, 128, 175, 208
June, 255
Kay, 255
Lucy, 207
Judson, Mickey, 178

K

Keller, Josiah, 7, 78
Keyport, 84, 132, 134
King George, Tallis, 239, 245
Kingston School Board, 191, 193
Kingston., 132, 167, 193, 225
Kitsap Community Action Agency, 171
Kitsap County
    tax foreclosures, 94. 112. 113
Kitsap County Commissioners, 151, 151, 157
Kitsap County Health Board, 19, 151

L

La-Hash, 106
Lambert
    Henry, 15, 93, 99, 105, 153
    Mary Ann, 11
land, 89-114
    lost in tax foreclosures, 94, 112, 113
    native concept, 90
    purchased by S'Klallam, 94-100
Lane, Barbara, 2, 17, 27, 53
Law, Frank, 107
leadership, 159-162
Leonard, Reverend Karl, 150, 157
Liberty Bay, 50
Lip Lip, 44
Little Boston community, 115-142
Little Boston Pentecostal Tabernacle Church, 211, 237
Little Boston School Board, 191
Littleman
    George, 14, 99
    Mary, 14, 25, 99
    Susie, 25, 95
Loeffler, Shirley, 132

Lofall, 98
logging, 57
longhouse, 97, 117
Lord Jim Balch, 101
Lower Elwha Klallam Tribe, 1, 25, 56, 136, 147, 172, 178
Lummi Reservation, 89, 97

M

Magnuson, Senator Warren, 19, 151, 168
Makah Tribe, 14, 17, 42, 93, 97, 121, 206
Makris
  Gus, 224
  Janis, 249
  Jewel, 173
marriage, 95, 119, 121, 122
Martha John Creek, 97
Martinez, Ruth (Henry), 13, 94, 138, 186
Matheson, Emily, 207
Mats Mats, 175
Mattson, Laurie, 244
McGrady, Karron, 254
Mead, James, 94
Merriam Report, 190, 198
Middle Creek, 45
Moon, Ed, 228
Moon, Scott, 228
Moran, Kate (Anderson), 36, 120, 122, 131, 132, 208, 209, 256
Muckleshoot Tribe, 52
musicians, 135

N

National Health Service Corps, 214
Naval Ammunition Depot, 134
Neah Bay, 31, 42, 43, 52, 89, 132
Nicholson, Helen (Jones), 167
Nick's Lagoon, 35
Nisqually Tribe, 52, 227
Nolan, Fred, 175, 179
Northwest Federation of American Indians, 106, 109
Northwest Indian College, 199
Northwest Intertribal Court System, 239

O

P

Price
    Ellen, 255
    Herman, 255
    Joe, 255
    Laura, 253, 254
Prince of Wales, 10. 101
Puget Mill Company, 5-7, 37
    acquisition of land, 78, 90
    promise made to S'Klallam people, 75, 76
    refusal to sell land, 102
    sale of land for reservation, 145, 146
Pulsifer
    Bill, 44, 98, 105, 108
    George, 37, 108
    Lizzie, 98
    Louisa, 15, 77, 96, 118, 202, 249
    Newton, 93, 113
Pumpkin Junction, 63
Purser
    Aaron, 140, 157, 171-174, 225
    Bud, 83, 130, 209, 224, 242
    Calvin, 224
    Craig, 52, 174
    Ed, 16, 72, 83, 84, 97, 137, 140, 160
    Eugene, 168, 217, 227
    Geraldine, 167
    Irene (Fulton), 17, 35-37, 41, 45, 68, 75, 83, 97, 122
    Irene (Jackson), 46, 61, 63, 64, 67, 98, 122, 123, 132, 139, 159, 209, 212, 214, 220, 256
    Jelmer, 123
    Julia (Sigo), 138, 153
    Nettie, 123, 153
    Penny, 256
    Richard, 16, 153
    Rose (Wellman), 28, 41, 47, 83, 85, 119, 124, 129, 135, 136, 139, 156, 169, 170, 173,
        208-210, 214, 226, 239, 248, 255
    Rudy, 72, 84, 85, 209, 224, 225, 227
    Rudy Jr., 141, 228
    Stan, 199
Puyallup Reservation, 209
Puyallup River, 8, 17, 31
Puyallup Tribe, 51, 52
Pysht, 101, 111
Pysht Tim, 111

Q

Quilcene, 53, 93, 101, 119
Quileute Tribe, 102
Quimper, 37
Quinault Reservation, 42, 207
    allotments for S'Klallam on, 102-107
Quinault Tribe, 59

R

Rafeedie, Judge, 56
Redtail Creek, 57
Rentola, Esko, Reverend, 213, 237
Ritchie, William, 109
Robb, Bill, 178
Roblin, Charles, 6, 109
Roosevelt, Eleanor, 150
Rudd, Pat, 167

S

S'Klallam Appropriations Act of 1925, 110-112
    as bar to I.R.A. organization, 145
S'Klallam Tribe
    1914 Council, 103-105
    1926 claims payment, 110-112
    Claims Committee, 111
    communities in 1911, 101
    Enrollment Committee, 1926, 111
    General Council, 178
    Indian Claims Commission Council, 178, 179
    language, 121, 122, 254
    lobbying campaign 1900s-1920s, 106-109
    payment roll, 1926, 110-112
    population loss from smallpox, 207
    settlements at treaty times, 1, 25
    skilled canoe handlers, 16, 17
    spiritual healing practices, 205
    traditional medicines, 204
    treaty signatories, 24, 25
Salisbury Point, 56
salmon, 17, 24, 26, 32-34, 44, 50-58, 86
    commercial sales of, 53-55, 259
    First Salmon Ceremony, 68
    salted, 40
    smoking, 36, 119

trolling, 43
Salmon Bank, 33, 99
Sampson, Ed, 235
San Juan Island, 14, 17, 33, 37, 95
    Kanaka Bay, 99
Scow Bay, 10, 46, 60, 101
Seabeck, 9, 35, 50
Seabeck mill, 9, 14, 85
Seachord, Candi (Ives), 239, 249
secret society, 119
self-determination, 235, 236
Self-Governance Demonstration Project, 240-246
Sequim Bay, 207
shellfish, 4, 32, 45, 91, 145, 159
    barnacles, 32, 202
    "Clam ball," 223-225
    clam chowder recipe, 252
    clambake, 47, 48, 250, 260
    clams, 32, 39, 45, 148
    cockle, 44
    commercial sales of, 55, 75, 132
    crab, 44, 47, 56, 250
    geoduck, 56
    importance of clams, 46-48
    sea cucumbers, 41
    sea urchin, 32
    treaty rights affirmed, 55, 56
Shine Creek, 57
Shorewood, 63
Sigo, 138
    John, 229
    Louise, 93
Skagit Tribe, 14
Skokomish Reservation, 9, 11, 15, 16, 23, 91, 97, 101, 106, 136, 202
Skokomish River, 35, 41
Skokomish Tribe, 2, 13, 22-24, 27, 44, 56, 59, 62, 86, 89, 94, 96, 135, 177, 226, 249
Skookum John, 15, 106, 108, 159
Skunk Bay, 39, 148
Sly, Joe, 93
Small Tribes of Western Washington, 172
smallpox, 79, 205, 206
Smith Island, 58
Snohomish Tribe, 15, 22, 109
Solomon,
    Alice, 13, 94, 97
    Old, 13, 35, 86, 94, 108
    Susie, 13, 67, 108

sovereignty
 federal governmental encroachment on, 144
 treaty right to, 22
Sparks
 Barbara, 128
 Bill, 122
 Carl, 128, 153, 170, 173
 Charlie, 15
 Cubby, 98, 229
 Delores, 98
 Fannie, 15
 George, 15, 43, 108, 126, 128, 153
 Josephine (Purser), 98, 128, 173, 256
 Louisa, 8, 15, 106
 Maxine, 98
 Patti, 170
spirituality, 117, 129
Squaxin Tribe, 35
Stan Purser Memorial Pow Wow, 199
Steelhead, 26, 34
Ste-tee-thlum, 11, 25
Stevens, Gina (Jones), 175, 199, 249
Stevens, Isaac, 4
storytelling, 184
Strait of Juan de Fuca, 15-17, 33, 36, 53, 58, 101, 119
Sullivan
 Barbara, 174
 Chad, 197
 Con, 39, 59, 63, 121, 224, 227, 229
 Cyrene "Dolly" (George), 96
 Daryl, 88, 227
 Diane, 236
 Frank, 96, 132, 153, 160, 164, 168, 169, 171, 174, 191, 195, 225
 Jeromy, 17i4. 246
Suquamish, 10, 98, 132
Suquamish Tribe, 2, 5, 16, 56, 59, 89, 96, 121, 143, 177, 224, 227, 229
survey
 public domain, 90
Swain, Leonidas, 188
Swift, Francine (Jones), 249

T

T'what-ski, 25
Tahuya, 35
Talbot, Frederic, 74
Tom